FIVE STRANDS OF FICTIONALITY

Five Strands of Fictionality

The Institutional Construction
of Contemporary American Writing

DANIEL PUNDAY

THE OHIO STATE UNIVERSITY PRESS | COLUMBUS

Copyright © 2010 by The Ohio State University.
All rights reserved.

Library of Congress Cataloging-in-Publication Data
Punday, Daniel.
  Five strands of fictionality : the institutional construction of contemporary American fiction / Daniel Punday.
     p. cm.
  Includes bibliographical references and index.
  ISBN-13: 978-0-8142-1114-4 (cloth : alk. paper)
  ISBN-10: 0-8142-1114-3 (cloth : alk. paper)
  ISBN-13: 978-0-8142-9212-9 (cd-rom)
  1. American fiction—History and criticism—Theory, etc. 2. Postmodernism (Literature)—United States. 3. Fiction—History and criticism. 4. Barth, John, 1930– —Criticism and interpretation. I. Title.
  PS374.P64P86 2010
  813'.5409—dc22
                        2009021042

This book comes in the following editions:
Cloth (ISBN 978-0-8142-1114-4)
CD-ROM (ISBN 978-0-8142-9212-9)
Paper (ISBN: 978-0-8142-5678-7)
Cover design by Jason Moore
Text design by Juliet Williams
Type set in Adobe Minion Pro

CONTENTS

Acknowledgments		vii
INTRODUCTION	Fictionality Today	1
CHAPTER 1	Myth and the Institutional Construction of Postmodernism in *The Friday Book*	31
CHAPTER 2	Folk Culture, the Archive, and the Work of the Imaginary	59
CHAPTER 3	Fiction, Fraud, and Fakes	87
CHAPTER 4	Style and Symptom in Postmodern Science Fiction	125
CHAPTER 5	Role-Playing Games, Possible World Theory, and the Fictionality of Assemblage	151
CHAPTER 6	Institutional Sutures in Electronic Writing	177
CONCLUSION	Fictionality in the Public Sphere	207
Works Cited		219
Index		233

ACKNOWLEDGMENTS

A book like this, which covers so much ground and draws from so many sources, clearly can only be written by someone lucky enough to have the guidance and help of many people. First and foremost I would like to thank Judith Burdan, who was a constant source of information about the eighteenth-century novel, which provides the basis for much of the recent and best work on fictionality. As a colleague with an office just down the hall from my own, Judith provided a sounding board for many of the ideas in this book. She was generous with her time and patient with my attempts to bend research in her field to my own goals in this book.

Several other people provided guidance and inspiration on particular occasions. This project had its genesis in a summer program at the School of Criticism and Theory at Cornell University lead by Catherine Gallagher, which provided me with a powerful introduction to theories of fictionality from a New Historicist perspective. Discussing this project on several occasions with Brian McHale helped to refine the shape of the argument. A conference session on electronic literature with Marie-Laure Ryan and Nick Montfort helped me to clarify my ideas about institutional sutures that are a key element of the sixth chapter. April Gabbert and Rafael Velez provided invaluable advice about the varieties of role playing games discussed in the fifth chapter. I initially presented much of the material in this book at various annual Narrative conferences, and it is no exaggeration to say that so eclectic a book would not be possible without the equally eclectic collective intelligence of the scholars who attend that conference each year.

This book manuscript has benefited from the constructive advice and editing of many people. Sandy Crooms deserves special thanks for guiding the book through the review and editing process at The Ohio State University Press. The Press's readers, including Marcel Cornis-Pope, provided tremendously helpful guidance about how to clarify and frame the significance of the book's argument. Earlier, readers for *American Literature* and *Poetics Today* provided valuable advice for refining the arguments that became chapters 1 and 5 (respectively) of this book. In particular, Meir Sternberg's precise and detailed editing work on my discussion of role playing games significantly improved the clarity of chapter 5.

My thanks, finally, to Sam Punday, who helped me play the computer games that inspired the last chapter.

INTRODUCTION

Fictionality Today

The world, we are told, is becoming more fictional than it used to be. Walter Truett Anderson's overview of contemporary culture, *Reality Isn't What It Used to Be* (1990), nicely captures this popular perception that the fictive has somehow wormed its way into spheres of contemporary life where it traditionally was not welcome. Public life today, Anderson remarks, is characterized by "curious fiction-fact cocktails" like staged political photo ops and based-on-actual-events television movies.[1] Anderson describes the common belief that our experience of reality is more manufactured than it used to be—more heavily influenced both by direct political manipulation as well as by indirect seepage of television and film into popular consciousness.

Anderson is, of course, drawing on a tradition for characterizing the nature of contemporary media culture—especially in America—whose basic

1. Walter Truett Anderson, *Reality Isn't What It Used to Be: Theatrical Politics, Ready-to-Wear Religion, Global Myths, Primitive Chic, and Other Wonders of the Postmodern World* (San Francisco: Harper & Row, 1990), 129.

premise has largely gone without saying. This tradition has its roots in a series of books published in the 1960s that attempted to define the changes in culture wrought by the expansion of media. Marshall McLuhan's announcement at the beginning of *Understanding Media* (1964) that "[r]apidly, we approach the final phase of the extensions of man—the technological simulation of consciousness, when the creative process of knowing will be collectively and corporately extended to the whole of human society" is perhaps the most celebrated of these attempts to define the new media landscape.[2] From the first, these changes in media have been understood to challenge our usual distinction between truth and lie. Guy Debord's *The Society of the Spectacle* (1967), for example, asserts that "the spectacle, though it turns reality on its head, is itself a product of real activity. Likewise, lived reality suffers the material assaults of the spectacle's mechanisms of contemplation, incorporating the spectacular order and lending that order positive support. Each side therefore has its share of objectivity reality. And every concept, as it takes its place on one side or the other, has no foundation apart from its transformation into its opposite: reality erupts within the spectacle, and the spectacle is real."[3]

Daniel Boorstin's *The Image: A Guide to Pseudo-Events in America* (1961) is even more explicit in linking media changes to the complication of truth. Boorstin defines a pseudo-event as planned, "primarily . . . for the immediate purpose of being reported or reproduced," which frequently functions as self-fulfilling: "The hotel's thirtieth-anniversary celebration, by saying that the hotel is a distinguished institution, actually makes it one."[4] Boorstin's primary critique is of news media, which he feels has allowed the demand for entertainment to blur the line between invented and genuine events, but he recognizes that the shift is part of a larger American culture: "I am thinking not only of advertising and public relations and political rhetoric, but of all the activities which purport to inform and comfort and improve and educate and elevate us: the work of our best journalists, our most enterprising book publishers, our most energetic manufacturers and merchandisers, our most successful entertainers, our best guides to world travel, and our most influential leaders in foreign relations" (5). Boorstin's analysis is by now old hat, and yet it reminds us how long the same basic feeling that contemporary

---

2. Marshall McLuhan, *Understanding Media: The Extensions of Man* (1964; repr. Cambridge, MA: MIT Press, 1994), 3–4.

3. Guy Debord, *The Society of the Spectacle,* trans. Donald Nicholson-Smith (1967; repr. New York: Zone Books, 1994), 14.

4. Daniel J. Boorstin, *The Image: A Guide to Pseudo-Events in America* (1961; repr. New York: Atheneum, 1975), 11, 12.

reality has become fictional has been with us. In his stringent critique of Jean Baudrillard, Christopher Norris pauses to admit that "one could hardly deny that Baudrillard's diagnosis does have a bearing on our present situation in the 'advanced' Western democracies. That is to say, it speaks directly to a widespread sense that we are living in a world of pervasive unreality, a world where perceptions are increasingly shaped by mass-media imagery, political rhetoric and techniques of wholesale disinformation that substitute for any kind of reasoned public debate."[5]

When philosophers and social critics claim that contemporary, postmodern culture is fictional because our sense of reality has been consciously manipulated, they are adopting one out of a variety of other ways that they might define the fictional. Although the popular imagination sometimes associates fiction and the merely untruthful, we need to circumscribe our definition of fiction carefully if we are to understand the unique position of fictionality in contemporary American culture. As Michael Riffaterre opines at the beginning of *Fictional Truth* (1990), "The only reason that the phrase 'fictional truth' is not an oxymoron, as 'fictitious truth' would be, is that fiction is a genre whereas lies are not. Being a genre, it rests on conventions, of which the first and perhaps only one is that fiction specifically, but not always explicitly, excludes the intention to deceive."[6] I am interested not so much in the apparent shift in our sense of reality—a shift that books aimed at a popular audience like Anderson's characterize—as in the conventions and the institutions behind them that define the *discursive* uses of fiction. In other words, what is accomplished today by arguing about fictionality? Failing to define the work of fictionality in these sorts of critiques of postmodernism dooms us, I think, to very slippery terminology that has often made these critiques either circular or misinformed. An example of the sort of dead end that I have in mind is provided by Hayden White, in an essay on the "modernist event" for a recent collection on contemporary history. Surveying recent critical as well as popular history, White sees only the loss of categories:

> But the dissolution of the event as a basic unit of temporal occurrence and building-block of history undermines the very concept of factuality and threatens therewith the distinction between realistic and merely imaginary discourse. This dissolution undermines the founding presuppositions

---

5. Christopher Norris, *What's Wrong with Postmodernism: Critical Theory and the Ends of Philosophy* (Baltimore: Johns Hopkins University Press, 1990), 171.
6. Michael Riffaterre, *Fictional Truth* (Baltimore: Johns Hopkins University Press, 1990), 1.

of Western realism: the *opposition* between fact and fiction. Modernism resolves the problems posed by traditional realism, namely, how to represent reality realistically, by simply abandoning the ground on which realism is construed as an opposition between fact and fiction.[7]

In characterizing postmodernity as the dissolution of the line between fact and fiction, White seems to block a serious discussion of how the discourse of fictionality can continue to be used in critical and creative writing. Even a quick glance at writing on postmodernism over the last two decades reveals that fictionality has continued to be a vital issue that generates a great deal of interest, debate, and, above all, writing. More productive than dismissing the opposition between fact and fiction is to ask what work the issue of fictionality does today.

What Is Fictionality?

In 1967, on the cusp of postmodern culture, Frank Kermode remarked, "nobody, so far as I know, has ever tried to relate the theory of literary fictions to the theory of fictions in general."[8] Although the years since have produced just such a theory, Kermode's handling of the concept of the fictional suggests the dynamics of the term. For Kermode, the fictional must be distinguished from myth: "Fictions can degenerate into myths whenever they are not consciously held to be fictive" (39). Fiction is defined here as something we are always aware to be untrue. Because myths imply belief, they need no other justification. Not so for fiction: "Fictions are for finding things out, and they change as the needs of sense-making change. Myths are agents of stability, fictions the agents of change" (39). Kermode neatly brings together two key components of fictionality: the irony that seems to come with it, as we say or consider obviously untrue things, and the fact that fictionality must have some purpose beyond itself. While one needs no reason to believe something, one quite clearly needs a reason to entertain the untrue.

---

7. Hayden White, "The Modernist Event," in *The Persistence of History: Cinema, Television, and the Modern Event*, ed. Vivian Sobchack (New York: Routledge, 1996), 18. Although White's focus seems to be on modernism, he makes clear that "this aspect of modernism . . . informs the creation of the new genres, in both written and visual form, of post-modernist, para-historical representation" (18).

8. Frank Kermode, *The Sense of an Ending: Studies in the Theory of Fiction* (London: Oxford University Press, 1967), 36.

In distinguishing the fictional from the mythical, Kermode argues that fictionality performs a service of some sort. This definition of fiction as an intellectual tool has its most thorough articulation in Hans Vaihinger's influential *The Philosophy of "As If"* (1911). He introduces his study of the "theoretical, practical and religious fictions of mankind" with a definition of fiction based on its productive effect: "By fictive activity in logical thought is to be understood the production and use of logical methods, which, with the help of accessory concepts . . . seek to attain the objects of thought."[9] Vaihinger goes on to describe reason itself in instrumental terms: "It must be remembered that the object of the world of ideas as a whole is not the portrayal of reality—this would be an utterly impossible task—but rather to provide us with an *instrument for finding our way about more easily in this world*" (15[10]). Like Kermode, Vaihinger describes fiction as a tool for accomplishing something. Vaihinger makes clear that fiction functions as a tool when he distinguishes it from the merely hypothetical. As two concepts associated with modern methods of finding out about the world, these are easily confused. And yet, for Vaihinger, the fictional does not depend upon eventual proof. Indeed, fictions are intentionally simplified or falsified for the purpose of inquiry: "They [fictions] are, or at least should be, accompanied by the consciousness that they do not correspond to reality and that they *deliberately substitute a fraction of reality for the complete range of causes and effects*" (20). One of Vaihinger's more straightforward examples of such fictions is in law: "in the new German Commerical Code, Art. 347, we find a provision that goods not returned to the sender within the proper time are to be regarded *as if* the recipient has definitely authorized and accepted them" (35). It is because such legal maneuvers are fictions and not hypotheses that eventually proving, for instance, that in fact the recipient has not authorized the receipt of goods makes no difference to the application of the law in a particular case.

For Vaihinger, fictionality is particularly modern and specifically associated with modern science: "The scientifically valuable fiction is only a recent growth. If the hypothesis, which is, after all, a very simple method, a form of thought lying near the surface, has but recently been correctly applied and developed in science, and if we have had to wait for modern science to show us how hypotheses are to be built up and how valuable they are for serious research, we may assume that the fiction, which presupposes the

---

9. Hans Vaihinger, *The Philosophy of "As If": A System of the Theoretical, Practical and Religious Fictions of Mankind*, trans. C. K. Ogden, 2d ed. (1911; London: Routledge & Kegan Paul, 1935), 12.
10. All italics in quotations are original.

artificial and sophisticated form of thought, came into us much later" (135). Vaihinger echoes Kermode, in fact, when he associates fiction used in these scientific terms with "a freedom and independence of logical thought . . . an emancipation from ordinary prejudices, such that we can only expect to find a productive utilization of this method where the logical function has really freed itself from the idea of its identity with reality, and where it is more or less aware of the chasm between its own operations and the actual state of affairs" (136). Vaihinger traces the development of the fictional through the Greeks into the modern use in law, mathematics, and science.

Fictionality, then, depends on a certain way of thinking about how we come to know the world. Behind any theory or use of fictionality is an implied epistemology that has to explain why making something up can be useful. Debates about this issue are, of course, usually traced back to Plato and Aristotle and carried forward into Renaissance attempts to justify the value of poetry as a means of moral instruction. Central in this genealogy and typical of the problems of defining the issue of fictionality in ahistorical terms is Sir Philip Sidney's "The Defense of Poesie" (1595). There is, in fact, some reason to be suspicious about whether Sidney himself is actually discussing the fictional when he is describing poetry. Sidney's address to the question of whether poets are liars is both the best-known part of this famous essay, and the point at which his departure from the fictional is clearest:

> To the second [charge against poets] therefore, that they should be the principall lyers, I answere *Paradoxically*, but truly, I think truly: that of all writers under the Sunne, the *Poet* is the least lyer: and though he wold, as a *Poet* can scarcely be a lyer. The *Astronomer* with his cousin the *Geometrician*, can hardly escape, when they take upon them to measure the height of the starres. How often thinke you do the *Phisitians* lie, when they averre things good for sicknesses, which afterwards send *Charon* a great number of soules drownd in a potion, before they come to his Ferrie? And no lesse of the rest, which take upon them to affirme. Now for the *Poet*, he nothing affirmeth, and therefore never lieth: for as I take it, to lie, is to affirme that to bee true, which is false. So as the other *Artistes*, and especially the *Historian*, affirming manie things, can in the clowdie knowledge of mankinde, hardly escape from manie lies.[11]

Sidney here distinguishes poetry, which makes no truth claim, from history and science, which do. What is remarkable about this well-known passage is

11. Sir Philip Sidney, *The Prose Works of Sir Philip Sidney*, ed. Albert Feuillerat, vol. 3 (Cambridge: Cambridge University Press, 1963), 28–29.

that lies are defined by Sidney not as intentional falsehoods, but rather as a deviation from the facts of the world. Errors, in other words, are lies. Indeed, it seems clear for Sidney that no science or history can ever be true—that is, safe from being turned into a lie—because of the "clowdie knowledge of mankinde." Because no fact can be certain, knowledge about the world is always subject to sliding into lie. Hence poetry appears to be an especially important form of knowing and transmitting moral lessons.

In suggesting that there is ultimately no truth to which the poetic can be contrasted, I would argue that Sidney cannot be said to have a theory of fictionality. Fictionality depends on an understanding how we know the world, and part of that understanding depends on our ability to sort the true from the false. Steven Shapin notes that in the seventeenth century scientific inquiry and proof was imagined in very different ways from today. According to Shapin, at the heart of such inquiry was the figure of the gentleman: "The concept and practice of truth were inscribed at the heart of traditional honor culture. The social practices mobilized around the recognition of truthfulness, the injunction to truth-telling, and the interpretation of why gentlemen were, and ought to be, truthful were central to the very notions of both honor and gentility."[12] Because of this equation between truth and gentility through the insistence on honor, only the gentleman could claim the truth. Not only does this understanding of truth exclude a wide range of observations and inquiries, but it defines the nature of scientific study along the model of polite conversation: "Conversation is not viewed as the means to an end, rather its pleasurable continuance *is* the end to which artful human endeavor strives. An unproblematically existing world—indeed, 'any world'—is 'sufficient to provide the indispensable environment for friendship as long as it accords with the requirements of pleasant company.' The conception of truth appropriate to conversational settings *is* a tolerant one. Matters that 'are the case' need only be so 'for all practical purposes.'"[13] This understanding of science as endless conversation has a great deal in common with Sidney's defense of poetry, where the truth of observations is constantly being redefined. Shapin notes, among other things, that this model of conversation places far more emphasis on believability than on verifiability. Shapin cites Lord Chesterfield's admonition to avoid the fabulous: "Chesterfield said that if he himself had actually witnessed anything 'so very extraordinary as to be

---

12. Stephen Shapin, *A Social History of Truth: Civility and Science in Seventeenth-Century England* (Chicago: University of Chicago Press, 1994), 67.

13. Ibid., 119; citing Niklas Luhmann, "The Differentiation of Advances in Knowledge: The Genesis of Science," in *Society and Knowledge: Contemporary Perspectives in the Sociology of Knowledge*, ed. Nico Stehr and Volker Meja (New Brunswick, NJ: Transaction Books, 1984), 103–48.

almost incredible, I would keep it to myself, rather than, by telling it, give any one body to doubt for one minute my veracity.'"[14] Such an understanding of truthfulness as likelihood clearly runs counter to our modern understanding of scientific inquiry. If, as Shapin argues, the seventeenth century does not share our modern understanding of truth as objective, observable by all, and disprovable, then we can say that it cannot have an understanding of fictionality as an invention that intentionally departs from the true. Thus Sidney frames his defense of poetry in terms of poetry's affirming nothing rather than as an intentional departure from the true. According to the more narrow definition of fictionality that I am using, Sidney does not have a theory of fictionality because he does not have a compatible understanding of truthfulness.

If my more narrow definition of fictionality is accepted it will mean rejecting some recent attempts to speak about fictionality as a transcultural embrace of revolutionary creativity. I have in mind, in particular, recent studies that cast fictionality as a force that runs throughout the history of literature. Wolfgang Iser, for example, follows critics like Kermode in defining fiction as the self-conscious departure from the true: "Unlike such non-literary fictions [such as 'the founding of institutions, societies, and world pictures'], the literary text reveals its own fictionality."[15] Fictionality here forces us to reflect back on our traditional ways of thinking about the world: "Self-disclosure of fictionality puts the world represented in brackets, thereby indicating the presence of a purpose that proves to be the observability of the world represented. Observability requires a stance, the necessity of which causes attitudes to be adopted by the recipient, who is made to react to what he or she is given to observe. Thus the purpose of the self-disclosing fiction comes to light" (16). Although Iser's claim may apply to modern fictions, he is eager to trace its lineage back to the Renaissance pastoral: "What perhaps makes pastoral poetry unique in literary history is the fact that it thematizes the act of fictionalizing, thereby enabling literary fictionality to be vividly perceived. This perception forms the basis of pastoralism as a literary system no longer bounded by genres, and thus it seems plausible that pastoral poetry lost its place of importance at the moment when the function of literary fictionality no longer needed to be exhibited" (24–25). I have suggested, however, that so broad a concept of doubling fails to account for the cultural assumptions about truthfulness and knowability that define the conditions of

---

14. Shapin, *Social History of Truth*, 81; citing Philip Dormer Stanhope, Earl of Chesterfield, *Letters to His Son and Others* (London: J. M. Dent, Everyman's Library, 1984), 149.

15. Wolfgang Iser, *The Fictive and the Imaginary: Charting Literary Anthropology* (Baltimore: Johns Hopkins University Press, 1993), 12.

fictionality.[16] Fictionality and the imagination must be located, instead, in the very precise contours of modern thinking about truth and the knowability of the world.

Fictionality as a Literary Institution

Fictionality functions, then, as one tool of inquiry. And yet, when critics characterize postmodern culture as more suffused with fiction than it used to be, it is clear that they are not trying to characterize a shift in our methods of scientific or legal thought. Quite the contrary, the claim that our contemporary sense of reality has been "fictionalized" instead suggests a dangerous movement of entertainment and aesthetics into an area of contemporary life where it does not belong. Raymond Federman begins his introduction to the influential anthology *Surfiction* (1975) by summarizing the "usual clichés" about the fictionality of contemporary life: "Writing about fiction today, one could begin with the usual clichés—that the novel is dead; that fiction is no longer possible because real life happens, everyday, in the streets of our cities, in the spectacular hijacking of planes, on the Moon, in Vietnam, in China (when Nixon stands on the Great Wall of China), and of course on television (during the news broadcasts)."[17] Federman goes on to suggest that this state of fictionality is a reason not to reject the novel but rather to embrace a particular form of experimentalism that "exposes the fictionality of reality" (7). When he cites the novel-is-dead cliché, Federman is drawing on an idea that had circulated within American literary culture for several decades. Alain Robbe-Grillet's dismissal of the traditional novel was published in translation in the *Evergreen Review* in 1957, and the idea that the novel is dead becomes a convenient straw man upon which writers and critics will draw for the next twenty years.[18] Ten years after Robbe-Grillet, Louis Rubin uses the "Curious Death of the Novel" as an occasion to criticize reviewers who dismiss contemporary writing because they come to it expecting to see more of the same modernist writing by Joyce, Faulkner, and Proust.[19]

    16. So it is, too, that Luiz Costa Lima's attempt in *The Dark Side of Reason: Fictionality and Power*, trans. Paulo Henriques Britto (Stanford: Stanford University Press, 1992), to locate fictionality in the rise of late medieval subjectivity is historically too broad.

    17. Raymond Federman, "Surfiction—Four Propositions in Form of an Introduction," *Surfiction: Fiction Now . . . and Tomorrow*, ed. Raymond Federman (Chicago: Swallow Press, 1975), 5–6.

    18. Alain Robbe-Grillet, "A Fresh Start for Fiction," *Evergreen Review* 1, no. 3 (1957): 97–104.

    19. Louis D. Rubin, Jr., *The Curious Death of the Novel: Essays in American Literature* (Baton Rouge: Louisiana State University Press, 1967).

The fictionality that Federman and others associate with contemporary culture and with the apparent obsolescence of the traditional novel arises not from a change in scientific or legal inquiry, but from the apparent proliferation of the spectacle. When Federman describes the blurring of reality and fiction, it is clear that he has in mind a kind of media-saturated event. Stephen Paul Miller has argued that "[t]he seventies was the decade when Americans brought self-surveillance to a high level. The decade began with Nixon spying on Ellsberg 'spying' on Johnson—with a culture and a counterculture fearful of one another's external surveillance, and it ended with virtually all aspects of American culture adapting themselves to a barely questioned corporate reality. It was almost as if Richard Nixon's overt surveillance and self-surveillance were ingested by the nation as a whole during Watergate and shortly thereafter internalized."[20] Watching and being watched, according to this characterization, stand behind the general feeling that life has become more fictional. Much the same feeling is implied by Boorstin's and Debord's early studies of the media spectacle. What strikes me as interesting in these characterizations of contemporary culture is that the death of the novel and the expansion of fictionality continue to function for these writers as comprising a fascinating theme and, in particular, an occasion for their own arguments about writing and the literary institutions that surround it. Throughout all of these characterizations of contemporary culture as more fictional is the underlying belief that fictionality becomes noticeable when it moves out of its traditional boundaries. Federman is quite explicit about this when he suggests that this expansion of fictionality in a contemporary society of spectacle means that "life has become much more interesting, much more incredible, much more dramatic than what the moribund novel can possibly offer."[21] To some extent, that fictionality becomes noticeable when it appears where we don't expect it should cause no surprise; however it also seems clear to me from this passage that this expansion of fictionality is being made to do certain types of rhetorical work by Federman. For him, the expansion of fictionality is an opportunity to reconsider the nature of literary institutions and our expectations about the traditional referentiality of realistic fiction. In many ways, this shift in topic is remarkable, since the connection between the two ideas seems quite tenuous once we pause to consider it: an increasing presence of spectacle in contemporary life means (according to Federman) that writing should become less beholden to mimesis. The logic of the connection seems to rely on the only partially stated belief that

20. Stephen Paul Miller, *The Seventies Now: Culture as Surveillance* (Durham: Duke University Press, 1999), 1.
21. Federman, *Surfiction*, 6.

the traditional institutional and disciplinary boundaries separating news and entertainment, fiction and politics have become blurred. Once this happens, literary "fiction" is free to take on different tasks than it traditionally addresses.

Fictionality becomes in contemporary discourse, then, an occasion to rethink institutional and disciplinary boundaries. Although Federman's appeal to fictionality may seem idiosyncratic, I would argue that fictionality routinely raises such questions, and that in fact precisely this reference back to its institutional context is what connects the scientific and literary appeals to fictionality. Vaihinger describes classifications as "semi-fictions" because they have a different relation to truth: they are, he says, "conscious mistakes" because they serve purely practical purposes.[22] Such classifications seem to me the very essence of institutions, which create categories to make possible institutionally sanctioned behaviors (from scientific observation to bureaucratic red tape).[23] In fact, in the most sophisticated handling of the concept by new historicist critics, fictionality works to reorder disciplinary boundaries. Lennard Davis frames his influential discussion of fictionality in the early novel as a struggle between genres. For Davis, the novel emerges against the backdrop of history and news:

> Authors who denied their authorship and insisted on the factuality of their works were, I would argue, attempting to make a statement about the real difficulties of finding their place in the midst of a discourse that was in the active process of rupture. As the news/novels discourse grew into specialized subdiscourses of journalism, fiction, and history, novelists still saw themselves as part of a news-synthesizing and disseminating system, but the works they were writing, while embodying the qualities of recentness, immediacy, voyeurism, memorialization, preservation, transcription, and dissemination, no longer could be seen as news.[24]

The relationship between news and novels is a question not only of genre but also of different ways of granting authority to the writer, and different ways

---

22. Vaihinger, *Philosophy of "As If,"* 80.

23. I have in mind here Foucault's description of the "formation of objects" in *The Archeology of Knowledge and the Discourse on Language,* trans. A. M Sheridan Smith (New York: Pantheon, 1972). As he explains there, social objects (his example is madness) depend on "authorities of delimitation" (41) that then make possible "systems according to which the different 'kinds of madness' are divided, contrasted, related, regrouped, classified, derived from one another as objects of psychiatric discourse" (42).

24. Lennard J. Davis, *Factual Fictions: The Origins of the English Novel* (Philadelphia: University of Pennsylvania Press, 1996), 191–92.

of evaluating the work produced. Davis notes that one of the reasons that novelistic discourse expands is because of the threat of legal action against purveyors of news (100). Likewise, observes Davis, the rise of the novel depends on the growing legitimacy of print as a "guarantor of immortality, fame, and public existence" (138).

Much as Federman does, Davis uses fictionality as a lens through which to describe the shift in disciplinary and institutional boundaries. Thus, while changes in fictionality reflect different ideas about the true and the invented, debates about fictionality themselves—in cultural critiques, for example, that bewail the loss of confidence in reality—are ways of sorting out relations between disciplines. If this is the case, we can reinterpret Clifford Siskin's influential discussion of how literary writing and "novelism" came to function as a cultural model for understanding the nature of writing in general. Siskin's *The Work of Writing* examines the proliferation of discourse in and about the novel in the late eighteenth and early nineteenth centuries, especially in the context of changes in the nature of work: "What changed—strikingly and fundamentally—were that society's ways of knowing and of working; the eighteenth and early nineteenth centuries in Britain saw the simultaneous advent of modern disciplinarity, on the one hand, and modern professionalism, on the other."[25] According to Siskin, literary writing—"writing about writing"—comes to function as an important site where changing attitudes about writing and, by implication, about these shifts in labor and professionalism, are worked through. Siskin describes novelism as "the now habitual subordination of writing to the novel" (172). More specifically, he argues that "[b]y ordering our experiences with an understanding of writing, novelism—as the discourse of and about novels—produces and reproduces private, public, and professional norms" (173).

In the framework of my discussion, we might say that Siskin's novelism is another way of using fictionality to reflect on disciplinary boundaries. Siskin notes the paradox of novelism's social usefulness: "The tendency *not* to engage writing as a productive, material practice arose, in fact, from the very set of social relations to which, in the eighteenth century, writing became indispensably related: the reorganization of work into mental versus physical labor" (24). The novel is valuable precisely because it both reflects on the productivity of writing while at the same time putting the practical concerns of work and materialism at a distance; the novel is, as Siskin remarks, "safe" (26). Key to its ability to reflect these concerns in a safe way is the novel's fictionality:

25. Clifford Siskin, *The Work of Writing: Literature and Social Change in Britain, 1700–1830* (Baltimore: Johns Hopkins University Press, 1998), 2.

When certain disciplines *"fiction" in writing*—and thus enact the imperative of improvement as the transformative discovery of "truth"—we call it *scientificity*. But what do we call it when other disciplines *write fiction*—and thus enact the imperative of improvement as . . . amusing occasions for self development? *Novelism*, I am suggesting, is a term that can help us to come to terms with our disciplinary fates. By paralleling it to *scientificity*, we can see that just as, within the sciences, the "fiction" has been subsumed within the "writing," make the scientific disciplines appear as simply hard and factual, and thus consequential, so, within the humanities, "writing" has been subsumed within the "fiction," casting those disciplines as soft and ambiguous, and thus less relevant to the "real" world. (188–89)

Siskin suggests that, while fictionality may have a function within a wide range of texts, in literary writing fictionality is given a metonymic function for the whole. More generally, the disciplines that grow up around this kind of writing will reflect more general forces that shape the process of sorting writing and defining the relevance of imagined states of affairs as a way of knowing.

We can say, then, that when critics and philosophers describe contemporary culture as more fictional than it used to be, they are at least in part suggesting the awareness of institutional structures at work within the representation of reality. As Siskin suggests, fictionality comes to stand as a marker for a whole series of debates about the institutions that shape the creation, transmission, and reception of information.[26] This anxiety about knowing translates into arguments about the nature of literary study. Over the last three decades, the nature of literary study has been redefined by the models that it has borrowed from other fields—first the structuralism borrowed from linguistics and anthropology in the 1960s, and more recently the history, sociology, and gender theory borrowed in the 1980s and '90s. At the same time, however, literary theory has become an increasingly important flashpoint in debates about the nature of contemporary culture. Frederic Jameson has argued more generally that the interest in theory represents a

---

26. In this regard we might link the recent popularity of political books accusing others of spreading lies—like Al Franken's *Lies (and the Lying Liars Who Tell Them): A Fair and Balanced Look at the Right* (New York: Dutton, 2003) and Ann Coulter's *Slander: Liberal Lies about the American Right* (New York: Crown, 2002)—as reflecting doubt about our traditional ways of verifying information and the disciplinary authority of who gets to define truth. As broader reflection on this trend, see Cass Sunstein's *Republic.com* (Princeton, NJ: Princeton University Press, 2001), which argues that the Internet supports the splintering of public sphere into independent subgroups who need not engage in political discourse that does not reflect their personal disposition.

breakdown in traditional disciplinary structures and boundaries: "A generation ago there was still a technical discourse of professional philosophy—the great systems of Sartre or the phenomenologists, the work of Wittgenstein or analytical or common language philosophy—alongside which one could still distinguish that quite different discourse of the other academic disciplines—of political science, for example, or sociology or literary criticism. Today, increasingly, we have a kind of writing simply called 'theory' which is all or none of those things at once."[27] Jameson equates the "dedifferentiation of fields" (73) with postmodernism. This dedifferentiation leads in a fairly straightforward way to undermining the authority of particular disciplines. Steven Connor notes the ironies of disciplinary specialization by literary critics during the twentieth century, seeing both the loss of belief in a general "public sphere" to which literature is relevant and an expansion of the "power and influence of literary and cultural institutions."[28] Connor explains this duality:

> If criticism has withdrawn in one direction from the close, enraptured study of patterns of alliteration in Spenser or the details of Manet's brushwork, then it has markedly expanded its competence to talk about pornography, pinball and the semiotics of the privy, in allegiances between subjects that share a body of legitimating theoretical material. There are, or have been, real gains and challenges in this "deconstruction" of disciplinary boundaries, but, separated from a much more intense determination to interfere with and reconstruct the functions of the university, or of the academic system as a whole, these can become merely incidental mutations in a system that is becoming increasingly operationalized. (15)

Although the phenomenon of the canon debates of the early 1990s has received a number of different interpretations, I would suggest that one part of those debates is (implicitly) about the nature and cultural role of fictionality. Indeed, if we consider Harold Bloom's foray into the canon question, *How to Read and Why* (2000), one of the things that is most remarkable is how important fictionality is by its absence. Bloom defines the value of reading as essentially selfish, clearly marginalizing the questions of history and culture that most critics have found compelling over the last two decades: "Ultimately we read—as Bacon, Johnson, and Emerson agree—in order to

---

27. Fredric Jameson, *The Cultural Turn: Selected Writings on the Postmodern, 1983-1998* (London: Verso, 1998), 3.
28. Steven Connor, *Postmodernist Culture: An Introduction to Theories of the Contemporary*, 2d ed. (London: Blackwell, 1997), 11, 12.

strengthen the self, and to learn its authentic interests. We experience such argumentations as pleasure, which may be why aesthetic values have always been deprecated by social moralists, from Plato through our current campus Puritans. The pleasures of reading indeed are selfish rather than social. You cannot directly improve anyone else's life by reading better or more deeply."[29] Bloom describes unmediated conversation between author and reader: "find what comes near to you that can be put to the use of weighing and considering, and that addresses you as though you share the one nature, free of time's tyranny. Pragmatically that means, first find Shakespeare, and let him find you" (22). This is an image of reading without fictionality, without the issue of the hypothetical or the invented, without a concern for how the created becomes truthful. And it is precisely by pushing the question of the fictional out of the debate about literary meaning that Bloom hopes to recover a nondisciplinary understanding of reading. For all that Bloom's book is a disciplining artifact (it teaches the reader "how to read" after all), the assumption in such passages is that true reading is a movement beyond any particular methodology to a direct understanding. In books like Bloom's, it is clear that literary study is being made to stand in for a number of shifts in American culture that it has almost no causal connection to, and which it exemplifies in only very tangential ways. The link between literary study and the insidious cultural malaise implied by books like Allan Bloom's *The Closing of the American Mind* (1987) should be obvious by now: literature is the discipline that studies the use and nature of fictionality, and when fictionality seems to be expanding within a culture, it is literary studies that deserves the blame.[30] This is why, it seems to me, that some of the most broadly accepted responses to the traditionalist position embodied by both Blooms is Gerald Graff's contention that teachers of literature should "teach the conflicts" between canons and interpretations.[31] In other words, Graff would have us foreground precisely the disciplinary structure that *How to Read and Why* ignores.

What is especially paradoxical about this equation between literary studies and the reckless use of fictionality is that fictionality is best defined by the operation of an institution that legitimizes the creation of invented stories.

29. Harold Bloom, *How to Read and Why* (New York: Scribner, 2000), 22.
30. Allan Bloom, *The Closing of the American Mind* (New York: Simon and Schuster, 1987).
31. Gerald Graff, *Beyond the Culture Wars: How Teaching the Conflicts Can Revitalize American Education* (New York: W. W. Norton, 1992); as an example of Graff's influence, note Gregory Jay's general focus on conflicts in *American Literature and the Culture Wars* (Ithaca, NY: Cornell University Press, 1997).

If there are many such institutions currently operating within American culture, the interest in fictionality in contemporary literary study, ironically, reveals to the point at which this field is most interdisciplinary. Literary studies, in other words, is exemplary within the American cultural landscape by being particularly eclectic in its disciplinary nature. Literary study thus becomes most representative of fictionality when it ceases to be any one distinct field of study. This is implied by Samuel Weber in *Institution and Interpretation:*

> It is no accident that what we call the crisis of professionalism has, at least within the academic world, been felt with special intensity in and around the discipline of literary studies. Ever since the New Criticism, the work of the literary critic has been constantly confronted with the ambivalent process of symbolization and of signification, inasmuch as criticism has tended to define itself more as a practice of reading and of reinscription, than as one entailing the acquisition or transmission of knowledge.... If this is one cause of that lack of consensus and of scientificity that characterizes the unruly discipline of literary studies, it may also turn out to have been a unique opportunity to pursue questions that other, more homogeneous disciplines are far less willing or able to raise: above all, the question of the conditions of consensus and of dissension, and of their relation to language.[32]

Literary studies are at the most powerful in raising these sorts of questions about knowledge and disciplinarity, when they are addressing the issue of the fictional.

American Fictionality

Fictionality reflects broad cultural issues that have special power in American literary culture. Indeed, in his influential history of the profession, Gerald Graff notes that from its inception the study of "American literature" in the university has been marked by heightened disciplinary awareness. Graff notes that from the outset "[a]cademic Americanists tended to be more sensitive than their antiquarian colleagues to critical trends outside the university."[33] Early studies of American literature imagined the transformation of

---

32. Samuel Weber, *Institution and Interpretation: Expanded Edition* (Stanford: Stanford University Press, 2001), 160.

33. Gerald Graff, *Professing Literature: An Institutional History* (Chicago: University of Chicago Press, 1987), 213.

literary studies: "the initial aspirations of American literature studies were tied to a quest for cultural synthesis" (215). Although Graff notes that American literature did not succeed in creating a "reorganization of knowledge" (224), it is clear that American literature as a field of study within the university has always had a particular interdisciplinary quality that seems naturally to raise questions about the boundaries between institutions.

The interdisciplinarity of American literary study reflects in part the tendency in America to view fiction as part of an individual's economic life. Indeed some of the best work on American literature of the last two decades has focused on the role of the marketplace and capitalism in the formation of modern ideas of fictionality. In *The Incorporation of America* (1982), Alan Trachtenberg notes the tension between idealism and market forces in American realism: "Although gentility had strengthened its hold on institutions of education and art, publishing and philanthropy, nevertheless critics and editors frequently took a defensive tone, challenged as much by new currents of art and literature as by vulgar politics and business. 'Realism' seemed such a threat, the term naming not so much a single consistent movement as a tendency among some painters and writers to depict contemporary life without moralistic condescension."[34] In William Dean Howells's criticism, in particular, "The 'real' his touchstone of value, 'false' became his deepest term of disdain, directed especially against those 'innutritious' novels 'that merely tickle our prejudices and lull our judgment'" (185). Thus, as a response to sentimentalism, realism "was a corrective to faulty vision, a way of disclosing what is really *there*" (185). In this environment, the image of the artist as a businessman selling his wares on the open market plays a surprisingly important role. Trachtenberg notes that "Howells was especially vexed by the apparent anomaly of serious literature, fictions with truth-telling claims, in a culture ruled by business values, by images of success and failure" (193). In the end, Howells's attitudes prove more ambiguous: "For the burden of Howells's essay is that the artist *must* be a businessman in a business world, must sell his wares not as a wage slave but as an independent entrepreneur, directly into a competitive market. This is precisely the goal of Howells's realism: to take a competitive stance among competing modes, and yet insist on it as the only true mode, the only serious fiction. Thus, Howells's realism bears the mark of the very competition it condemns as alien to art and the instinct of equality" (196–97). Fiction's vocation to address the real, Trachtenberg argues, is formulated by Howells as a matter of market competition.

34. Alan Trachtenberg, *The Incorporation of America: Culture and Society in the Gilded Age* (New York: Hill and Wang, 1982), 182.

This tradition of treating fiction as a business functioning within the "marketplace of ideas" is an important framework for the development of contemporary uses of fictionality. Walter Benn Michaels has explained the implications of this way of thinking about American writing in a way that helps us to see clearly its relationship to the issue of fictionality. According to him, capitalist economies link economic success with self-representation: "These [economic] fears and desires were themselves made available by consumer capitalism, partly because a capitalist economy made it possible for lower-class women to wear nice clothes and for middle-class men to lose their jobs, but more importantly because the logic of capitalism linked the loss of those jobs to a failure of self-representation and linked the desirability of those women to the possibility of mimesis."[35] If competing on the job market involves effective self-representation, then producing consumer goods likewise involves representation, since "the logic of capitalism produces objects of desire only insofar as it produces subjects, since what makes the objects desirable is only the constitutive trace of subjectivity those objects bear" (20).

We can see the position of writing described by Michaels as inherently connected to modern American corporate culture. Indeed, Michaels's description of the "fictitious" nature of the corporation obviously shares many qualities with fictional writing: Michaels discusses a contemporary debate (1911) about the existence of the corporation by Arthur Machen:

> It asserts both that a corporation is "artificial" and that it is "imaginary or fictitious," when, in fact, what is "artificial is real, and not imaginary: an artificial lake is not an imaginary one"; it asserts that a corporation is "created by the state" and "fictitious," whereas something that has been created must be "real"; and it asserts that a corporation is "composed of natural persons" and is "imaginary or fictitious," whereas "neither in mathematics nor in philosophy nor in law can the sum of several actual, rational quantities produce an imaginary quantity." All these contradictions revolve around what is said to be "fictitious" in the corporal identity, and since what is "fictitious" is the characterization of the corporation as a person, the way to eliminate the contradiction, Machen argues, is to try to hang on to the notion of the corporation's real and independent existence while getting rid of the idea that this independent existence is personal. (198)

---

35. Walter Benn Michaels, *The Gold Standard and the Logic of Naturalism: American Literature at the Turn of the Century* (Berkeley: University of California Press, 1987), 19.

Michaels concludes that these same issues translate to creative writing; according to Frank Norris, "The poet, then, is the paradigm of the corporate person, writing the paradigmatic corporate act" (211–12). More generally, "The corporation, the 'artificial person,' incarnates (for better or for worse) this transcendence of the limits that make up 'natural' persons. And in doing so, it represents what I take to be the central problem for naturalism, the irruption in nature of the powerfully unnatural" (212). Writing in America at the turn of the century, then, is marked by concern with the fictional that is defined by issues of markets, consumers, and products.

When critics struggle to define the nature of literary study in America during the twentieth century, it is against the backdrop of the tendency in American culture to define literature instrumentally. Over the last two decades, for example, work on the Book-of-the-Month Club has shown that reading is imagined in terms of both self-improvement and efficiency. Joan Shelley Rubin's *The Making of Middlebrow Culture* describes the appeal to efficiency:

> As one advertisement for the supplement proclaimed, *Books* presented "the complete picture of current literature" so that readers would not "miss" the works they "want to read." Moreover, in much the same way Frederick Winslow Taylor's ideology of "scientific management" used the rhetoric of self-fulfillment to organize the individual for industrial productivity, this information served the priorities of a consumer society, in which "using books efficiently" . . . came before the slow accretion of liberal culture. "The less time you have for reading," the same ad phrased it, "the more important it is for you to consult 'BOOKS' in order that none of your reading time may be wasted."[36]

The language of "using" reading for the purposes of self-definition seems to me to be deeply connected to the theoretical issue of fictionality—in what circumstances can the untrue be useful? If we have any doubt that such concerns lurk just below the surface of much contemporary writing, we might note Robert Coover's introduction to the Fiction Collective anthology *Statements 2* (1977): "America is, at best, a strange place for an artist to work in. On the one hand there is the illusion of artistic freedom, constitutionally protected; on the other, there's the operative dogma of the marketplace: will it sell? In America, art—like everything else (knowledge, condoms, religion,

---

36. Joan Shelley Rubin, *The Making of Middlebrow Culture* (Chapel Hill: University of North Carolina Press, 1992), 69–70.

etc.)—is a product. The discovery of this is the capstone to the artist's alienation process in America."[37]

Fictionality and the Postmodern

We can say, then, that the issue of fictionality emerges as a component of contemporary, postmodern culture in America for reasons that reflect broad resonances between the speculative nature of the American nation and the problematic awareness of disciplinarity. When critics argue about postmodernity and its tortured relationship with "reality," they usually suggest some sort of shift in cultural or philosophical belief. According to this reading, we have lost confidence in our ability to grasp facts and history objectively because of the pernicious influence of deconstruction, and this loss of confidence defines postmodernity. I have suggested here, instead, that we should see the expansion of fictionality in contemporary culture as reflecting a variety of forces inherent to the nature of disciplines in America. By this definition, then, postmodernity is less a cause of the expansion of fictionality, or even an effect of our loss of confidence in reality, and more another name for the period in which the nature of disciplinarity emerges as an observable fact within American culture.

There are a number of reasons why this definition of postmodernity should be taken seriously, despite its departure from conventional ways of thinking about the period. The first reason is the fact that postmodernity—while frequently described in global terms—has distinctly American roots. As Hans Bertens notes, "The debate on postmodernism as it has been variously defined since the 1960s has its origins in American literary and cultural criticism and it is from there that it moves into all the other fields and disciplines where it has in the last twenty-five years [from 1995] manifested itself."[38] As Bertens suggests, to describe postmodernity as a general philosophical discovery equivalent to poststructuralism and embodied in Baudrillard is largely to miss the cultural framework in which it appeared. By my interpretation, it is natural that postmodernity should be imagined and defined in America first, since the conflict between disciplines that gives us our sense of fictionality and defines postmodernity seems to be especially strong in American culture.

In recent years, postmodernism's relation to the conflict of disciplines

---

37. Robert Coover, "Statement," in *Statements 2: New Fiction*, eds. Jonathan Baumbach and Peter Spielberg (New York: Fiction Collective, 1977), 7.
38. Hans Bertens, *The Idea of the Postmodern: A History* (London: Routledge, 1995), 17.

has been recognized. Discussing the concept of postmodernism, John Frow summarizes the challenge for a theory:

> There are two main reasons why the concept of postmodernism is logically incoherent. The first has to do with the question of exemplification. The literature on postmodernism is notorious for its contradictory assumptions, rarely made explicit, about what is contained in the set of the postmodern....
>
> The second, and related, area of incoherence concerns the problem of periodization.... [T]he concept of period has a totalizing force: it "depends upon the taxonomical privileging of one ensemble of cultural practices—identified as the distinctive or definitive one—over a plurality of others," and it assumes some logical affinity between these practices.[39]

These incoherences lead Frow to conclude that postmodernism as a concept makes sense less as an attempt to describe an historical event or group of objects, and more as a kind of discursive game. Frow writes, "the concept of the postmodern obeys a discursive rather than a descriptive necessity: its function is that of a logical operator, establishing categorical polarities which then allow—in a tautologous and self-justifying circuit—the construction of fictions of periodization and value, fictions that have no content other than the structure of binary opposition itself" (36). Postmodernism here is a kind of critical or cultural game, a form of debate with no end beyond itself.

What strikes me as more important about Frow's argument is that it helps us to explain why postmodernism is so relentlessly linked to the fictional. Indeed, even in the brief passage that I have quoted—and in a very offhand way—Frow suggests that these games played by critics of postmodernism are a matter of "the construction of fictions." While the language here may appear coincidental, it is telling, since it reminds us that the issue of fictionality appears when disciplinary boundaries are in question. It seems natural that Frow should describe theories of postmodernism as *fictions* because precisely the sort of disciplinary and institutional squabbling that characterizes these debates is the very thing to which fiction points. Postmodernism, then, is more fictional than previous periods not because we live in an age more suffused with entertainment and political spin—although these may be the case—but because it represents a time when the institutions that justify knowledge and that organize disciplines for creating and disseminating that knowledge are especially subject to debate.

39. John Frow, *Time and Commodity Culture: Essays in Cultural Theory and Postmodernity* (Oxford: Clarendon Press, 1997), 26–28; citing David Bennett, "Wrapping Up Postmodernism," *Textual Practice* 1, no. 3 (1987): 256.

INTRODUCTION

The Goals and Methods of This Project

My goal in this project is to describe the operation of fictionality in contemporary (post-1960) American fiction and culture. I have suggested why fictionality will emerge as a particularly powerful issue in literary studies. There is a great deal of irony in the particularly literary sources of contemporary fictionality, since the concept of the fictional will interest writers and critics precisely because it seems to draw into question the distinction between disciplines. It should be clear that this is not a study of contemporary ideas of creativity or imagination in general. Such a study would necessarily be cross-disciplinary and very broad indeed in its sources. Some of the best work on the concept of fictionality has been just this sort of project; Vaihinger's *Philosophy of "As If"* is the obvious example.[40] My goals in this book are more modest. As I have suggested, fictionality has had so powerful an influence on literary studies not because it is a cultural condition, but because it provides a way of talking about how disciplines produce knowledge and truth. While there may well be similarities between the models of fictionality that I am discussing in literary studies and inquiries in the hard or social sciences, for example, my interest is in tracing the literary roots of our thinking about fictionality.

I likewise have avoided any extended analysis of fictionality as a principle in media other than writing. Although the recent popularity of "reality television" might make this choice seem counterintuitive, for example, my interest is in how fictionality is imagined in relationship to literary institutions and disciplines. The appeal to "reality" in recent television shows like *Survivor* reflect changes in television demographics and economics, and in fact harks back to the live drama and quiz shows that have been part and parcel of television entertainment since its inception.[41] In other words, it seems to me that these shows have developed not by appealing to literary categories or by working to define institutional or disciplinary boundaries, but because of forces more direct and pragmatic. The types of nonliterary, game or filmic "texts" that I do discuss in this project—role-playing games and science fiction films, in particular—warrant the attention of this project only when they are framed by changes in literary institutions that they reflect or prompt.

40. When such work has been done in the past, it is frequently pitched at a general audience and more sweeping in its claims that is entirely convincing. For an example of this sort of work, see Mark Pesce, *The Playful World: How Technology Is Transforming Our Imagination* (New York: Ballantine, 2000).

41. James Friedman describes television as "real from the start" in his introduction to *Reality Squared: Televisual Discourse on the Real* (New Brunswick: Rutgers University Press, 2002).

My assumption in this study is that institutions are always multiple and in flux. It is for this reason that I have focused specifically on the metaphor of five "strands" of contemporary fictionality. I believe that literary institutions are in fact marked by the contention between several different ways of legitimating the fictional, and that the contention between these strands marks a larger struggle between central and peripheral positions in regards to contemporary literature. In using the term *position* I am of course invoking Pierre Bourdieu's work on institutions, which has been so influential over the last decade. Bourdieu describes art as reflecting institutional definitions, and suggests that the current art field produces the value of the work by locating it within a structure of social and economic forces: "The producer of the *value of the work of art* is not the artist but the field of production as a universe of belief which produces the value of the work of art as a *fetish* by producing the belief in the creative power of the artist."[42] Bourdieu specifically describes this field as a series of positions:

> The field is a network of objective relations (of domination or subordination, of complementarity or antagonism, etc.) between positions—for example, the position corresponding to a genre like the novel or to a subcategory like the society novel, or from another point of view, the position locating a review, a salon, or a circle as the gathering place of a group of producers. Each position is defined by its objective relationship with other positions, or, in other terms, by the system of relevant (meaning efficient) properties which allow it to be situated in relation to all others in the structure of the global distribution of properties. (231)

According to this way of thinking about institutions, artistic or literary quality is produced by institutions, and those institutions in turn define a variety of positions that may be adopted in relation to that quality and to other positions. Even cynical critics should recognize, however, that literature (more, perhaps, than other forms of art) plays a broader role within culture than merely as a relay within the circulation of symbolic value, which complicates any straightforward application of Bourdieu's theory of position making. Indeed, literary fiction constantly promises to move beyond the narrow confines of academic interest to address common readers and broad social topics. It is after all fiction, and not sculpture or painting, that gets dragged to the beach for summer reading, that prompts reading groups to sprout up and

---

42. Pierre Bourdieu, *The Rules of Art: Genesis and Structure of the Literary Field*, trans. Susan Emanuel (Stanford: Stanford University Press, 1995), 229.

that (for better or worse) routinely gets translated into movies. If our everyday reception of fiction is not innocent of literary institutions, an account of those institutional forces must recognize their liminal nature—the fact that fiction constantly promises to transcend its institutions. This is, after all, why canon debates as literary fiction invoke such passion.

In such cases, institutions influence our interaction with fiction in more subtle ways than Bourdieu's language of positions and force fields suggests. In particular, institutions work to define the material "stuff" of the culture that then seems to circulate without reference to those institutions. In *The Imaginary Institution of Society*, Cornelius Castoriadis describes how institutions "materialize" the whole society: "[A]t the same time or beyond the name, in totems, in the gods of the city, in the spatial and temporal extension of the person of the King, the institution is constituted, grows heavier and materializes, that posits the collectivity as existing, as a substance defined and enduring beyond its perishable molecules, and that replies to the question of its being and its identity by referring them to the symbols that unite it to *another* 'reality.'"[43] Castoriadis goes on to note that this "mythical" national identity "nonetheless proves more solid than any other reality" (148). The concept of the "civil imaginary," which has been used by a variety of critics interested in national identities, is deeply connected to the functioning of social institutions. As Castoriadis implies, the very function of the institution is to create such imaginary entities even at the moment when institutions seem to promise nothing but function ("institutions fill vital functions without which the existence of society is inconceivable" [116]). Institutions, in this sense, "cannot be reduced to the symbolic but they can exist only in the symbolic; they are impossible outside of a second-order symbolism" (117). The objects materialized by the institution become the means by which symbolism and function are joined, and thus best embody the institution as a whole. In this sense, as well, institutions are always on some level *fictional* in that they necessarily imagine objects and events. This is why, as I have suggested, fictionality and institutions are inherently connected.

Critics working on the nature of institutions have noted their problematic claims to permanence. Homer Brown, for example, describes a duality in the concept of institution: "Institution, then, designates at once an act, an action, a process and the product of that action or process—at once action and stasis, lingering effect, or remainder as such."[44] In large part this seems to be the case because institutions always presuppose a form of practice and

---

43. Cornelius Castoriadis, *The Imaginary Institution of Society*, trans. Kathleen Blamey (Cambridge, MA: MIT Press, 1987), 148.

44. Homer Obed Brown, *Institutions of the English Novel: From Defoe to Scott* (Philadelphia: University of Pennsylvania Press, 1997), 3.

behavior that they "institute." Indeed, elsewhere Bourdieu is more explicit in arguing that institutions are inherently linked to practices: "The theory of practice as practice insists, contrary to positivist materialism, that the objects of knowledge are constructed, not passively recorded, and, contrary to intellectualist idealism, that the principle of this construction is the system of structured, structuring dispositions, the *habitus,* which is constituted in practice and is always oriented towards practical functions."[45] The literary institutions through which the issue of fictionality is usually discussed reflect the same dynamics of position taking and are subject to the same sorts of change that come naturally with practice. I have in mind, then, an inquiry that reflects broadly Raymond Williams's influential account of culture in *Culture and Society:*

> The history of the idea of culture is a record of our reactions in thought and feeling, to the changed conditions of our common life. Our meaning of culture is a response to the events which our meanings of industry and democracy most evidently define. But the conditions were created and have been modified by men. Record of the events lies elsewhere, in our general history. The history of the idea of culture is a record of our meanings and our definitions, but these, in turn, are only to be understood within the context of our actions.[46]

It seems that one of the central conditions of culture is our understanding of fictionality, and that in turn this definition is depended upon and fought over by a variety of institutional forces that address the literary. The resulting definitions of fictionality will be multiple and frequently overlapping, and these definitions in turn will produce different sorts of literary and cultural actions, from protocols for reading to the construction of canons. In defining fictionality in this way, I join a group of critics who see literary institutions as multiple rather than monolithically hegemonic. In their introduction to *Cultural Institutions of the Novel,* Deidre Lynch and William Warner note that approaching institutions in this way allows us to see their contingency and to recognize that literary forms like the novel are sites where different groups accomplish social work that may be indirect: "The global dissemination of novel reading and novel writing has, however, made 'the' novel a discursive site where the relations among nations are brokered. By bringing the question of genre back into the foreground of novel studies, by attending

---

45. Pierre Bourdieu, *The Logic of Practice,* trans. Richard Nice (Stanford: Stanford University Press, 1990), 52.

46. Raymond Williams, *Culture and Society, 1780–1950* (New York: Columbia University Press, 1983), 295.

to transnational institutions of the novel, this collection finds new ways to analyze the productive powers that novels exercise in culture."[47]

I particularly want to emphasize that these definitions of fictionality are porous and subject to multiple, overlapping uses by groups and institutions that may initially seem to be quite different from each other. My decision to refer to these definitions of fictionality as "strands" in this book is meant to capture this interaction between different uses and groups operating within and outside of contemporary American literary culture. Each of these strands involves defining the nature and value of the fictional differently, and each represents a different position in relation to our traditional ways of thinking about literature as timeless, appropriate for university study, a vehicle for personal development, and so on. Terry Cochran has noted that literature has "been at the (ideological) center of knowledge institutions, along with what one might call the configuration of knowledge that accompanies them,"[48] and each of the strands of contemporary fictionality can be read as a response to this conventional way of thinking about literature. Some of these strands will embrace the conventional understanding of the value of literature, others will critique that understanding, and still others will operate from a position outside of our standard literary practices altogether. I have organized this book to move through my five definitions of fictionality operating in American culture in terms of their relationship to traditional literary institutions and practices, starting with the most conventional in the first chapter and moving to the least conventional in the fifth. But I want to emphasize that these definitions are strands within a whole culture rather than mutually exclusive definitions, and that frequently the power of a literary work emerges from the interaction between several strands. In this regard, this book rejects one of the most common ways of thinking about literature and institutions—as a way of policing boundaries. Bourdieu writes for many critics when, in *The Rules of Art*, he describes advocates for different definitions of art engaged in a zero-sum game of boundary policing: "Each is trying to impose the *boundaries* of the field most favourable to its interests or—which amounts to the same thing—the best definition of true membership of the field (or of titles conferring the right to the status of writer, artist or scholar) for justifying its existence as it stands."[49] The picture that I hope to describe of American literary culture is based, instead, on the interrelation of multiple

---

47. Deidre Lynch and William B. Warner, "Introduction: The Transport of the Novel," in *Cultural Institutions of the Novel*, eds. Deidre Lynch and William B. Warner (Durham, NC: Duke University Press, 1996), 3.

48. Terry Cochran, *Twilight of the Literary: Figures of Thought in the Age of Print* (Cambridge, MA: Harvard University Press, 2001), 40.

49. Bourdieu, *Rules of Art*, 223.

groups and boundaries, and porous relationship between the definitions of the fictional.

My first chapter both introduces the initial definition or strand of fictionality circulating within contemporary culture and also provides an explanation of why fictionality is important to our understanding of literary institutions. Specifically, I use debates about postmodernism in fiction to show what happens when we attend to the institutional forces at work on contemporary literature. John Barth's literary essays in *The Friday Book* provide the occasion for this discussion. As a text constructed at the height of the concept of postmodernism in fiction (1984) looking back on essays written as much as twenty years earlier, Barth's book exemplifies the institutional work of defining postmodernism. The definition of fiction that Barth ends up offering in this collection of essays—and, indeed, in his writing as a whole—is as a form of myth. What we find when we look at these essays is that the definition of fiction as a kind of myth is itself a struggle to understand the occasions that give shape to creative writing. Fiction is mythical for Barth to the extent that fiction is able to escape from its occasion and touch on universal tensions and dynamics within writing. What is especially important about the example that Barth provides in this opening chapter is that it makes very clear that an attempt to understand contemporary writing without reference to these sorts of institutions is deeply flawed. In particular—as I show in this chapter—attempts to think about postmodernism in fiction on the model of poststructuralism that became so popular with critics during the 1990s ultimately cannot account for the purpose and vocation of the writing of fiction. In many ways this first chapter functions as a sort of archeology of the concept of postmodernism indebted to critics like Hans Bertens, which attempts to return to the motivations and intellectual backdrop that invigorated the early definitions of postmodern. Allowing ourselves to forget these institutional contexts, I argue, makes us ultimately unable to understand the work that the concept of postmodernism did for Barth, and the ways that it has been adopted and transformed to do work for subsequent critics.

Barth's definition of fiction as a kind of myth also shows the ultimately conservative nature of this way of thinking about contemporary writing. In the first chapter I trace the roots of Barth's definition back to mid-century American intellectual obsessions with existentialist psychoanalysis, and note that the institutions in which Barth places himself reflect these philosophical dispositions. As a result, Barth's canon of contemporary, postmodern writing reflects traditional gender and class biases. I conclude the first chapter by noting the counterexample of Toni Morrison's definition of her novels as a folktale, which I suggest is a clever intervention into the inherited tradition of associating fiction and myth. In chapter 2 I follow up the alternative understanding of fictionality more systematically, and offer the definition of fiction as an archive as a second strand of contemporary fictionality. I develop this explanation of the archive by balancing Alice Walker's literary archive against Andy Warhol's media-defined imaginary. Thinking about fiction as providing an archive of materials defines the nature of literary study in a very different way than the canon the Barth discusses. Rather than gesturing back to some fixed body of texts that serve as a reference point from the past, the archive emphasizes future work and the way that new forms of imaging will be produced. In doing so, the archive provides a different way of thinking about the American imaginary and a different definition of literary invention.

In chapter 3 I turn to a particularly important and broad definition of fiction that runs throughout a great deal of contemporary writing: as a lie. Indeed, defining fiction as a lie is as old as our notion of the poetic itself. In a contemporary context, I suggest, definitions that embrace fiction as a lie do so in part in response to Freudian theories that see all subjectivity as self-deceived, but also as a way of adapting to the changing nature of American publishing. My interest in this chapter is particularly on metafiction, which foregrounds the actions of the writer in producing the text. These narratives treat either the space of the page or the book itself as an artifact. This artifact, in turn, comes to stand in for all the institutionally sanctioned forms of writing. Ultimately, I suggest, these narratives justify their particular form of fictionalizing by using these spaces as allegories, and by conspicuously obeying the traditional forms of writing in letter rather than in spirit.

Chapter 4 examines the way that science fiction has been positioned within this contemporary American landscape. Science fiction embodies many of the most conventional definitions of fictionality inherited from the nineteenth century: it seems to present a possible future for the sake of investigation and learning. In the context of postmodern American culture, however, the idea of modeling such possible futures is deeply problematic. In this regard, the attempt to define a uniquely postmodern form of science fiction around the work of William Gibson and the general category of "cyberpunk" writing reveals the tension between postmodernity and these traditional definitions of fictionality. More importantly, we can see evolving in critical celebration of this cyberpunk writing a definition of fiction that focuses on the style of the work as a general reflection of the culture. I open my discussion in this chapter in fact by focusing on a work that reached a broader audience even than cyberpunk writing—the 1999 hit science fiction movie *The Matrix*. This film nicely embodies the way that critics and reviewers have tried to define the nature of fictionality in such speculative genres, and the contradictions in the way that the film presents its hypothetical future reveals both the nature and the limitations in this type of fictionality. Defining science fiction as relevant because of its symptomatic style is not only evident in this film and in cyberpunk, but is a background definition of fictionality in many works of postmodern fiction. Such a definition of postmodern fiction reflects the attempt to position this writing in the institutional landscape as distinct from other forms of writing, but it also reveals our own anxieties about the nature of literary study in general. To read a work as a symptom of a culture is to sidestep the question of who is qualified to interpret a work, and to straddle broad cultural worries about whether literary study as a whole demands particular forms of disciplinary training.

In chapter 5 I turn to another point of interaction between a subgenre of contemporary writing and a critical methodology that responds to many of the same anxieties. The role-playing game is, I argue, a remarkable use of contemporary fictionality. What is especially interesting about it in the context of this study is that it adopts a position outside of literary institutions from which to imagine and use fictionality. As I describe in this chapter, these games draw from a variety of popular literary genres like science fiction and fantasy writing. The games themselves allow players to combine these works by defining parameters through which the characters and situations that circulate through different works can be standardized for comparison. The result is a form of gameplay that is fundamentally intertextual—players combine genres and favorite stories in order to play in a quasi-literary world. And yet, this very way of playing with these works is fundamentally irreverent and foregoes any claim to literary seriousness. In contrast to science fiction's ability to symptomize the culture discussed in chapter 4, the use of subliterary genres in this chapter is considerably less invested in any idea of literary value. This way of playing with texts and the understanding of fictionality upon which it depends is, in other words, fundamentally and self-consciously outside of the category of literature.

In this fifth chapter I discuss how this attitude towards subliterary texts may in fact reflect an attempt to reclaim a particular kind of agency that we have seen to be a hallmark of all of the definitions of fictionality that I have described in this book. Although the pressures that produce this desire for agency and its supporting definition of fictionality are broader than literary categories—since they reflect economic changes during modern industrialization—they also have direct effects on how literary analysis is understood. In particular, I focus on the appeal to possible world theory in some current narrative theory as a form of criticism that adopts the irreverent attitude of these games towards literary categories. This possible world theory also shares much of the focus on "portable" textual objects and situations that characterize role-playing games. This theory, in other words, reflects how the role-playing game's explicitly anti-literary form of fictionality can be translated back into engagement with literary criticism. The result is a form of fictionality that stands in perhaps the most complex relationship towards literary institutions that I discuss in this project.

In chapter 6 I apply these five strands of fictionality to a form of nascent literary activity—electronic writing—to show the interaction and competition between these definitions. As critics, writers, and readers all try to figure out how computers can be used to present a literary experience, they engage in an ongoing debate about how well terms like text, narrative, and reading apply to electronic works. More importantly for this book, they also struggle to decide under what broad category these works should be considered. Is it a kind of literary text (a story) or is it a game? In examining electronic works, I offer the concept of the "suture" introduced by Jacques Lacan but refined by Ernesto Laclau and Chantal Mouffe to describe the way that texts designed to be read electronically work to position themselves between two institutional definitions: literary text and game. After describing how this suturing works, I then turn to five different electronic works—some hypertext narratives, some computer games—that appeal to the different strands of fictionality that I have described in this book. These electronic works particularly allow us to see how these different strands of fictionality interact and frequently become meaningful by contrast to the other definitions of fictionality entertained and rejected by these works. I conclude my sixth chapter by briefly discussing the influential early CD-ROM computer game *Myst*, which (not quite coherently) combines nearly all of the types of fictionality that I have been describing in this book. *Myst* had the influence that it does, I argue, in part because it creates a space in which these different types of fictionality and different ways of thinking about what fictional stories are good for can be weighed and considered.

Why is fictionality in American culture "stranded" today? Is it just a matter of conflicting forces struggling to define fiction? Is it a moment before a more fully defined understanding of fictionality emerges? Although I offer no predictions about fiction in the future, this study shows that, in the end, the multiplicity of these definitions is empowering. As my conclusion suggests, the conflict over the nature and usefulness of fictionality can actually make possible discourse on topics that might otherwise be limited by the expectations of professionalism and disciplinarity.

CHAPTER 1

Myth and the Institutional Construction of Postmodernism in *The Friday Book*

Unlike avant-garde writing in its classic formulation, postmodern fiction in America has developed not in resistance to literary institutions but in the midst of them. As critics have regularly noted, the writers who have come to be considered postmodernists began to write before the term existed and in isolation from each other.[1] Stephen Koch remarked in *TriQuarterly* in 1967 that "a major obstacle to our movement away from an infantile literary mentality has been the failure to establish a community of artists and readers worthy of the name."[2] If a community of postmodern writers

---

1. Robert Coover remarks about the isolation of postmodern writers at a symposium on contemporary fiction: "We felt that we were all alone. No one was reading us, nor was anyone writing anything remotely like the sort of writing we were doing until, in the little magazines, we began slowly to discover one another. Few of us knew one another at the time we began writing. There was no manifesto, no group, or no school" ("'Nothing but Darkness and Talk?': Writers' Symposium on Traditional Values and Iconoclastic Fiction," *Critique* 31 [1990]: 233).

2. Stephen Koch, "Premature Speculations on the Perpetual Renaissance," *TriQuarterly* 10 (Fall 1967): 18.

developed—and there have certainly been associations between certain writers, such as the founding of the Fiction Collective in the mid-1970s as an alternative to traditional publishing methods—those communities have come after these writers have already launched their careers, after they have taken up at least some role within literary institutions as novelists, editors, and university teachers.[3]

Remarkably, few critics have looked at this process of the institutional formation of postmodern fiction. The way that institutions have worked to shape our understanding of contemporary fiction is the subject of this book, and the changing fortunes of the term *postmodernism* is a good example of what attention to the issue of fictionality can do for us. Most critics today still continue to describe postmodernism in fiction through a collection of qualities that certain works have, looking for some underlying family resemblances that define this writing. Other critics have recognized the ways in which postmodernism as a literary concept has been constructed, but attribute the agency in this construction to critics themselves. That is, such studies assume that a large body of writing exists to which critical concepts are applied more or less fairly by critics with particular theoretical and institutional agendas. Brian McHale opens his 1992 book, *Constructing Postmodernism,* with just this sort of assertion: "No doubt there 'is' no such 'thing' as postmodernism. Or at least there is no such thing if what one has in mind is some kind of identifiable object 'out there' in the world, localizable, bounded by a definite outline, open to inspection, possessing attributes about which we can all agree."[4] Even a sophisticated discussion of postmodernism like McHale's misses what seems to me most remarkable about postmodern fiction in America: the fact that these writers are not the passive victims of categorization but rather agents themselves within the complex dance of movement definition and canon formation.[5]

---

3. Ronald Sukenick's cultural history of the New York Beat and post-Beat art scene, *Down and In: Life in the Underground* (New York: Beech Tree Books, 1987), for example, treats the Beat movement as the last avant-garde movement and thus the last group of writers unified around a common aesthetic of resistance.

4. Brian McHale, *Constructing Postmodernism* (London: Routledge, 1992), 1.

5. The few critics who have recognized the role of the institution in the formation of the concept of postmodernism have tended to use this relationship to dismiss the concept altogether. Mark McGurl concludes *The Art Novel: Elevations of American Fiction after Henry James* (Princeton, NJ: Princeton University Press, 2001) by treating Barth's *Lost in the Funhouse* as the very embodiment of the institutionalization of writing: "Reading this disillusioning passage, where fiction, as metafiction, has become rhetorically indistinguishable from literary criticism, one is tempted to say that the programmatic 'technicality' of the metafictional experiments of American professor-writers such as Barth and Barthelme and Coover should be read, in a sense, as *instances* of the bureaucratic-technical discourse produced in the postwar American university—even as they must also be seen as *aestheticizations* of that discourse" (179).

MYTH AND POSTMODERNISM IN *THE FRIDAY BOOK*

In this opening chapter I will show that fictionality is a lens through which to examine the role of particular *literary* institutions in the formation of the concept of postmodernism. In particular, I will discuss the issue of fictionality through its construction in John Barth's collection of literary essays, *The Friday Book*. I am interested in how the concept of the fictional is made to do a certain kind of work that transforms the institutions from which this writing emerges. Not only does Barth define one of the principal ways of thinking about contemporary fictionality, but the origins and afterlife of his definition provide a model for the institutional conflicts that will shape all the other definitions discussed in this book.

Forgetting Fictionality

When critics describe the aesthetic and cultural impetus for postmodernism in fiction, they usually point to qualities that have more in common with visual art or architecture than with earlier theories of fiction. Typical in this regard is Andreas Huyssen's influential *After the Great Divide* (1986). Huyssen finds his model of genuine postmodern avant-garde in Warhol and pop art. Huyssen wants to distinguish the academic institutionalization of postmodernism within the framework of poststructuralist theory from an earlier period of experimental writing and engagement in popular culture.[6] For him, pop art at its best attempts the classic avant-garde goal of reestablishing links between art and everyday experience; it is "an ally in the struggle against traditional bourgeois culture, and ... many people believed that Pop art fulfilled Marcuse's demand that art not be illusion but express reality and the joy in reality" (145–46). Huyssen's primary argumentative move is to find a certain strain of postmodernism that critiques literary and art institutions. Drawing on the tradition of Dada and surrealism, Huyssen's central inspiration for this avant-garde definition of postmodrnism is Marcel Duchamp (see especially 146–48). To think of postmodernism in fiction within an avant-garde framework has meant, then, to define postmodernism in essentially medium-independent terms.

Such medium-independent definitions of postmodernism have become increasingly prominent. Linda Hutcheon's well-known overview of the concept, *A Poetics of Postmodernism* (1988), takes its orientation from architecture rather than from fiction itself, implying that there is an aesthetic

---

6. Andreas Huyssen, *After the Great Divide: Modernism, Mass Culture, Postmodernism* (Bloomington: Indiana University Press, 1986), 166.

framework that transcends particular media.[7] Likewise, Fredric Jameson's influential *Postmodernism* is subtitled, after all, "The Cultural Logic of Late Capitalism."[8] In such theories, postmodernism is first and foremost a reflection of its culture. Indeed, it is characteristic of most recent work on postmodernism in fiction to see such writing as primarily a response to or product of a particular cultural moment. To find writers who treat postmodernism as a style of writing—as a mode chosen to some extent freely by writers—we must go back to an earlier wave of criticism. Philip Stevick's *Alternative Pleasures* (1981), Alan Wilde's *Horizons of Assent* (1987), and Brian McHale's *Postmodernist Fiction* (1987) all treat postmodernism in fiction as essentially a style that is chosen, even if that style reflects cultural issues of the time.[9] Hans Bertens reviews such works and notes, "This investment in the political [in recent work by critics like Jameson] goes a long way towards explaining why the relatively few serious attempts to come to terms with postmodernism along formalist lines have had so little impact after the very first stages of the debate."[10] While none of these books looks at the institutional formation of postmodernism in fiction, all of them remind us that recent work on postmodernism understands such writing first and foremost as a product of a "cultural logic." When such cultural logics are used to define postmodernism, the specific qualities of fictionality fall into the background.

Writers of postmodern fiction who turn to other art forms like film and music encourage such medium-independent definitions of postmodernism. When Ronald Sukenick describes postmodernism in fiction, he draws on jazz innovation as a model: "It was the genius of Henry Miller... to employ for the first time since Rabelais (with—as far as I can recollect at the moment—the possible exception of Sterne) what might be called a free-form style of composition whose main technique is improvisation, and the great exemplar of which is jazz."[11] Many writers besides Sukenick have turned to

---

7. Linda Hutcheon, *A Poetics of Postmodernism: History, Theory, Fiction* (New York: Routledge, 1988).

8. Fredric Jameson, *Postmodernism: Or, the Cultural Logic of Late Capitalism* (Durham: Duke University Press, 1991).

9. Philip Stevick, *Alternative Pleasures: Postrealist Fiction and the Tradition* (Urbana: University of Illinois Press, 1981); Alan Wilde, *Horizons of Assent: Modernism, Postmodernism, and the Ironic Imagination* (Philadelphia: University of Pennsylvania Press, 1987); Brian McHale, *Postmodernist Fiction* (New York: Methuen, 1987).

10. Hans Bertens, *The Idea of the Postmodern: A History* (London: Routledge, 1995), 14.

11. Ronald Sukenick, *In Form: Digressions on the Act of Fiction* (Carbondale: Southern Illinois University Press, 1985), 6. In fairness I should note that in other places Sukenick emphasizes the verbal construction of the fictional text. Like Federman, who is discussed later, Sukenick appeals to other media while remaining concerned with issues of written narrative that keep him implicitly if not always explicitly connected to the issue of fictionality.

jazz as a way of thinking about the process of reading and composition. Ishmael Reed remarks in a 1973 interview, "It's obvious that there's something different when you come to the fiction of people like Clarence Major, Baraka, Wright, or Barthelme. Major was influenced by painters. Baraka was influenced by music, jazz and be-bop music. And Barthelme certainly uses a different art form in his work. . . . I think what will happen is that more writers will try to collaborate with other fields of art. Maybe this is what the new fiction is all about."[12] Such an interest in other arts and how they might provide a way of organizing writing is quite common in contemporary fiction; Richard Kostelanetz is axiomatic in asserting that "an operational truth is that advanced artists are likely to find their most productive inspirations in sources outside their own medium."[13] While a transmedia aesthetic might have developed in America, and while this aesthetic might be important in its own right as part of the contemporary artistic scene, this aesthetic does little to help us to understand what it means to create fiction instead of, say, poetry or film. Because fiction remains an institution in the broadest sense—a category that shapes everyday readers' expectations while it also organizes the economics of publishing and criticism—radical experimentation with the page in the tradition of concrete poetry had little sustained effect on American writing through the 1980s and '90s.[14]

What seems to me to be missing in these accounts of postmodernism is an explanation of what it means to be writing fiction today. As I noted in the introduction, New Historicist criticism has made clear that the "rise of the novel" is not the ascendancy of a certain aesthetic goal, but rather the gradual acceptance of principles by which fiction can be distinguished from both the real and the untruthful. As Catherine Gallagher argues, "Before the mid-eighteenth century . . . there was no consensus that all those genres shared a common trait; instead they were classified according to their implied purposes (moral fables, for example), their forms (e.g. epic), or their provenance (e.g. oriental tales). That discursive category we now call fiction was a 'wild

---

12. Joe David Bellamy, *The New Fiction: Interviews with Innovative American Writers* (Urbana: University of Illinois Press, 1974), 131.

13. Richard Kostelanetz, "Introduction," in *Breakthrough Fictioneers: An Anthology*, ed. Richard Kostelanetz (West Glover, VT: Something Else Press, 1973), xvii.

14. In this regard, Kostelanetz is right to note that much of our thinking about postmodern writing has been hemmed in by narrow definitions of what it means to produce "experimental" or "innovative" writing. His calls for radically innovative fiction that draw more on the tradition of concrete poetry, however, have never gained a foothold either in popular reading or in academic criticism—in part, perhaps, because they so completely reject the institutional conditions in which fiction is produced and read. For his statement of these transmedia principles, see his introduction to *Breakthrough Fictioneers;* for his analysis of literary institutions, see *The End of Intelligent Writing: Literary Politics in America* (New York: Sheed and Ward, 1974).

space,' unmapped and unarticulated."[15] Historicist critics like Gallagher and Lennard Davis have shown that the gradual acceptance of fiction depended upon sorting fiction from news, history, and science.[16] Gallagher argues that critics who ask about the sudden interest in realism are making a mistake: "We should ask, not why the novel became the preferred form of fiction, but why fiction became a preferred form of narrative" (164). Critics of contemporary fiction make the same mistake when they look for aesthetic principles in postmodernist fiction that echo Warhol without first asking what contemporary fiction itself means.

It is through a definition of fictionality that the novel becomes an institution in the broadest sense. As Homer Brown has remarked, "If it is part of the business of an institution to attempt to control its own proper contexts, institution also, as Bourdieu has pointed out, institutes or legitimates a difference, an exclusion. Watt's and McKeon's institutions of the novel seem set to allow them to use a sort of generic cleansing to exclude it from any contamination by the curiously dreaded term 'romance.'"[17] And because this sorting function occurs today at the nexus of a number of different institutions—entertainment media, universities, publishing houses—it is a point at which the institutional pressures on contemporary writing are most powerful and productive. We can see just this struggle to differentiate fiction from everything else in Raymond Federman's definition of "surfiction," which I discussed in the introduction as a prime example of the use of fictionality to characterize postmodernism:

> Just as the Surrealists called that level of man's experience that functions in the subconscious SURREALITY, I call that level of man's activity that reveals life as a fiction SURFICTION. Therefore, there is some truth in that cliché which says that "life is fiction," but not because it happens in the streets, but because reality as such does not exist, or rather exists only in its fictionalized version. The experience of life gains meaning only in its recounted form, in its verbalized version, or, as Céline said, some years ago, in answer to those who claimed that his novels were merely autobiographical: "Life, also, is fiction . . . and a biography is something one invents afterwards."[18]

---

15. Catherine Gallagher, *Nobody's Story: The Vanishing Acts of Women Writers in the Marketplace, 1670–1820* (Berkeley: University of California Press, 1994), xvi.

16. Lennard J. Davis, *Factual Fictions: The Origins of the English Novel* (Philadelphia: University of Pennsylvania Press, 1996).

17. Homer Obed Brown, *Institutions of the English Novel: From Defoe to Scott* (Philadelphia: University of Pennsylvania Press, 1997), xii.

18. Raymond Federman, "Surfiction—Four Propositions in Form of an Introduction," in *Surfiction: Fiction Now . . . and Tomorrow*, ed. Raymond Federman (Chicago: Swallow Press,

Although Federman frequently appeals to other media like visual art and music to define contemporary writing, in this passage we can see him struggling with the concept of fiction and trying to define it against all the changes in how we think of truth and history.

This is why we have failed to account adequately for the emergence of the concept of postmodernism in fiction. If we think of postmodernism in fiction as essentially a written version of a Warhol painting, then we flatten not only the aesthetic differences between fiction and painting, but—and more importantly, I think—the very distinct role that fictionality plays in the contemporary novel and the institutions in which the novel is entangled.

Barth's Occasional Writing

While doing interviews leading up to the publication of his 1966 novel *Giles Goat-Boy,* John Barth repeatedly told the story of how his methods of writing were changed by a critic of his previous novel, the *Sot-Weed Factor* (1960). Here's how Barth tells the story in a 1964 interview with the then *Wisconsin Studies in Contemporary Literature:* Barth offers that "It's quite curious how perceptive people—reviewers, critics, knowledgeable students—will point out things to you about your books and the connection between them and other works that you simply didn't know about, and yet which, once you've seen them, you know that you're not ever going to make anybody believe you didn't have in mind when you wrote your book." He goes on to explain the genesis of *Giles:*

> Somebody told me that obviously I must have had in mind Lord Ragland's twenty-five prerequisites for ritual heroes when I created the character of Ebenezer Cooke in *The Sot-Weed Factor.* I hadn't read Raglan, so I bought *The Hero,* and Ebenezer scored on twenty-three of the twenty-five, which is higher than anybody else except Oedipus. . . . Well, subsequently I got excited over Ragland and Joseph Campbell, who may be a crank for all I know or care, and I really haven't been able to get that business off my mind—the tradition of the wandering hero. The only way I could use it would be to make it comic, and there will be some of that in *Giles Goat-Boy.*[19]

1975), 7–8; Federman's ellipsis.
    19. John J. Enck, "John Barth: An Interview," *Wisconsin Studies in Contemporary Literature* 6 (1965): 12.

Barth's comments on mythic patterns within his writing struggle to define the relationship between what an author creates and what he or she produces accidentally or inherits; in a general way, Barth is concerned here with the limits of his own fictionalizing. Although *Giles* is rarely considered Barth's best novel—indeed, many consider it his worst—it does mark a transition in his career from the existentialist style of novels like *The End of the Road* (1958) to the more obviously postmodern works like *Lost in the Funhouse* (1968), *Chimera* (1972), and *LETTERS* (1979).[20] Indeed, if we look back on the publishing history of the short stories that Barth produces leading up to the collection of explicitly metafictional stories, *Lost in the Funhouse*, we notice that the only short stories published before *Giles* are the relatively modernist "Water-Message" and "Ambrose His Mark" in 1963.[21] The stories that we most associate with Barth as a metafictionalist—works like the title story, "Menelaiad," and "Title"—were all published after *Giles*. So when Barth speaks about this review changing his way of thinking about his writing, he certainly seems to be pointing to some genuine shift in his writing style.

What seems especially important in this incident is the way that it gets at the question frequently ignored by so many critics and theorists of postmodernism: what is the nature and purpose of the fictional in writing today? Barth's account of his own self-discovery finds this answer precisely in institutional frameworks like critical reviews and interviews with academic journals. In other words, when Barth tries to talk about how he developed the particular way that he thinks about fictionality as a postmodern writer, he does so by appealing to the institutional conditions of his career. In this regard, it should be no surprise that the novel that stands at this transition point, *Giles Goat-Boy*, is a satire about an institution—in this case, the American university. The play between mythic fictionality and literary institutions is illustrated well by Barth's collection of essays, *The Friday Book* (1984). As a collection constructed in the heyday of postmodernism as a concept, organizing material written much earlier (starting in 1960), Barth recontextualizes these earlier statements. We can see him working to reconstruct the rise of the term *postmodernism* in the introduction to a 1963 essay: "Reread-

---

20. While *Giles*'s elaborate allegory is usually considered to be less effective in raising metafictional concerns than the shorter works that followed, it seems quite clear that *Giles* is the transition point in his writing. Indeed, Campbell's diagram of the hero's cycle of events reoccurs thirteen years later in *LETTERS* ([1979; Normal, IL: Dalkey Archive, 1994], 647), and it seems clear that the kinds of structural patterns that he discovers in writing *Giles* are important to his subsequent writing.

21. Barth notes in his 1968 introduction to the collection that these two stories are "the earliest-written, [and] take the print medium for granted" (*Lost in the Funhouse: Fiction for Print, Tape, Live Voice* [1968; New York: Anchor, 1988], xi).

ing the result twenty earlier later, I hear what we call the 1960s beginning to rumble in its latter pages. And I confess to being tantalized by how nearly I uttered, at the end, the now talismanic word *postmodern*. Oh well."[22]

I would like to suggest that Barth develops an understanding of what it means to write fiction precisely by working through the institutional occasions of his writing and by searching for principles that appear within those occasions. Indeed, to read Barth's 1984 introductions to individual essays is to be struck by the accidental quality of many of the occasions that gave rise to his essays. Asked to write a foreword to a Tobias Smollett's novel, Barth observes, "I responded that I had in fact neither read anything at all of Smollett's nor ever written a literary essay. *They* responded, in effect, Why not try both? I did" (30). Asked to contribute to *Book Week,* Barth notes, "As I had never tried my hand at a newspaper piece, I agreed to give it a go" (55). Such events are both accidental and deeply institutional—forms of academic and literary production that, while disconnected from Barth's own immediate interests and studies, nonetheless occur as classic manifestations of the profession to which he belongs. Indeed, remarkable in *The Friday Book* is the fact that for all the accidental and occasional quality of many of these essays, none of the occasions that give rise to his writing are disconnected from literary activities. While Barth may veer off into politics in one speech, that speech itself is delivered as a commencement address at a university. While Barth's interest in sailing may lead him to write the foreword to a book on the Chesapeake Bay, that foreword becomes a meditation on representing the landscape. Barth's essays, then, are always occasioned by institutions of writing, educating, and publishing.

The story that Barth tells about these occasions is always the same one: the discovery of some principle at work within the seemingly accidental. Barth's send-up of the convention on bookish "front matter" is typical in this regard; his title is *The Friday Book, or, Book-Titles Should be Straightforward and Subtitles Avoided.* Even in such an innocuous and straightforward parody of the occasion of book titling, Barth's play with rules and principles for writing is evident, since he appeals to what *should* happen here. The trend continues as he moves into sections "The Title of This Book," "The Subtitle of This Book," and "Epigraphs," each of which offers a list of rules by which novels should be introduced: "Comic works need not bear comic titles.... A catchy title may serve a catchy book.... But better a book more engaging than its title ... than a title more engaging than its book" (vii). The search for principles amid the apparently accidental occasion continues as Barth

22. John Barth, *The Friday Book: Essays and Other Nonfiction* (Baltimore: Johns Hopkins University Press, 1984), 30.

moves into more serious and traditionally literary essays. In "How to Make a Universe," Barth consigns critics the role of "anatomist of literature," but then goes on to search for principles himself: "The first law of embryology, for instance—that ontology recapitulates phylogeny—is as poetic a fancy as anything in literature. I wish I'd thought of it. And the second law of thermodynamics, the principle of universal entropy, informs the whole show with a splendid dying fall. My point is that this grand and complex entity after all *is*, as *Huckleberry Finn* finally is, beyond philosophy, theology, literary criticism, and the sometimes torturing attempts of its inhabitants to understand it and their place in it" (24). Barth's opposition between the accidental quality of particular literary jobs—the task of the critic to be an anatomist and to seek to explain a book—is finally transcended by the poetic principle embodied in the work. And this play between the accidental occasion and the discovered principle is one that runs throughout Barth's essays in this collection.

To transcend the occasion of writing is the very thing that defines the fictional for Barth. Indeed, as he is narrating the historical occasions surrounding his writing (the Vietnam War, campus protests) he remarks that his own writing at the time, the cluster of novellas *Chimera*, "has nothing to do with politics at all" (97). As this observation suggests, Barth is eager to put aside the entanglement of the everyday world in order to define fiction as something that transcends its occasions. Barth repeatedly asserts that fiction arises out of a particular occasion but leaves that occasion behind. His treatment of poetry in *The Friday Book*, conversely, is quite different. One of the few occasions where he talks about poetry is in the essay titled "A Poet to the Rescue," which is introduced by stories of poets intervening into political events. Barth's treatment of poetry here is primarily at the level of the word and phrase—his main focus is on the palindrome—and it is clear that his interest in poetry is quite different from his concern for fiction. Poetry is occasional while fiction transcends its occasions. The other essay in which Barth discusses poetry is equally occasional in its focus. In "The Prose and Poetry of It All, or Dippy Verses" Barth defends his novel *Sabbatical* from a reviewer who accuses him of inserting "dippy verses" into the work. He does this by relentlessly explaining the occasion from which these poems were created by the novel's characters. There are no principles for the creation of poetry, no interest in patterns that emerge from them; instead, Barth is content to focus entirely on occasion—why they were created and what they say about their creators. Quite in contrast to fiction, poetry appears to Barth to be inherently occasional.

His denial of fiction's involvement with its occasion accounts for the controversy surrounding Barth's best-known essay, "The Literature of Exhaustion." This essay seems to arise clearly and directly out of its cultural occasion, out of the sense that the novel had come to some sort of dead end because of changes in our sense of reality and the gradual diminution of literature's importance amid the explosion of entertainment options after the middle of the twentieth century. This indeed is precisely the way that most critics have understood Barth's essay and have accepted or rejected it as a statement about the "death of the novel." In his 1984 introduction to the essay, however, Barth is eager to distance himself from this reading: the essay "has been frequently reprinted and as frequently misread as one more Death of the Novel or Swan-Song of Literature piece. It isn't" (64). Indeed, throughout this essay Barth discusses "some old questions raised by the new 'intermedia' arts" (64)—in other words, aesthetic issues that transcend the particular cultural moment when he is writing. When Barth finally gets around to Jorge Luis Borges's writing—which provides him with his central example of the literature of exhaustion—he praises it for precisely the ability to escape the "felt ultimacies" of contemporary culture. Writing of Borges's *Tlön, Uqbar, Orbis Tertius*, Barth asserts, "like all of Borges's work, it illustrates in other of its aspects my subject: how an artist may paradoxically turn the felt ultimacies of our time into material and means for his work—paradoxically, because by doing so he transcends what had appeared to be his refutation" (71). Barth is frustrated by critics who misread his essay as another "death of the novel" argument precisely because to do so reinserts it firmly into the occasion of its composition.

This tension between occasion and transcendence in fiction is especially evident in the novel that Barth wrote while composing most of the essays contained in *The Friday Book*. At various points in his retrospective introductions to each of the pieces included in this collection, Barth is quite explicit in suggesting that the writing of the essays is deeply connected to the topic of *LETTERS*. As he describes one typical essay, "I wound up more or less reviewing My Fiction Thus Far: a kind of self-orientation prompted by the *LETTERS* project, which for better or worse—and against my personal shop rules—happened to involve a character from each of my previous six books" (130). The novel itself is an epistolary narrative organized around letters written by characters from Barth's earlier novels. In organizing all of these characters into a single narrative, Barth is not only connecting the stories and themes of his earlier books but also adopting an explicitly metafictional position, since an important part of his correspondence is exchanged between the author and characters who believe themselves to be real. Indeed, the subtitle of the novel is "An old time epistolary novel by seven fictitious drolls &

dreamers each of which imagines himself factual." In returning to his earlier novels, Barth is obviously interested in finding underlying patterns within his writing. Doing so is explicitly an occasion for further invention. One of the key phrases that runs throughout the novel is the corporate slogan of Mack Enterprises: *Praeteritas futuras stercorant* [sic] (80), which Todd Andrews glosses as "the past (*a*) fertilizes the future, (*b*) turns into shit in the future, or (*c*) turns the future into shit" (81). This Latin phrase summarizes the ambiguous relationship between past and present that Barth pursues throughout the novel, trying to understand the way in which the future in enabled or foreclosed by its historical occasion. *LETTERS* itself repeatedly invokes the interrelation between fiction and history, focusing in particular on the fictive structures that occur at certain historical moments. Andrews, for example, remarks about events in his personal life, "All of which items, to be sure, have dramatic potential, and are almost fictional in their factual state. But I'm not an *homme de lettres;* my dealings are with the actual lives of actual people, and of my view of them is tragical, it's not exploitative" (97). The implication is that fiction *is* exploitive—transcending the particular occasion of this event for the sake of some literary use. It is clear here that Barth uses the historical occasions of his novel in much the same way that he uses the occasions for which his *Friday Book* essays are written: as instances in which structures that transcend the accidental will appear. And for Barth, those structures are inherent to fiction.

In this, Barth sounds Aristotelian, distinguishing between historical accident and the poetic truths of fiction.[23] And yet what is remarkable about Barth's essays is that such a classical way of thinking about the fictional seems to depend so relentlessly on the occasional. In Barth's idea that one transcends the occasions for writing to discover deeper principles at work, it is difficult not to hear a kind of anxious struggle to exclude the transient from the genuinely literary.[24] A parallel for Barth's struggle with and use

---

23. In the *Poetics*, Aristotle remarks, "The distinction between historian and poet is not in the one writing prose and the other verse—you might put the work of Herodotus into verse, and it would still be a species of history; it consists really in this, that the one describes the thing that has been and the other a kind of thing that might be. Hence poetry is something more philosophic and of graver import than history, since its statements are of the nature rather of universals, whereas those of history are singulars" ("Poetics," trans. I. Bywater, *The Complete Works of Aristotle*, ed. Jonathan Barnes [Princeton, NJ: Princeton University Press, 1984], 1451a39–1451b8; p. 2323).

24. Sukenick remarks about this search for truth amid social constructions in Barth's writing. He sees several possible responses to contemporary culture: "You become, then, a connoisseur of fiction, the expert in measuring and collecting and judging between and making distinctions among fictions. The other direction was to propose to yourself that fiction could tell some truth beyond your personal vision and beyond literature itself" (Tom LeClair and Larry

of the occasions of his writing is Derrida's treatment of the occasions of speech in his early discussion of Edmund Husserl, *Speech and Phenomena*. When Derrida describes the opposition between expression of an idea and the particular means of indication that are chosen to communicate this in Husserl's theory of language, he offers up an image of language that struggles to overcome its occasion. Despite the repeated attempts to define expression as prior to and independent of indication, "Every expression would thus be caught up, despite itself, in an indicative process."[25] We see the same curious dependence on occasion (indication) that Derrida attributes to expression in Barth's description of his writing. Barth never leaves the accidental behind to create the transcendental truth; rather, he constantly intertwines the accidental and the transcendental. The events of *LETTERS* are not only a repetition of earlier patterns but rather a repetition that reveals a structure within its particular occasion. Barth explains the distinction between reenactment and "mere repetition" in *The Friday Book:* "The spiral reenacts the circle, but opens out—if you're going in the right direction. The nautilus's latest chamber echoes its predecessors, but does not merely repeat them, and it is where the animal lives; he carries his history on his back, but as a matter of natural-historical fact, that history is his Personal Flotation Device, not a dead weight carrying him under" (170). While "mere repetition" feels accidental or occasional, the "natural historical fact" of mythical reenactment is more meaningful. But repetition is exactly what we are left with if we forget the occasion of writing. This is a point that Derrida makes when he notes that expression is defined precisely by its possibility of being repeated exactly: ideality, "which is but another name for permanence of the same and the possibility of its repetition, *does not exist* in the world, and it does not come from another world; it depends entirely on the possibility of acts of repetition" (52). When Barth rejects simple repetition, he is rejecting ideal patterns that are completely independent of their occasion. In other words, repetition is not enough for such facts to become mythical; they must, instead, become part and parcel of their occasion. The image of the spiral is not just a structure that reappears constantly but rather a structure that changes and develops by virtue of its occasion—feeding off its earlier appearances. Myth, then, captures precisely the ambiguity evident in Barth's definition of fictionality as curiously transcending and dependent on its occasions.

McCaffery, *Anything Can Happen: Interviews with Contemporary American Novelists* [Urbana: University of Illinois Press, 1983], 282).
    25. Jacques Derrida, *Speech and Phenomena and Other Essays on Husserl's Theory of Signs*, trans. David B. Allison (Evanston, IL: Northwestern University Press, 1973), 21.

CHAPTER 1

Myth in Mid-Century Literary Culture

After Barth's "discovery" of the concept in 1966, myth became an important theme within contemporary fiction. Although Robert Coover's interest in myth and ritual as a way of giving shape to social wholes is probably the best parallel to Barth's use, such appeals to myth are common throughout postmodern writing.[26] Thomas Pynchon's use of mythic patterns is especially prominent in *Gravity's Rainbow,* where critics have noted the importance of classical myths like the Orpheus story as well as obscure myths like the Rocketman subtheme. Donald Barthelme appeals to mythic figures in his early *Snow White* (1967) as well as in his late *The King* (1990).[27] Although his interest in myth is shared by many writers, Barth's particular way of defining myth as struggling against occasion works as much to exclude writers from the nascent canon of postmodernism as it does to define his own aesthetic practice. Barth's decision to frame postmodernism as a matter of transcending the occasional is especially remarkable because he associates fiction concerned with contemporary reality—writing, in other words, concerned with its occasion—with female writers. In his "Literature of Replenishment" essay, Barth dismisses in a single sentence "many of our contemporary American women writers of fiction, whose main concern, for better or worse, remains the eloquent issuance of what the critic Richard Locke has called 'secular news reports'" (195–96). It is clear from Barth's essay that he believes that such writing is, indeed, much more for the worse than for the better. But to characterize contemporary writing by women in this way, Barth needs to ignore the rewriting of myth and fairy tale that became the hallmark of feminist criticism, fiction, and poetry in the late 1970s.[28] Despite the multitude of texts written by women that seek to challenge received narrative plots and redeploy myths,[29] Barth continues

26. For an overview of Coover's use of myths, see Kathryn Hume, "Robert Coover's Fiction: The Naked and the Mythic," *Novel* 12 (1979): 127–48.

27. And certainly the frequent use of superhero stories within contemporary fiction—from Barthelme's "The Joker's Greatest Triumph" (in *Come Back, Dr. Caligari* [Boston: Little, Brown, 1964], 147–58) through Steve Katz's stories in *Creamy and Delicious: Eat My Words (in Other Words)* (New York: Random House, 1970) to Michael Chabon's *The Amazing Adventures of Kavalier & Clay* (New York: Picador, 2000)—should be seen as attempting to work through the narrative possibilities of mythic stories.

28. A number of feminist critics have noted how myth and fairy tales have provided female authors of the 1980s and '90s with a way to respond to received cultural beliefs; as Susan Sellers asserts, "Deconstruction or the reading of myth to expose its manipulations and suppressions is not enough; we must counter with our own mythopoeia" (*Myth and Fairy Tale in Contemporary Women's Fiction* [New York: Palgrave, 2001], 32).

29. This is perhaps most obvious in early feminist criticism that analyzes and adopts literary myths, like Sandra M. Gilbert and Susan Gubar's *The Madwoman in the Attic: The Woman*

to distinguish (male) postmodernism of myth from the occasional writing of women.[30]

Barth's definition of fiction as myth represents the most hegemonic way of thinking about contemporary writing—both in the sense that it is the most explicitly connected to established literary institutions, and in the sense that it draws most heavily on already-established ways of thinking about fiction. One of the reasons that Barth excludes from his definition of postmodern fiction a wide range of fiction produced by women is because he develops his theory out of the very (masculine) literary institutions and traditions current at the time of his writing. The shift in style that Barth describes in his writing is not a simple rejection of prior ways of thinking about fiction but rather a particular way of inhabiting conventional definitions of literature that nonetheless produces changes in the framework for thinking about fictional stories. When Barth describes myth in his writing, he defines the term in a way that had distinct currency in late 1950s American literary and popular culture.[31] One of the central thematic elements of *The End of the Road* (1958) is the "mythotherapy" recommended for Jacob Horner, a way of thinking about himself as the hero of his own life, and making up a grand overall narrative that makes individual choices and events meaningful.[32] The pages of mainstream intellectual journals like the *Partisan Review, The Hudson Review,* and *The Kenyon Review* are littered with such existentialist psychoanalysis, which is perhaps best embodied by popular intellectual studies like Viktor Frankl's *Man's Search for Meaning* (trans. 1959) or Jean-Paul Sartre's work. A good example of this sort of popular intellectual framework is Eleanor Hakim's 1966 essay in *Salmagundi*, "Jean-Paul Sartre: The Dialectics of Myth." Reading through Sartre's recently published autobiography, *The Words,* provides Hakim with an occasion to explore autobiography as an analogy for "the

---

Writer and the Nineteenth-Century Literary Tradition (New Haven: Yale University Press, 1979). It is also, however, an important theme in writing by women that attempts to tell what Molly Hite calls "the other side of the story," narratives that struggle to escape from "the prevailing constructions of gender and genre"; *The Other Side of the Story: Structures and Strategies of Contemporary Feminist Narrative* (Ithaca, NY: Cornell University Press, 1989), 6.

30. This is true even in essays written after this 1984 collection. In his later collection of essays, *Further Fridays: Essays, Lectures, and Other Nonfiction, 1984–94* (Boston: Little, Brown, 1995), Barth notes the emergence of a kind of realistic minimalism during the 1990s practiced by both male and female authors (72), but defines this style of writing as an alternative to postmodernism rather than using it as an opportunity to reconsider his definition of postmodernism itself.

31. In doing so, Barth passes on the opportunity to draw on other traditions that define the term differently. In *Women as Mythmakers: Poetry and Visual Art by Twentieth-Century Women* (Bloomington: Indiana University Press, 1984), for example, Estella Lauter defines contemporary feminist mythmaking based on the tradition of H. D.'s mythical poetry.

32. John Barth, *The End of the Road*, rev. ed. (1958; Garden City: Doubleday, 1967).

archetypal dynamics of mythology: the unraveling of the symbol clusters and constellations of those unconscious fantasies that constitute the original project of one's specific inner mythology."[33] Although published in the mid-1960s, all of the literary/cultural predispositions of the late 1950s are evident in this project: the starting point of existentialist subjectivity, the use of myth to describe psychoanalytic dependencies, and the broad gesture beyond the individual struggles with meaning to larger cultural archetypes.

Myth stands as a transitional concept between such established ways of thinking about literary fiction and the innovations that we will come to associate with postmodernism. A good example of the pressure from innovation exerted through the concept of myth in the 1950s is Leslie Fiedler's well-known *Love and Death in the American Novel* (1960), a work of psychoanalytic cultural criticism of literature that embodies the dispositions of the period.[34] Fiedler's anti–New Critical thematic reading of the American novel posits an essentially "boyish" quality to American writing, implying in the process its involvement in Freudian psychosexual dynamics: "The child's world is not only asexual, it is terrible: a world of fear and loneliness, a haunted world; and the American novel is pre-eminently a novel of terror. To 'light out for the territory' or seek refuge in the forest seems easy and tempting from the vantage point of a chafing and restrictive home; but civilization once disavowed and Christianity disowned, the bulwark of woman left behind, the wanderer feels himself without protection, more motherless child than free man."[35] Fiedler's implicit understanding of a kind of existentialism is evident here, but more striking is the way that he uses a psychoanalytic understanding of subjectivity to create thematic links between a wide range of American novels. As Fiedler suggests, the appeal of myth is its promise to step outside of a strictly textual interpretation of the work to consider the larger social and cultural "occasion" of subjectivity.[36] Indeed, in

---

33. Eleanor Hakim, "Jean-Paul Sartre: The Dialectics of Myth," *Salmagundi* 1, no. 2 (Winter 1966): 59.

34. Although this, Fiedler's best-known work, was published in 1960, his interest in myth is already well established in an essay like the 1952 "Archetype and Signature: The Relationship of Poet and Poem," in *The Collected Essays of Leslie Fiedler*, vol. 1 (New York: Stein and Day, 1971], 529–48.

35. Leslie A. Fiedler, *Love and Death in the American Novel* (New York: Criterion Books, 1960), xxi.

36. This is why, while Northrop Frye's influential archetypal theory of literature, *Anatomy of Criticism: Four Essays* (Princeton, NJ: Princeton University Press, 1957) might come to mind first as an example of mid-century mythical criticism, Fiedler's work is a better example of the trends within 1950s literary culture—he is so much more a transitional figure between academic and popular culture. Indeed, myth seems to mark precisely the possibility of moving between popular and academic culture.

his preface to *Love and Death,* Fiedler remarks that "the 'text' is merely one of the contexts of a piece of literature, its lexical or verbal one, no more or less important than the sociological, psychological, historical, anthropological, or generic" (viii).

It is clear here that a psychoanalytically inflected understanding of myth allows Fiedler to emphasize broader social patterns. Nonetheless, as the existential subjectivity that runs throughout his book suggests, he remains committed to a kind of individualism. This paradoxical attempt to marry myth and individualism is evident in other prominent psychoanalytical/mythical theories of the 1950s. Probably the most influential such theory is Norman O. Brown's *Life Against Death* (1959). Like Herbert Marcuse's *Eros and Civilization* (1955), Brown's book seeks to link individual psychosexual dynamics with broad cultural patterns.[37] Indeed, the subtitle of Brown's book is "The Psychoanalytical Meaning of History." The way in which this link is made is explicit at the outset of the book: "In the new Freudian perspective," he remarks on the first page, "the essence of society is repression of the individual, and the essence of the individual is the repression of himself."[38] The balance that Brown, Marcuse, and Fiedler all evidently try to strike is one between the individualism of subjectivity implied by existentialism and the broader social patterns postulated by myth. Mythical patterns evolve in these mid-century theories out of the individual's contact with the social whole—out of what we can call the occasion of society. All of these stories take a step beyond pure focus on the individual—or the individual text for that matter—and instead try to reestablish a relationship between individual and society.[39]

In trying to step outside of the work to its occasion, these mythic theories are also working to change the occasion for the study and discussion of fiction. Ihab Hassan is quite explicit in arguing that the problem of literary change emerges around postmodernism. At the beginning of his well-known

---

37. Herbert Marcuse, *Eros and Civilization: A Philosophical Inquiry into Freud* (Boston: Beacon, 1955).

38. Norman O. Brown, *Life Against Death: The Psychoanalytical Meaning of History* (Middletown, CT: Wesleyan University Press, 1959), 3.

39. In this regard, it is worth noting that myth plays a very different role in other, less traditional literary journals at the time. In a countercultural journal like the *Evergreen Review,* myth is more often discussed as an alternative to existentialist thinking. Indeed, in 1961 it published a translation of Octavio Paz's "The Dialectic of Solitude," which uses myth as one component of the dialectic that he discusses. For him, "The dual significance of solitude—a break with one world and an attempt to create another—can be seen in our conception of heroes, saints and redeemers. Myth, biography, history and poetry describe a period of withdrawal and solitude—almost always during early youth—preceding a return to the world and to action" (*Evergreen Review* 5, no. 20 [September/October 1961]: 107–8).

essay, "POSTmodernISM: A Paracritical Bibliography" (1971), Hassan raises the question of how to imagine change and overcome what he describes as the two urges evident in thinking about literary change: to deny change or constantly to reinvent the past.[40] An essay published a decade later, "Ideas of Cultural Change," asserts bluntly that "[w]e speak much of change and have no theory of it."[41] In trying to imagine literary change, appeals to myth play an important role. Indeed, if we compare Hassan's *Radical Innocence* (1961) and *The Dismemberment of Orpheus* (1971) we can see the same transformation of myth that we can observe in Barth's essays. *Radical Innocence* treats contemporary American fiction primarily in the terms that we can recognize in Barth's early, existentialist period. Focusing on writers like J. D. Salinger and Saul Bellow, Hassan describes the contemporary novel through the representation of "the modern self in recoil." Myth appears here (Hassan cites Campbell's *Hero with a Thousand Faces*, for example) to introduce the issue of the individual bereft of religious values and social meaning.[42] Although already engaged with myth as an existentialist theme, *Radical Innocence* is essentially a conservative work of literary history, since it depends on the themes and literary topoi that are well established at the time.[43]

The Dismemberment of Orpheus, conversely, marks a change in the structure of literary study and definition. In this 1982 "postface" to the work, Hassan explicitly defines the radical challenge to the institutions for studying fiction that he offers: "in the question of postmodernism, there is a will and counter-will to intellectual power, an imperial desire of the mind, but this will and desire are themselves caught in a historical moment of supervention, if not exactly obsolescence. The reception or denial of postmodernism thus

---

40. Ihab Hassan *Paracriticisms: Seven Speculations of the Times* (Urbana: University of Illinois Press, 1975), 39–40.

41. Ihab Hassan, "Ideas of Cultural Change," in *Innovation/Renovation: New Perspectives on the Humanities,* ed. Ihab Hassan and Sally Hassan (Madison: University of Wisconsin Press, 1983), 15.

42. Hassan writes at the end of his discussion of Campbell, "Yet if the contemporary hero seems mythic in the sacrificial quality of his passion, his actions have the concrete self-definition of an existential encounter" (*Radical Innocence: Studies in the Contemporary American Novel* [Princeton, NJ: Princeton University Press, 1961], 114).

43. In this regard I would contrast Hassan's work to other early theories of postmodernism that search for continuities between contemporary and earlier American literature by trying to define common concerns and topoi. Tony Tanner, for example, introduces *City of Words: American Fiction 1950–70* (New York: Harper & Row, 1971) by using Richard Poirier's *A World Elsewhere: The Place of Style in American Literature* (New York: Oxford University Press, 1966) to establish a "distinctive American tradition" of creating an environment of freedom apart from the everyday world. Although this type of analysis can be insightful, the urge to place postmodernism within earlier traditions seems to me fundamentally different from the appeal of myth.

remains continent on the psychopolitics of academic life."[44] Hassan is right to attach this observation not to *Radical Innocence* but to *Dismemberment*, because it is in the latter that he works to change how contemporary writing is studied. He does this by stepping outside of the conventions of literary history that are so clear in *Radical Innocence*, and instead adopting an explicitly mythical style through which he will discuss postmodernism: "The signing body of Orpheus holds, then, a contradiction—between the dumb unity of nature and the multiple voice of consciousness—that the song itself longs to overcome" (6). Along with this mythical framework, Hassan turns to a much wider range of sources that emphasize the larger cultural occasion for contemporary writing. Where in *Radical Innocence* he frames the discussion by reference to psychoanalytic existentialism as the condition for the hero of the contemporary novel, in *Dismemberment,* Hassan draws on a much wider range of contemporary theorists like Barthes and Maurice Blanchot as well as Norman Brown. What seems to me important is that for Hassan the mythical style that he adopts in his writing of the early 1970s challenges the study of contemporary fiction. For him, myth transforms the academic and publishing institutions that surround this writing.[45]

Hassan's attempt to change the study of fiction is, like Barth's definition of postmodernism, limited by the traditional roots of his own understanding of myth. Just as I have suggested that Barth's definition of myth as transcending occasion works to exclude a whole range of contemporary writing by women, so too Hassan's interest in cultural occasion is limited by his implicit sense of what sorts of materials and theories are relevant to understanding postmodernism. Thus, psychoanalysis and continental philosophy figure largely in his understanding of postmodern culture, but gender, race, or the economics of contemporary writing fail to register as significant issues even within his

44. Ihab Hassan, *The Dismemberment of Orpheus: Toward a Postmodern Literature*, 2d ed. (Madison: University of Wisconsin Press, 1982), 262.

45. One way that we can think about this reorientation is how it shifts the locus of discussion of contemporary literature from mainstream intellectual journals like *Partisan Review* to new and more explicitly academic journals like *TriQuarterly,* which was launched in 1964 by explicitly embracing academic culture: "One thing is clear—its [the university's] scope has been immeasurably increased—not only does everyone end up at college, but as institutions, universities have been made responsible for everything from driver training to the preservation of grand opera.... Still, leisure does strange things to people. And the university's function, most magnificently conceived, has after all been roughly akin to the artist's, in that it is pledged to the damnation of spurious order, and devoted to questions that society will not, alone, ask itself" (Charles Newman, "Foreword," *TriQuarterly* 1 [Fall 1964]: 5). Academic culture is imagined here as a locus for the artful and eclectic useful of a wide variety of contemporary issues—precisely the qualities that postmodernism sought to define against the hegemony of mid-1950s literary culture.

wider range of reference. These limitations seem to me implicit in Barth's essays as well, and the work that he accomplishes in defining postmodernism must be seen as less an expression of some sort of new postmodernist thinking and more a transformation of terms already at work within the various literary institutions through which his career moves.[46] His appeal to myth draws on terms already current within academic and popular literary institutions of the 1950s and '60s; at the same time, in using myth like Fiedler and Hassan, he is subtly redefining the framework in which fiction is to be understood.[47] Barth's use of myth in *Giles* and afterwards certainly embodies some qualities that we associate with postmodernism: the interest in the relativity of knowledge, the problematization of history, the questioning of individuality. It also allows him to think about what we would now call the metafictional quality of his writing—the self-conscious use of past literary models, the tendency for the text to turn back on itself and comment on its patterns, and so on. Because myth draws attention to the occasion of writing, it ultimately raises issues about discourse that dovetail easily with the poststructuralist framework in which so much postmodern writing will be read in the following decades. But it does all these things by using concepts at work within literary institutions and reaccenting them, giving them a different purpose within the writing and discussion of fiction. As a concept for understanding fiction, myth acts on and through institutions to transform and rejuvenate Barth's writing. In other words, it accomplishes *work*. In looking at the development of the novel in the eighteenth century, Clifford Siskin uses a similar notion of work to describe how forms of writing create ways of reading and organize institutions around themselves in order to produce more writing: "Writing induced a fundamental change in readers—leading them to behave as writers—which, in turn, induced more writing. Writing's capacity to produce change, in other words, was, in this basic way, historically crucial to what I have been calling its *proliferation*—the production of more writing."[48] Barth's turn to myth does not merely solve rhetorical

46. This is why, it seems, that definitions of postmodernism that emphasize the breakdown of the separation between popular and literary styles of writing miss the point at least in part. While it may be true that postmodernism does question why some types of writing are valued, it also seems clear that some attempts to integrate more popular cultural materials specifically work to transform the occasion for discussing contemporary fiction.

47. In contrast, we might note criticism by women authors who complain that their inability to inhabit literary institutions in even this partial way has made the acceptance of women's writing so difficult to achieve. In fact, Joanna Russ argues that it is because science fiction has a different institutional structure (as "outsider" art) and a different set of received literary myths that it has been more accommodating to feminist narrative (*To Write Like a Woman: Essays in Feminism and Science Fiction* [Bloomington: Indiana University Press, 1995], 90).

48. Clifford Siskin, *The Work of Writing: Literature and Social Change in Britain, 1700–1830* (Baltimore: Johns Hopkins University Press, 1998), 4.

problems or offer an opinion about the coming postmodernism in fiction; instead it redefines the relation between fiction and its institution, and thus provides the conditions for more writing.

How Myth Became Passé (for Critics)

In the middle to late 1960s, then, the concept of myth did a certain kind of institutional work in defining the nature of fiction. As I noted in the introduction, some of the most recent work on postmodernism has recognized the pragmatic function of the term *postmodernism*. John Frow, for example, has recently argued that we should see debates about postmodernism not as arguments about how a neutral object should be defined and categorized, but as "nothing more and nothing less than a genre of theoretical writing."[49] Describing these debates as a form of discursive "game" (23), Frow goes on to argue that "the concept of the postmodern obeys a discursive rather than a descriptive necessity: its function is that of a logical operator, establishing categorical polarities which then allow—in a tautologous and self-justifying circuit—the construction of fictions of periodization and value" (36). It seems clear that the concept of postmodernism, framed using myth, does a certain kind of intellectual work for Barth as he shuttles between his 1960s and '70s essays and their collection in 1984, and that the nature of this work changes in subsequent uses of the term *postmodernism*.

To understand what happens to myth as a definition for postmodern fiction in the decades that follow Barth's essays, we might consider Gerald Graff's comments about Barth at a conference in 1981. Graff remarks that Barth's observations about postmodernism in "The Literature of Replenishment" leave largely undiscussed the limitations of our "reasonable working definition of the *Zeitgeist*."[50] Graff admits that asking for such a definition is unfair: "I wouldn't put so much pressure on the shorthand (as I've been calling it) if it weren't that we've lately been asking this shorthand to carry a great deal of argumentative freight in our discussion of literature and, particularly, in our quarrels about where the contemporary arts are, or ought to be, headed" (156). Graff's observation seems to me to reflect the spirit of a great deal of the criticism of postmodernity that has followed. Essays like "The Literature of Exhaustion" and Barth's own struggles toward a mythical basis for his writing ultimately do not answer the questions about contem-

---

49. John Frow, *Time and Commodity Culture: Essays in Cultural Theory and Postmodernity* (Oxford: Clarendon Press, 1997), 15.

50. Gerald Graff, "Under Our Belt and Off Our Back: Barth's *Letters* and Postmodern Fiction," *TriQuarterly* 52 (Fall 1981): 156.

porary culture that most interest academic critics. It would be fair to say, I think, that postmodernism as a concept has shifted in its institutional role as its usefulness has changed. Where Barth saw postmodernism as an occasion to rejuvenate his own writing through a reconceptualization of fictionality, critics of the 1980s and '90s have seen in it the opportunity to define and critique contemporary culture.[51] Barth himself has remarked in 1998 about the way that the term *postmodernism* has drifted in recent years, becoming "stretched out of shape": "I would say the definitions advanced by such European intellectuals as Jean Baudrillard and Jean-François Lyotard have only a kind of a grand overlap with what I mean when I am talking about it [postmodernism]."[52]

The moment that myth emerged in theories of postmodernity, it was already moving away from an account of contemporary fictionality and towards other institutional uses that will become the hallmark of postmodernity in the 1990s. Early in her 1988 synthesis of the various strands of postmodernism—a synthesis that did a great deal to frame the discussion of the concept for the next decade—Linda Hutcheon defines postmodernism through Roland Barthes's semiology:

> Perhaps it is another inheritance from the 1960s to believe that challenging and questioning are positive values (even if solutions to problems are not offered), for the knowledge derived from such inquiry may be the only possible condition of change. In the late 1950s in *Mythologies*, Roland Barthes had prefigured this kind of thinking in his Brechtian challenges to all that is "natural" or "goes without saying" in our culture—that is, all that is considered universal and eternal, and therefore unchangeable. He suggested the need to question and demystify first, and then work for change. The 1960s were the time of ideological formation for many of the postmodernist thinkers and artists of the 1980s and it is now that we can see the results of that formation.[53]

There are fairly simple ways in which debates about postmodernism draw on this type of Barthesian myth as a primary example. When John Duvall introduces a recent collection of essays on postmodernism and history, he uses

---

51. This essay is especially interesting in comparison to Graff's comments on *The End of the Road* thirteen years earlier, "Mythotherapy and Modern Poetics," where Barth's concept of mythotherapy becomes the occasion to critique New Critical analysis of poetry (*TriQuarterly* 11 [Winter 1968]: 76–90).

52. Charlie Reilly, "An Interview with John Barth," *Contemporary Literature* 41 (2000): 607.

53. Hutcheon, *A Poetics of Postmodernism*, 8.

myth as an embodiment of the discursive construction of reality that is taken to be an essential part of the postmodern condition: "Historian Neill Asher Silberman's embrace of Disney's America—Jameson's degraded historicism writ large—fittingly summarizes the mood of recent Republican Congresses: since all public history is mythologizing and commercialized anyway, why not privatize, have Disney do it instead of the National Parks Service?"[54] Myth as it is being used by Hutcheon and Duvall has some relationship to the cultural occasion for writing in which Barth is interested, but it is less a matter of the usefulness of made-up stories than a lens for reading culture. Because myth does different work for these critics, it should be no surprise that other terms have replaced myth as tools for cultural analysis. Thomas Docherty's influential anthology, *Postmodernism* (1993), for example, frames debates about postmodernism through Adorno and Horkheimer's *Dialectic of Enlightenment*.[55] The rise of Adorno as a major figure in debates about postmodernity during the 1990s derives from his materialist rather than semiotic definition of culture. As my discussion of Hassan's early 1970s essays on postmodernism suggest, this shift is implicit within the way that postmodernism as a concept operates on literary institutions at the very outset. If Hassan works to integrate a wider range of materials in order to think about literary change, it is no surprise that attention naturally gravitates towards cultural patterns and away from primarily literary issues like fictionality.[56]

In this chapter I hope that I've shown, however, that myth once did real work in helping critics and writers to think about contemporary writing and the institutional distinctions between fiction and history, philosophy, and news.[57] If we go back to the earliest theories of postmodernism in writing, we notice that myth conceived in the Freudian framework discussed in the previous section is an accepted part of such theories. In *The Fabulators* (1967), Robert Scholes tells a story about the rejuvenation of allegory as a contemporary mode of writing. In a far-off land of Fiction, storytellers decide to borrow their ideas from historians and philosophers. Scholes's story ends,

54. John N. Duvall, "Troping History: Modernist Residue in Jameson's Pastiche and Hutcheon's Parody," in *Productive Postmodernism: Consuming Histories and Cultural Studies*, ed. John N. Duvall (Albany: State University of New York Press, 2002), 5.

55. Thomas Docherty, ed., *Postmodernism: A Reader* (New York: Columbia University Press, 1993).

56. It is for this reason, I think, that Hassan embraces link between postmodernism and poststructuralism in his 1982 preface to *Dismemberment of Orpheus*. Deconstruction comes across here as simply one of many cultural sources that Hassan is eager to use to talk about changing literary institutions, even though in other ways those sources ultimately help to hide the work of transforming institutions that he is trying to accomplish in this book.

57. A good example of this struggle from the other side of this line—from journalism and the nonfiction novel—is provided by Mas'ud Zavarzadeh in *The Mythopoeic Reality: The Postwar American Nonfiction Novel* (Urbana: University of Illinois Press, 1976).

The Historians and Social Scientists got tired of having other folks put their Ideas into stories. They decided to muscle in on the story racket themselves. So they climbed out of the bog and invaded the fertile fields of Fiction, and everybody who stayed on in the territory they occupied had to agree to write non-Fiction novels. At the same time the Philosophers and Theologians got a whole new batch of Ideas called Existentialism and Wittgenstein which frightened them so much that they lit out for the highest peaks leaving Ideas strewn all over the foothills. But some Philosophers got to like that territory so much that they wouldn't leave. They were still there when the refugees from Realism started to pour in and take over. Finally, in order to stay, they had to agree to show these refugees a new way to do Allegory with all these new Ideas. A few of the refugees had smuggled some Ideas called Jung and Freud with them, and when the leftover Philosophers saw them they said they weren't Social Science Ideas anyway, but things those rascals had stolen from Theology and Philosophy to begin with. So they took all the old and new Ideas they could find and began trying to work out a new kind of Allegory.[58]

Scholes's story is one that I have been developing in a different way, a shift from existentialism through a new conception of fictional writing that ends—unsurprisingly—with *Giles Goat-Boy* as the culminating example. It is an unremarkable part of the mid-1960s landscape that critics have largely forgotten that this transformation was imagined as a different way of thinking about the nature and purpose of writing. And, indeed, a yearning for a more satisfying definition of fictionality reappears in surprising places. Kathy Acker's early writing, for example, was fairly explicit about embracing poststructuralist thinkers like Foucault and Gilles Deleuze and Félix Guattari,[59] and most of her early novels reflect a kind of fractured and strongly problematized sense of subjectivity that we associate with postmodernism as it came to be defined in the 1990s. Later in her career, however, Acker expressed dissatisfaction with the essentially negative poetics of her early writing, and instead became fascinated with myth as personal and aesthetic principle. In an interview, she describes in *Empire of the Senseless* (1988), "The search for a myth to live by. The purpose is constructive rather than deconstructive as in [her earlier novel] *Don Quixote*."[60] Acker certainly seems to be announcing

58. Robert Scholes, *The Fabulators* (New York: Oxford University Press, 1967), 98–99.
59. Kathy Acker, "Devoured by Myths: An Interview with Sylvère Lotringer," in *Hannibal Lecter, My Father*, ed. Sylvère Lotringer (New York: Semiotext(e), 1991), 10.
60. Ellen G. Friedman, "A Conversation with Kathy Acker," *Review of Contemporary Fiction* 9, no. 3 (Fall 1989): 17.

a turn back to the principles for thinking about fictionality as a form of myth that I have described in this chapter. Acker develops this myth by invoking the traditional image of the sailor, free to travel anywhere on a whim and unbounded by convention or social bonds. In particular, Acker insists that the sailor rejects material possession for the sake of imagination and exploration.[61] Acker's image of the sailor may seem romantic—and this is no doubt one of the reasons that she refers to it as a myth—but she is well aware of the fundamentally problematic nature of this way of life. Acker notes that the motto of the sailor is "any place but here" (156), a concise statement of how imaginative myths do not translate to stable, pragmatic, political structures. In his discussion of Acker's novel, Robert Siegle explains this well: "Stability is to be found [not] in the status of intellectual or political mastery.... It is found in the constancy of change, fluidity, a very female voyaging in which no preetablished metaphysics, demystified or not, rules. This state 'occurs only imaginarily' because it is *not* a state but an ongoing voyaging that does not stop."[62] More explicitly than Barth, Acker shows that this myth is unable to transcend time and occasion.[63]

The struggle to define fictionality, then, is an inherent part of the institutional construction of contemporary writing. I hope to have shown that the fate of contemporary fiction and the theoretical debates that have grown up in the wake of the concept of postmodernism have been in large part determined by the way Barth initially framed the subject. This framing, in turn, was made possible and effective in part because he was able to draw upon and reinterpret a concept of myth already current within literary institutions. Alternate definitions have struggled either to reconcile themselves to the model they have inherited from Barth, or to break free and create their own. One way to understand feminist struggles with the concept of postmodernism in fiction is as a dissatisfaction with the available models of fictionality circulating within these institutions and inherited from realism, modernism, and Barth's quirky definition of postmodernism.[64] In this sense, one of the reasons for Toni Morrison's extraordinary success in forcing literary

61. Kathy Acker, *Empire of the Senseless* (New York: Grove, 1988), 214.
62. Robert Siegle, *Suburban Ambush: Downtown Writing and the Fiction of Insurgency* (Baltimore: Johns Hopkins University Press, 1989), 114.
63. I discuss Acker's definition of myth as a critique of representation in "The Local Site and Materiality: Kathy Acker's *Empire of the Senseless*," *Genders* 27 (1998), http://www.genders.org/g27/g27_theories.html.
64. On struggles to define the relationship between postmodern fiction and feminist writers, see Hite's *The Other Side of the Story*, Patricia Waugh's *Feminine Fictions: Revisiting the Postmodern* (London: Routledge, 1989), and Magali Cornier Michael's *Feminism and the Postmodern Impulse: Post-World War II Fiction* (Albany: State University of New York Press, 1996).

institutions to recognize the aesthetic seriousness and sophistication of contemporary women's writing is her ability to inhabit and redefine conventional definitions of fictionality.[65] In a 1981 interview, Morrison describes the use of myth and folklore in her writing: "I think the myths are misunderstood now because we are not talking to each other the way I was spoken to when I was growing up in a very small town."[66] These myths are part of the "folklore of [her] life" and appear "everywhere—people used to talk about it, it's in the spirituals and gospels" (255). We might think, for example, of Morrison's brilliant critique of authorial omniscience in *Jazz*, a novel that has met with a mixed reception from critics and reviewers.[67] The most powerful and disturbing element of Morrison's storytelling is how the narrator admits in the end that she simply did not know her characters as well as she thought she did: "So I missed it altogether. I was sure one would kill the other. I waited for it so I could describe it. I was so sure it would happen. That the past was an abused record with no choice but to repeat itself at the crack and no power on earth could lift the arm that held the needle."[68] Against such a traditional understanding of authorial control and knowledge she offers the gossip that makes up her story. Indeed, the shocking thing about this novel is that the author herself is swept up into the community of the novel, made an object of the characters' observation and subjected to the same partial knowledge shared by all of the characters in the community: "I thought I knew them and wasn't worried that they didn't really know about me. Now it's clear why they contradicted me at every turn: they knew me all along. Out of the corners of their eyes they watched me. And when I was feeling most invisible, being tight-lipped, silent and unobservable, they were whispering about me to each other" (220).

How is this folkloric definition of fictionality different from myth? Most obviously, such an understanding of fiction does not require us to transcend occasion. Based on this understanding of folklore, Morrison defines her writing as "village literature": "fiction that is really for the village, for the tribe. Peasant literature for *my* people, which is necessary and legitimate but which also allows me to get in touch with all sorts of people" (253). Much as

---

65. On the shift in Morrison's reputation and her position relative to (white) mainstream literary institutions, see Dane Johnson, "The Rise of Gabriel García Márquez and Toni Morrison," in *Cultural Institutions of the Novel*, eds. Deidre Lynch and William B. Warner (Durham, NC: Duke University Press, 1996), 129–56.
66. LeClair and McCaffery, *Anything Can Happen*, 254.
67. For an overview of the reception of Morrison's novel, see Tracey Sherard's "Women's Classic Blues in Toni Morrison's *Jazz*: Cultural Artifact as Narrator," *Genders* 31 (2000): par. 4. http://genders.org/g31/g31_sherard.html.
68. Toni *Morrison, Jazz* (New York: Knopf, 1992), 220.

Barth inhabits and reshapes conventional definitions of myth in 1966, Morrison molds the association of myth and contemporary writing in a new way to create a "legitimate" village literature. In this dance between writing and category, fictionality and legitimacy, we see the ongoing struggles to define contemporary writing. Just as Barth does, contemporary writers like Acker and Morrison suggest that myth is essential to thinking about the *productive* uses of contemporary fictionalizing, and makes clear that any understanding of contemporary or postmodern writing needs to ask about the condition of fictionality today.

CHAPTER 2

Folk Culture, the Archive, and the Work of the Imaginary

Although both were published in 1975, Alice Walker's "In Search of Zora Neale Hurston" and Andy Warhol's *The Philosophy of Andy Warhol* could not, at first glance, be less alike. Walker's search for Zora Neale Hurston is a quest for an authentic folk culture suppressed by racist literary and ethnographic powers; Warhol's "philosophy" is a celebration of mass media and the easy acceptance of the stereotypes of American life. And yet, for all their differences, both are engaged in the project of defining the American imaginary, of understanding the models and images that give shape to contemporary life. In the process of responding to such media images, these two essays represent an attempt to define the uses of invented stories that break sharply from the particular mid-1950s literary culture that I have discussed in the previous chapter. John Barth's definition of fiction as myth reflects, I argued in chapter 1, a hegemonic position that is shaped directly by the academic status quo—particularly the previous decade's existentialist psychoanalysis. At the end of that chapter, however, I noted attempts to break from this traditional genealogy and the literary institutions on which it depends—especially Toni Morrison's interest in folklore. Morrison suggests that alternatives to mythic fictionality need not come from within literary and academic institutions. Walker and Warhol—although in very different ways—struggle to think about the use of the fictional that responds to the challenges of contemporary media culture by looking outside of literary institutions for inspiration. As a result, the definition of fictionality that we see here will function in contemporary culture in a very different way, and will launch from a different point of departure.

What is especially interesting about both Warhol and Walker is that they both take positions more distinctly outside of the institutions with which they are involved (art and literature, respectively) than Barth did. Where Barth participated in institutional occasions at every turn, Warhol and Walker hold their respective institutions at arm's length. And yet, at the same time, Warhol and Walker are fundamentally still involved with those institutions. Indeed, for all of the satire of artistic institutions implicit in Warhol's work, no artist depended more on artistic institutions, nor can there be much doubt that Warhol's work has become part of our standard histories of contemporary art. Likewise, balanced against her critique of how American literary culture has neglected Hurston is the fact that Walker herself has achieved all the honors and recognition that come with literary success. Both Warhol and Walker have achieved their place within their respective institutions precisely because they so wholeheartedly criticized and in the process rejuvenated them. In particular, Walker's search has become a model for a whole generation of writers and critics, for whom the rediscovery of suppressed writing by women and minorities is the paradigmatic responsibility of socially engaged literary history. Walker's essay provides some of the groundwork for the revisionist literary history embodied in the *Heath Anthology of American Literature*. Indeed, in recovering neglected texts and placing them alongside the traditional "masterpieces" of American writing, the *Heath* has set the tone for the teaching of American literature in the university classroom for the last decade. Even the more traditional *Norton Anthology of American Literature* has begun to look like the *Heath* in its more recent editions. The *Heath*'s principal editor, Paul Lauter, describes the goals of such an anthology as "a broad platform in this process of canon change, a kind of still point in the changing cultural world, from which future departures will undoubtedly be made. Such volumes force on us very different conceptions of American literary and cultural history, simply in order to account for the existence, much less the characteristics, of such texts."[1] It should be clear that the definition of

---

1. Paul Lauter, *Canons and Contexts* (New York: Oxford University Press, 1991), 162.

fictionality that circulates within the folkloric framework departs from the model of postmodernism that I discussed in the previous chapter. We can see this simply by examining the works that anthologies like the *Heath* include. Jeffrey Nealon notes that the *Heath*'s goal of including a wide range of contemporary texts and of rejecting any particular universal standards paradoxically ignores particular postmodernist texts that challenge those standards not on the basis of ethnicity or gender but through poststructuralist theory of language. "The diversity hailed by the *Heath Anthology*," Nealon remarks, "then, seems to rest in opening up a kind of epiphanic white experience to many other groups. What is diversified here are the groups who can legitimately express a similar experience of personal feeling."[2] As Nealon rightly notes, defining fictionality as an archive of cultural resources and forms is no less artificial than defining it as the kind of psychoanalytically informed existentialist myth that provided Barth's model in the previous chapter.

The appeal to such neglected texts embodied in Walker's essay and the *Heath Anthology* has a complex if not contradictory relationship to literary institutions. In an essay a few years later, Walker describes her search for Hurston as the product of a need for source material for her own writing: "I became aware of my need of Zora Neale Hurston's work some time before I knew her work existed. In late 1970 I was writing a story that required accurate material on voodoo practices among rural Southern blacks of the thirties; there seemed none available that I could trust."[3] Hurston represents for Walker such an archive of material from which her own writing can be developed. In the years that have followed Walker's essays, just this sort of definition of fiction as the product of folk materials has emerged within popular and academic culture. Indeed, Ann duCille has defined "hurstonism" as a crucial experience of discovery and identification by a generation of writers interested in African American studies.[4] Others have described the battle to claim Hurston's legacy; as Michele Wallace asks, "Who owns Zora Neale Hurston?"[5] This makes Warhol and Walker different from the writers that I will discuss in later chapters, who reject literary institutions in a stronger way (without implying a positive direction for reform) or who simply stand out-

---

2. Jeffrey T. Nealon, *Double Reading: Postmodernism after Deconstruction* (Ithaca, NY: Cornell University Press, 1993), 156.

3. Alice Walker, "Zora Neale Hurston: A Cautionary Tale and a Partisan View," *In Search of Our Mothers' Gardens: Womanist Prose* (San Diego: Harvest, 1984), 83.

4. Ann DuCille, "The Occult of True Black Womanhood: Critical Demeanor and Black Feminist Studies," in *Female Subjects in Black and White: Race, Psychoanalysis, Feminism*, eds. Elizabeth Abel, Barbara Christian, Helene Moglen (Berkeley: University of California Press, 1997), 21–56.

5. Michele Wallace, *Invisibility Blues: From Pop to Theory* (London: Verso, 1990).

side of the institutions altogether. They are, in this regard, the first step away from the most conventional understanding of fictionality that I described in the previous chapter.

Although we might follow Morrison's use of folklore as a way to grasp this strand of contemporary fictionality, it seems to me that Walker's intervention in the American literature canon offers a more useful window into contemporary literary culture. Walker represents a particularly interesting point of intersection between the creative and the critical wings of the literary institution, and their meeting in her essay on Hurston has had a more direct impact on literary criticism and canonicity. In this chapter, I would like to suggest that we can gain perspective on Walker's definition of fiction by comparing it to Warhol's *Philosophy*. Warhol reflects many of the same concerns that Walker expresses, but his broader interest in media and social performance allows us to extend Walker's insights to our national narratives in general.

Walker's Lies

Walker's brief essay describes her journey to Hurston's hometown of Eatonville in 1973 to find her grave and mark it with a tombstone. In essence, Walker is juxtaposing two stories in this essay. The first is obviously the search for Hurston's tomb and the exploration of contemporary Eatonville, many of whose citizens have no knowledge of Hurston's life or writings. The second, which becomes clearer and more explicit in her essay "Zora Neale Hurston: A Cautionary Tale and a Partisan View," two years later, is a narrative about Hurston's disappearance from the literary canon and the need to reevaluate her writing. In Walker's earlier essay, this future use of Hurston is almost entirely in the background; why Walker wants to find Hurston is allowed to remain vague. Indeed, the larger purpose of the journey is implied only in the quotations that Walker inserts without commentary between sections of the narrative. Some of these quotations come from Hurston's contemporaries; others reflect the responses of Walker's own contemporary students and scholars, who frequently comment on the elusive nature of Hurston's biography or the problems of her reception. Over the course of the essay, it becomes clear that Walker wants to sort out this biography and overcome the prejudice that pushed Hurston to the margins of African American literature.

Walker combines these two narratives using the story of the journey to accomplish the goal of correcting Hurston's critical neglect. The story itself does not explain the origins of Walker's interest in Hurston. Nor does it discuss in any detail the task of getting to Eatonville. Nearly all of the narrative concerns Walker's encounters with the citizens of Eatonville. These encounters fall into one of two types. The first functions as a testimonial to the way that Hurston has been neglected as an important figure in twentieth-century writing. Walker travels, for example, to the house that Hurston lived in only to discover that the young people who live in the house across the street know nothing about Hurston:

> I go up to them to explain. "Did you know Zora Hurston used to live right across from you?" I ask.
> "Who?" They stare at me blankly, then become curiously attentive, as if they think I made the name up. They are both Afroed and he is somberly dashikied.
> I suddenly feel frail and exhausted. "It's too long a story," I say. . . . [6]

This exchange comes late in the narrative, and is clearly meant to instance Hurston's neglect as well as the task of resuscitating her reputation. The other type of encounter that Walker describes concerns meetings with people who had firsthand experience with Hurston in the past. She meets Mathilda Moseley, who appears in one of Hurston's books, as well as the daughter of the director of the funeral home that buried Hurston. Both provide apparently misleading information about the circumstances of Hurston's burial. All this seems to be cleared up when Walker meets Dr. Benton, who knew Hurston personally and seems to explain the actual conditions of her death and burial. The nature and order of Walker's encounters mirrors the structure of her narrative as a whole. The narrative gradually unpacks Hurston's life, pealing away indifference and misconceptions and progressing to those with personal knowledge who set the record straight.

Walker's narrative, then, is organized around a series of personal encounters that determine the trajectory for her quest to understand Hurston's life and death. What interests me in particular in this story is the way that Walker takes on a fictional identity to collect information. Walker introduces herself to Eatonville and all of the people that she meets as Hurston's illegitimate niece. Late in the essay Walker reflects on the ethics of her lie when talking to Benton: "I hate myself for lying to him. Still, I ask myself, would I have gotten this far toward getting the headstone and finding out about Zora Hurston's last days without telling my lie? Actually, I probably would have. But I don't like taking chances that could get me stranded in central Florida" (110). Walker's remark is strange because it so obviously calls into the question

---

6. Walker, "Looking for Zora," *In Search of Our Mothers' Gardens*, 113–14.

the whole structure of her story. In the process, Walker encourages us to consider the importance of this central lie to the journey and her narrative of it as a whole. Although the issue may seem tangential at first, in fact the idea of lying to get to the truth is, as I suggested in the introduction, the central one in fiction. And since Walker is recovering Hurston not primarily for the sake of the folklore that she offers but as source material for the writing of fiction, the lies that Walker tells are not irrelevant to her story but rather a foundational issue.

Walker's lies follow a trajectory linked to her quest to discover the truth of Hurston's life and burial. Walker opens her story by describing the simplicity and usefulness of her lie: "Because I don't wish to inspire foot-dragging in people who might know something about Zora they're not sure they should tell, I have decided on a simple, but I feel profoundly *useful*, lie" (95). Walker's lie here is a fiction in the most traditional sense: it is an invention deployed to get at some other truth. It also, however, raises some questions about Walker's project as a whole. From Walker's essay published four years later, we know that Hurston's writing represents authenticity and, especially, a kind of belonging that Walker is eager to recapture. Walker's mini-narrative of her discovery of Hurston's work leads her to "test" it on her relatives, "who are such typical black Americans they are useful for every sort of political, cultural, or economic survey" (84). Finding Hurston's stories well received by her relatives, Walker goes on to describe the "perfection" of these stories: "For what Zora's book did was this: it gave them back all the stories they had forgotten or of which they had grown ashamed (told to us years ago by our parents and grandparents—not one of whom could *not* tell a story to make you weep, or laugh) and showed how marvelous, and, indeed, priceless they are" (84–85). Precisely what makes Hurston's writing priceless is its ability to provide an archive of lost materials. Because this archive represents the basis for a community that may not even recognize itself as such, reading Hurston's work provides a moment of recognition on the part of Walker's family. Although she can see them as statistically average, it is only through the reading of Hurston's folktales that they are able to recognize themselves as members of this community. Indeed, this question of recognition is essential to Hurston's own problematic place within African American history. Hazel Carby suggests that Hurston is "a central figure in the cultural struggle among black intellectuals to define exactly who the people were that were going to become the representatives of the folk."[7] In

---

7. Hazel V. Carby, "The Politics of Fiction, Anthropology, and the Folk: Zora Neale Hurston," in *New Essays on Their Eyes Were Watching God*, ed. Michael Awkward (Cambridge: Cambridge University Press, 1990), 77.

Walker's essay, lying about her ancestry is a way to get at the truth of this folk culture.

For a while, Walker grows into this fictitious identity. In the middle of the story she lies for a second time but feels more comfortable: "By this time I am, of course, completely into being Zora's niece, and the lie comes with perfect naturalness to my lips. Besides, as far as I'm concerned, she *is* my aunt—and that of all black people as well" (102). Walker's acceptance of this identity may seem perfectly natural. As her comments on group recognition in her later essay suggest, the kind of imagined relation that Walker describes is precisely what her quest to Eatonville is all about. On further reflection, however, Eatonville itself functions as a deeply problematic site for her rediscovered community. It is precisely this community's not-knowing—its unfamiliarity with Hurston—that makes the lie necessary. And yet, this trip is obviously necessary to Walker. It is not enough to have discovered Hurston's writing and to have constructed a community around those stories by sharing them with friends and family; Walker demands, instead, the true discovery of the actual grave of Hurston. Such a discovery is an exemplary act of archival foundation—the establishment of a reference point from which future work and thinking can be charted. In *Archive Fever,* Derrida argues that the creation of the archive is always the foundation upon which future work is based. Derrida describes the archive as "a *pledge,* and like every pledge, a token of the future."[8] The archive functions as a pledge to the future by defining and granting legitimacy to a certain resource for future work: the archive presupposes "not the originary *arkhē* but the nomological *arkhē* of the law, of institution, of domiciliation, of filiation" (95). This is why, I think, Walker's response to Benton is so much a break from the way that her fictitious identity has functioned in the rest of the story. It is here for the first time that Walker expresses regret: "I hate myself for lying to him." In part, Walker's sense of guilt arises from the kindness that Benton shows: he "comes to [her] rescue" and defends her when she claims that she is illegitimate (110). But what seems to be more the source of Walker's guilt is that Benton clearly represents the truth that she has been seeking in the story. It is he who explains what seem to be the real circumstances of Huston's death and burial, and who dismisses the other accounts that Walker has gathered as fictions; he asks "indignantly," "Where did you get that story from?" (110). Benton calls on Walker to discard fictions for the sake of truth.

Walker's ambiguous relationship with the fictions that she creates in this

---

8. Jacques Derrida, *Archive Fever: A Freudian Impression,* trans. Eric Prenowitz (Chicago: University of Chicago Press, 1996), 18.

story says a great deal about the dynamics of fictionality as a site of cultural and discursive struggle. I have argued that the use of fictionality always reflects an institutional framework and the disciplinary practices that make those invented stories acceptable and useful. Walker's search for Hurston dramatizes just this movement into legitimacy. At first, Walker describes herself as without a context for understanding Hurston and without a community that knows what to do with her writings and life. In such a situation, fiction is impossible, and lies are a necessary evil designed to get at the truth. As Walker begins to develop a community around Hurston's life in the figure of Benton, truth becomes possible but lies are likewise more shameful. We might recall Michael Riffaterre's link between fiction and genre that I quoted in the introduction: "The only reason that the phrase 'fictional truth' is not an oxymoron, as 'fictitious truth' would be, is that fiction is a genre whereas lies are not. Being a genre, it rests on conventions, of which the first and perhaps only one is that fiction specifically, but not always explicitly, excludes the intention to deceive."[9] We might say that once Hurston has been recovered as a source and a fictionality based on these materials is possible, the lie told to make those materials available seems scandalous.[10] And yet, it should go without saying, Walker's ambiguous relationship to the lies that she tells is not some accidental quality of her style of writing; it is, rather, the very thing that makes Hurston's writing so important to her. The very folkloric archive that Walker is trying to develop in her search for Hurston's grave is entangled with ironies of lying and truth seeking that reflect the issue of fictionality.

The legitimacy that blossoms around Walker's quest arises not from the development of a traditional discipline or even institution. Although Walker does, indeed, mark Hurston's grave with a symbol of social legitimacy and biographical facticity, the story ends not by constituting a discipline for studying Hurston or even a method of accounting for her life. Instead, Walker has simply accomplished the task of marking a reference point for her own work, and in particular of identifying the existence of a certain body of materials. This is a significant departure from the types of legitimation that I described

---

9. Michael Riffaterre, *Fictional Truth* (Baltimore: Johns Hopkins University Press, 1990), 1.

10. In *Hard Facts: Setting and Form in the American Novel* (New York: Oxford University Press, 1987), Philip Fisher describes literary works whose original cultural effects are difficult to grasp because of how effectively they have transformed the cultural landscape: "The simple argument of this book is that within the 19th-century American novel, cultural work of this fundamental kind was often done by exactly those popular forms that from a later perspective, that of 20th-century modernism, have seemed the weakest features of 19th-century cultural life" (5). I am describing something of the same sort of difficult-to-grasp emergence of fictionality in Walker's writing.

in the previous chapter. Instead of arguing for a canon in relation to current literary culture, Walker inaugurates an archive from which future work can proceed.[11] The contrast to Barth's understanding of fictionality is striking: where Barth imagined fiction as a kind of mythical transcendence of its occasion, Walker sees an archival moment whose consummation is all in the future. In the context of Walker's very different relationship to traditional literary disciplines, it is no accident that the voice of truth that shames her fictions is embodied in a doctor; the opposition between traditional disciplinary authority and some other form of knowing is at the heart of Walker's essay.

Walker anticipates the discussion of the archive and canon that will develop in the next two decades in literary criticism. The starting point that she describes seems to be different from a simple canon—a collection of resources that are also a guide to study, a general structure for a discipline. In his article for *Critical Terms for Literary Study*, John Guillory notes that the canon is traditionally defined according to rule or measurement.[12] By focusing on the issue of judgment and exclusion, contemporary debates about the canon have depended upon a very specific and limited way of framing our use of prior writing materials. In his discussion of canon theory, Paul Lauter notes that the *Heath* tries to provide "materials" for answering questions about the formation of the canon,[13] but ultimately falls back in one way or another on the task of "reconstructing" the canon.[14] Although Walker does not articulate the theory behind her interest in Hurston, it seems clear that

---

11. A good example of this inauguration of the archive is provided by Joseph Tabbi, in his discussion of preserving materials for the future study of electronic literature, "Toward a Semantic Literary Web: Setting a Direction for the Electronic Literature Organization's Directory" (http://eliterature.org/pad/slw.html). Tabbi notes that any attempt to create a body of research material will necessarily involve including some and excluding other works, "Promoters of e-literature should avoid sounding too disappointed about the 'loss' of established works of e-lit whose platforms now are outdated." Instead, he emphasizes the importance of the founding act itself: "The recovery is itself a social and political act, since the only sure criterion for a work's importance is that someone, some group, cares enough to recognize and recover the work. This is a collective critical act that, like the recognition and reproduction of works by the dead, goes on after an author has completed a work."

12. John Guillory, "Canon," in *Critical Terms for Literary Study*, eds. Frank Lentricchia and Thomas McLaughlin, 2d ed. (Chicago: University of Chicago Press, 1995), 233.

13. Lauter, *Canons and Contexts*, 162.

14. Although Lauter sees *Reconstructing American Literary History* (ed. Sacvan Bercovitch [Cambridge, MA: Harvard University Press, 1986]) as ultimately conservative, he also concludes his discussion by asserting the continuing role of canons in academic study: "canons are socially constructed *by* people and *in* history . . . they have always changed and can be changed . . . they are deeply shaped by institutions and the material conditions under which writing is produced and consumed" (169).

hers is a story of an archive rather than a canon, and that the differences between the two have not been appreciated. If, as Derrida suggests, the very nature of the archive is to promise futurity rather than the dependence on the past that a canon implies, appeals to an archive model of fictionality sidestep the traditional structure of canons and truth legitimation. The degree to which such appeals really do break from disciplinary structures will be considered in the remainder of this chapter. In particular, we must account for the very structure of Walker's story: Why is the trip to Eatonville itself so important? Why work to find the actual grave of Hurston? In discussing the appeal of Hurston to later critics and writers, Hazel Carby has associated Hurston's writing with a certain colonial imagination that links traveler and explorer in "the romantic discovery by the writer of people and places unknown to the reader."[15] It is clear that Walker finds this site of discovery to be a principal attraction in Hurston's writing, extending Hurston's travels to become the very place of discovery and repository in Eatonville. Such a journey problematically leads Walker into the series of lies that she tells, but it also seems essential to the foundation of the Hurston archive and the promise of future writing. And yet, nothing in our models for fiction explain why the physical act of travel would be necessary to found such an archive. As I argued in the introduction, models of fictionality traditionally emphasize thought experiments and hypothetical conditions. This is especially the case with the sorts of "semi-fictions" like classifications that Hans Vaihinger associates with institutions. If Walker believes that the act of travel to a starting point is important to her use of Hurston for her own fiction, it seems that such an act marks the point at which her understanding of fictionality most clearly departs from traditional disciplinary definitions. It is the work of the physical journey that Andy Warhol helps to explain.

Warhol at Work

The Philosophy of Andy Warhol would seem an unlikely place to look for a theory of fiction, much less a commentary on Alice Walker's earnest attempt to understand the shared folklore of African American culture. Warhol's explicit rejection of struggles against stereotypes or social norms seems miles away from Walker: "I always go after the easiest thing, because if it's the easiest, for me it's usually the best."[16] While Warhol's tone throughout this

15. Carby, "The Politics of Fiction," 80.
16. Andy Warhol, *The Philosophy of Andy Warhol (From A to B and Back Again)* (San Diego: Harcourt, 1975), 83.

book is tongue-in-cheek, there can be no doubt that he takes a very different approach to the American imaginary. Like Walker, Warhol is fundamentally concerned with imagining American society. Warhol describes a vision of America with him as president: "We can start the country over from scratch. We can get the Indians back on the reservations making rugs and hunting for turquoise. . . . Can you see the Blue Room with Campbell's Soup Cans all over the walls? Because that's what Foreign Heads of State should see, Campbell Soup Cans and Elizabeth Taylor and Marilyn Monroe. That's America. That's what should be in the White House. And you would serve Dolly Madison ice cream. A, see yourself as others see you."[17] Warhol's description of America is striking because it addresses a topic very similar to what Walker struggles with: how do we recognize ourselves as part of American culture? While Warhol asks us to see ourselves as others see us, Walker quite explicitly asks her family to see themselves as Hurston sees them. Both likewise imagine community by delving into the past—Walker into the life of Hurston, Warhol into the absurd past of a pristine America inhabited only by television Indians and pop culture icons. Warhol's image of the American imaginary, however, is not part of some particularly literary activity but rather part of mundane social life. In other words, Warhol's account of imagining American culture moves from the restricted economy of Walker's essay on literature to the general economy of life in contemporary media culture.

Warhol opens his *Philosophy* by introducing the issue of social connections and cultural models that are such a fundamental part of his account of being an American. He describes the problems that arise from the fantasies that people develop around the future, especially around romance. Warhol notes in his discussion of love that "[p]eople have so many problems with love," and goes on to suggest that "[t]here should be courses on beauty and love and sex" (43). Warhol reconsiders, however: "But then I think, maybe it works out just as well that nobody takes you out of the dark about it, because if you really knew the whole story, you wouldn't have anything to think about or fantasize about for the rest of your life, and you might go crazy, having nothing to think about, since life is getting longer, anyway, leaving so much time after puberty to have sex in" (43). Warhol's approach to fantasy is exemplified by this passage; it is both a source of personal suffering as well as a compensation for the meaninglessness of life. Warhol locates these fantasies both in individual personal histories as well as in broad cultural images. He notes that "[w]ith everything changing so fast, you don't have a chance of

17. Ibid., 15. This passage occurs in dialogue between A (Warhol) and B and is attributed to B. Although not spoken by the Warhol voice, it seems that the general characterization of American culture is consistent with Warhol's view.

finding your fantasy image intact by the time you're ready for it. What about all the little boys who used to have fantasies about girls in beautiful lace bras and silk slips?" (52). Fantasies develop out of general cultural mores and media images, even though they leave individual and potentially quirky marks on people. By turning to the issue of desire, Warhol approaches contemporary culture and media exclusions in a fundamentally different way than Walker.

And yet Warhol's focus on desire in identification draws our attention to undercurrents in Walker's search for the archive. Derrida's discussion of the archive places desire at its heart.

> The *trouble de l'archive* stems from a *mal d'archive*. We are *en mal d'archive*: in need of archives. Listening to the French idiom, and in it the attribute *en mal de,* to be *en mal d'archive* can mean something else than to suffer from a sickness, from a trouble or from what the noun *mal* might name. It is to burn with a passion. It is never to rest, interminably, from searching for the archive right where it slips away. It is to run after the archive, even if there's too much of it, right where something in it anarchives itself. It is to have a compulsive, repetitive, and nostalgic desire for the archive, and irrepressible desire to return to the origin, a homesickness, a nostalgia for the return to the most archaic place of absolute commencement.[18]

The passion for something that slips away is clearly evident in Warhol's discussion of media images, but is also clear in Walker's search for Hurston's grave. Although Walker suggests that reading Hurston is a means of identifying with a group, the relationship between desire and identification—especially of Walker's own desire for Hurston's life story—is curiously neglected in her essay. And yet, clearly here is a story of passion that drives Walker beyond all boundaries of polite truth telling. Warhol's interest in desire and identification seems to me to be a way that we can understand the passion of Walker's own nostalgic quest for Hurston's grave and thus what drives our interest in archives in general.

Warhol is both attracted to and repelled by social fantasies. As he writes, "People's fantasies are what give them problems. If you didn't have fantasies you wouldn't have problems because you'd just take whatever was there. But then you wouldn't have romance, because romance is finding your fantasy in people who don't have it" (55). Elsewhere, Warhol is even more forceful in arguing that fantasies are not a matter of finding a partner who matches your

18. Derrida, *Archive Fever*, 91.

desire but rather of projecting desires in a fundamentally unstable way: "So today, if you see a person who looks like your teenage fantasy walking down the street, it's probably not your fantasy, but someone who had the same fantasy as you and decided instead of getting it or being it, to *look like it*, and so he went to the store and bought the look that you both like. So forget it" (53). Warhol describes social space so suffused by fantasies that individuals are left with only two choices: searching for their fantasies in others or imitating their fantasies in their own appearance. Very little room remains for simple identity or desire; rather, desire is always desire for a representation. Precisely this need for representation runs throughout Walker's search for Hurston—who, as we have seen, promises to allow for group identification in a way that Walker's friends and relatives immediately recognize. Indeed, it is precisely the representative quality of Hurston that lures Walker into telling lies about herself; I have already quoted Walker's remark that "as far as I'm concerned, she *is* my aunt—and that of all black people as well." Such a justification reads a historical figure symbolically and clearly substitutes for Hurston's literal identity a meaning very much invested in Walker's own need for a model.

Warhol, then, raises important questions about the simple narrative of discovery and identification that Walker offers us. The desire for identification that Walker wears so explicitly in her essay is shown to be a far from simple goal by Warhol. Warhol's central model for sexual fantasies is drag performance. He gives the following example:

> In *Women in Revolt,* Jackie Curtis ad-libbed one of the best lines of disillusionment with sex when he-as-she, portraying a virgin schoolteacher from Bayonne, New Jersey, was forced to give oral gratification—a blow-job—to Mr. America. After gagging and somehow finishing up, poor Jackie can't figure out if she's had sex or not—"This can't be what millions of girls commit suicide over when their boyfriends leave them. . . . " Jackie was acting out the puzzled thoughts so many people have when they realize sex is hard work just like everything else. (55)

This passage connects gender performance to the cultural and individual fantasies that I have already discussed. Sex represents for Warhol the point at which fantasies give way to the simple effort of work, of necessarily performing sexually. This performance is both a matter of the physical sexual act as well as the broader performance of gender and social identity. Warhol explains that good performers "are all-inclusive recorders, because they can mimic emotions as well as speech and looks and atmosphere—they're more inclusive than tape recordings or videotapes or novels. Good performers can somehow record complete experiences and people and situations and then pull out these recordings when they need them" (82). Although Warhol seems to feel that performance as a kind of work is most evident in explicitly physical acts, this passage makes clear that for him work is diffuse within social identity. A few pages later he offers what I take to be a general comment on this broad definition of work: "I suppose I have a really loose interpretation of 'work,' because I think that just being alive is so much work at something you don't always want to do. Being born is like being kidnapped. And then sold into slavery. People are working every minute. The machinery is always going. Even when you sleep" (96). Living, as Warhol says, is work. By this he seems to mean the work of performing social identities and fantasies; this work is always at odds with the fantasies built up by television and print media.

Warhol is not concerned with particular literary institutions. Nonetheless, his interest in the work of social performance should remind us of the emphasis on literary practice, of the disciplinary *habitus*, against which Walker's quest for an archive struggles. In trying to unpack the nature of desire and identification within a media environment, Warhol is obviously encouraging us to think about how our practices are structured. But it is also clear that Warhol's understanding of practice emphasizes not the conventions that give that shape but the work that it requires. Pierre Bourdieu's concept of the *habitus,* which provides the theory for so much recent work on literary institutions, is ultimately structuralist in nature—speaking of fields, structures, and formulae. Bourdieu describes the *habitus* in The Logic of Practice:

> The conditionings associated with a particular class of conditions of existence produce *habitus,* systems of durable, transposable dispositions, structured structures predisposed to function as structuring structures, that is, as principles which generate and organize practices and representations that can be objectively adapted to their outcomes without presupposing a conscious aiming at ends or an express mastery of the operations necessary in order to attain them. Objectively "regulated" and "regular" without being in any way the product of obedience to rules, they can be collectively orchestrated without being the product of the organizing action of a conductor.[19]

---

19. Pierre Bourdieu, *The Logic of Practice,* trans. Richard Nice (Stanford, CA: Stanford University Press, 1990), 53.

While Warhol is clearly also interested in the ways that actions are shaped unconsciously, his emphasis is less on the "structuring structures" than the effort that goes into practice. In this, it seems, Warhol offers an important supplement to the ways that we usually think about social performance—a supplement that will help to link fictionality and the civil imaginary.

Throughout *Philosophy* Warhol offers himself and his industrially inspired art as a kind of return to work and debunking of aesthetic "auras." Warhol defines himself as doing a kind of "business art": "Business art is the step that comes after Art. I started as a commercial artist, and I want to finish as a business artist. After I did the thing called 'art' or whatever it's called, I went into business art. I wanted to be an Art Businessman, or a Business Artist. Being good at business is the most fascinating kind of art" (92). Although Warhol is playing on a number of different senses of the word *artist* here, what seems most important is that he wants to pull emphasis in art away from aesthetic principles and back towards a calculus of simple production and work. Warhol tells the following story: "When Picasso died I read in a magazine that he had made four thousand masterpieces in his lifetime and I thought, 'Gee, I could do that in a day.' You see, the way I do them, with my technique, I really thought I could do four thousand in a day. And they'd all be masterpieces because they'd all be the same painting" (148). It turns out, as Warhol relays, he was unable to complete the four thousand paintings in a single day. Although he is clearly parodying clichés about what makes a masterpiece and why it is important that a particular work be unique, what seems especially important in this story is Warhol's insistence on returning artistic creation to work and production. Warhol concludes his discussion of fame earlier in the book: "So you should always have a product that's not just 'you.' An actress should count up her plays and movies and a model should count up her photographs and a writer should count up his words and an artist should count up his pictures so you always know exactly what you're worth, and you don't get stuck thinking your product is you and your fame, and your aura" (86).

In emphasizing the principle of work which runs contrary to the aura of fame, Warhol rejects the basis for much of the recent work on artistic institutions. Indeed, the issue that launched my discussion of Warhol in particular is the problem of the disciplinary structure of knowledge, a problem invoked by Walker's essay. For Warhol, work is an alternative to the social conventions that usually define the value of art. In particular, Warhol is proposing an alternative to the language of "cultural capital," which accepts the aura as a principal value in artworlds. Warhol's insistence on the gross work of artistic projection—on "business art"—is in fact a much stronger rejection of traditional ways of thinking about the value of art based on symbolic capital. Here's Bourdieu's definition of the "two economic logics" of art:

> These fields are the site of the antagonistic coexistence of two modes of production and circulation obeying inverse logics. At one pole, there is the anti-"economic" economy of pure art. Founded on the obligatory recognition of the values of disinterestedness and on the denegation of the "economy" (of the "commercial") and of "economic" profit (in the short term), it privileges production and its specific necessities, the outcome of any autonomous history. This production, which can acknowledge no other demand than one it can generate itself, but only in the long term, is oriented to the accumulation of symbolic capital, a kind of "economic" capital denied but recognized, and hence legitimate—a veritable credit, and capable of assuring, under certain conditions and in the long term, "economic" profits. At the other pole, there is the "economic" logic of the literary and artistic industries which, since they make the trade in cultural goods just another trade, confer priority on distribution, on immediate and temporary success, measured for example by the print run, and which are content to adjust themselves to the pre-existing demand of a clientele.[20]

Warhol's rejection of the aura is a rejection of the economy of symbolic capital. What he offers instead is a return to the principle of work, which is closer to the "immediate and temporary" demands of the art industry. Warhol's interest in work, however, attends more closely to the very material nature of production rather than to abstract demands like print runs and distribution. In this sense, Warhol's understanding of art has more in common with Evan Watkins's discussion of "work time" in English departments than with traditional analyses of discipline and institution. Watkins argues that the disciplinary structure of English can be studied not only as a collection of ideologies and practices but also as a much more material structure of work: "In this context, it matters less *how* you were taught Romantic poetry say—what socialization or countersocialization of expectations took place—than what grade you got at the end of the process. Thus so far from an abstraction, labor force seems appropriate enough to designate the activities of a large body of people who in the gross number terms of grades generate over and over, like the intellectual 'assembly line' to which it's often been compared, the discriminations on which economic opportunity in part depends."[21]

20. Pierre Bourdieu, *The Rules of Art: Genesis and Structure of the Literary Field*, trans. Susan Emanuel (Stanford, CA: Stanford University Press, 1995), 142.
21. Evan Watkins, *Work Time: English Departments and the Circulation of Cultural Value*

In *Philosophy,* Warhol implies that his own relentlessly mundane films are ways of exposing the machinery of social performance, the work of everyday life. Warhol explains:

> What I was actually trying to do in my early movies was show how people can meet other people and what they can do and what they can say to each other. That was the whole idea: two people getting acquainted. And then when you saw it and you saw the sheer simplicity of it, you learned what it was all about. Those movies showed you how some people act and react with other people. They were like actual sociological "For instance"s. They were like documentaries, and if you thought it could apply to you, it was an example, and if it didn't apply to you, at least it was a documentary, it could apply to someone you knew and it could clear up some questions you had about them. (48)

The description in this passage of what people "can do" seems to me another way of referring to the work of social performance. Warhol claims that his films achieve a documentary quality by making this work evident. It should be clear that Warhol has nothing in mind that would normally be considered sociological in the sense of providing an average experience. Such definitions of average experience depend heavily on the kinds of disciplinary conventions that we have already noted both Warhol and Walker seek to avoid. Instead the interest here is on the act or the mechanics of the performance. Warhol's description of *Tub Girls* makes the effort of the performance clear: "In *Tub Girls,* for example, the girls had to take baths with people in tubs, and they learned how to take baths with other people. While we were doing *Tub Girls.* They met in a tub. And the girl would have to carry her tub to the next person she'd have to take a bath with, so she'd put her tub under her arm and carry her tub" (48). Warhol's interest here is not in some kind of average way of taking baths, nor is the lesson (how to take baths with other people) likely to be of much practical relevance. Instead what seems to be interesting is the effort and mechanics of the task: what kind of tub to use ("We used a clear plastic tub") and how it is carried from bath to bath.

When Warhol chooses to focus on the work of social performance rather than on the structures that give it shape, he is anticipating the direction of American studies in the last decade. What Warhol does especially well is to link social performance to the objects that circulate within the American imaginary. Both are themes important to contemporary literary criticism,

---

(Stanford, CA: Stanford University Press, 1989), 6.

but the connection between these seem to be inadequately explained outside of Warhol's interest in work. We can see a general movement over the last decade from an interest in American "ideology" towards an idea of the American imaginary based on social practices. This is the way that Lauren Berlant describes the functioning of the "national symbolic" in Hawthorne's writing, which works to interpellate the reader into a national subject position; Hawthorne's project is "reconstructing the individual reader into a communal/national subject."[22] Berlant describes the national symbolic not just as a set of beliefs but as a set of objects linked to cultural practices: "'America' is an assumed relation, an explication of ongoing collective practices, and also an occasion for exploring what it means that national subjects already share not just a history, or a political allegiance, but a set of forms and the affect that makes these forms meaningful" (4). This interest in the imagined objects of American society is an essential component of Warhol's interest in the work of performance and the key to the importance of his way of thinking about society. When Simon During discusses the concept of the "civil imaginary," he captures just this sense of the social whole:

> The civil Imaginary is an attempt to order what Steele calls "the uncontrollable jumble of Persons and Things" in that society. Thus its purpose is in part ethical in the Foucauldian sense. It produces representations of manners, taste, behaviour, utterances for imitation by individual lives. Its sphere is secular—that is, not religiously enthusiastic. It is *not* political (it relies on what Habermas has called the modern split between politics and ethics), it is not dominated by the old caste system, not determined by classical and Renaissance *virtu*. Its prime value is a sociability which cannot be expressed in terms of moral laws.[23]

During distinguishes between what we would normally think of ideology—abstract principles and moral laws—and the "jumble" of objects that make up society. Such objects order behavior in subtle ways.

Those objects have a degree of materiality that seems to me to be an important supplement to theories of social practice. In this regard, we might place Warhol's interest in the work of social performance in the context of Judith Butler's discussion of materiality in gender performance. In particular, Warhol and Butler share an emphasis on the effort that social categories

22. Lauren Berlant, *The Anatomy of Nation Fantasy: Hawthorne, Utopia, and Everyday Life* (Chicago: University of Chicago Press, 1991), 45.
23. Simon During, "Literature—Nationalism's Other? The Case for Revision," in *Nation and Narration,* ed. Homi K. Bhabha (London: Routledge, 1990), 142–43.

demand. Butler, after all, opens *Bodies That Matter* by invoking the need for reiterating gender categories:

> "[S]ex" not only functions as a norm, but is part of a regulatory practice that produces the bodies it governs, that is, whose regulatory force is made clear as a kind of productive power, the power to produce—demarcate, circulate, differentiate—the bodies it controls. Thus, "sex" is a regulatory ideal whose materialization is compelled, and this materialization takes place (or fails to take place) through certain highly regulated practices. In other words, "sex" is an ideal construct which is forcibly materialized through time. It is not a simple fact or static condition of a body, but a process whereby regulatory norms materializes "sex" and achieve this materialization through a forcible reiteration of those norms.[24]

Like Warhol's *Philosophy*, this passage veers from a simpler and more familiar interest in social norms to attend to the work of performance that they demand. Perhaps more importantly for my analysis of the American imaginary in Warhol's writing, Butler likewise links this work to materialization. The objects of the social imaginary owe their materiality to this work. Thinking about American culture comprising such objects constantly involved with work reflects the archive rather than a discipline: where the archive emphasizes the work that it promises, the discipline implies a set of definitions and structures. The objects of the social imaginary, which have no existence outside of the social behaviors that constantly materialize them, capture this more sophisticated sense of how American social identity is shaped.

Accidental Lies and Becoming Fictional

How does this understanding of the American social imaginary lead to a theory of fictionality? Consider Warhol's appeal to the "leftover," which is a point at which the place of objects within a whole social space ultimately raises questions about truth and lying. Warhol begins by noting, "I always like to work on leftovers, doing the leftover things. Things that were discarded, that everybody knew were no good." Warhol gives an example:

---

24. Judith Butler, *Bodies That Matter: On the Discursive Limits of "Sex"* (New York: Routledge, 1993), 1–2.

> When I see an old Esther Williams movie and a hundred girls are jumping off their swings, I think of what the auditions must have been like and about all the takes where maybe one girl didn't have the nerve to jump when she was supposed to, and I think about her left over on the swing. So that take of the scene was a leftover on the editing-room floor—an out-take—and the girl was probably a leftover at that point—she was probably fired—so the whole scene is much funnier than the real scene where everything went right, and the girl who didn't jump is the star of the out-take. (93)

Warhol concludes by connecting this leftover scene to the issue of waste and productivity: "I'm not saying that popular taste is bad so that what's left over from the bad taste is good: I'm saying that what's left over is probably bad, but if you can take it and make it good or at least interesting, then you're not wasting as much as you would otherwise" (93). The "interesting" scene seems to me to echo Warhol's idea of mechanical, documentary scenes in films like *Tub Girls*. The leftover reminds us of the work of the original scene—the fact that all the actresses had to perform the scene just right, and that there were many chances to mess up. The outtake leftover, like the monotonous "documentary" about mundane actions, points out the mechanics of everyday performance.

When Warhol raises the issue of productivity and excess he connects his discussion of the leftover to his treatment of social space in *Philosophy*. One point at which this book explicitly discusses media is when Warhol claims that individuals can extend themselves beyond their own personal space: "Before media there used to be a physical limit on how much space one person could take up by themselves. People, I think, are the only things that know how to take up more space than the space they're actually in, because with media, you can sit back and still let yourself fill up space on records, in the movies, most exclusively on the telephone and least exclusively on television" (146). Warhol's description of media as a way of allowing people to take up more space than they would physically reflects his thinking about space as a medium for personal connections. His first chapter, in fact, opens by introducing the issue of this sort of social relation: "At a certain point in my life, in the late 50s, I began to feel that I was picking up problems from the people I knew" (21). He goes on to suggest that "these problems of friends were spreading themselves onto me like germs" (21). This observation becomes the occasion for Warhol to think about his own childhood and his love of solitude. He concludes the story by explaining that he escaped his friends' problems by buying a television: "I kept the TV on all the time, especially while people were telling me their problems, and the television I found to be just diverting enough so the problems people told me didn't really affect me any more. It was like some kind of magic" (24). Media here embody the power of individuals to extend their influence beyond its physical limits, but they also make personal connection seem less real. Television describes a kind of social relationship that lacks the immediacy that so troubles Warhol. Media fill up all available space, making it impossible for the "germs" of friends' problems to infect Warhol. At the same time, however, Warhol describes the beauty of empty space: "When I look at things, I always see the space they occupy. I always want the space to reappear, to make a comeback, because it's lost space when there's something in it. If I see a chair in a beautiful space, no matter how beautiful the chair is, it can never be as beautiful to me as the plain space" (144). Warhol concludes that "[e]verything in your closet should have an expiration date on it the way milk and bread and magazines and newspapers do, and once something passes its expiration date, you should throw it out" (145). Warhol understands his own artistic practice as filling space: "An artist is somebody who produces things that people don't need to have but that he—for *some reason*—thinks it would be a good idea to give them" (144). Warhol goes on to state the paradox more directly: "So on the one hand I really believe in empty spaces, but on the other hand, because I'm still making some art, I'm still making junk for people to put in their spaces that I believe should be empty" (144). Warhol's economy of artistic production as creating objects that fill up space is obviously connected to his understanding of the leftover as something recycled; reusing leftovers seems to be a way of decreasing the space used up by his art.

Warhol suggests that space must either be empty or uncomfortably full. Ironically, space can seem empty despite being filled with media images so long as those images create the feeling of the flat uniformity that he suggests helped him escape the "germs" of his friends problems. Warhol associates uniformity with mass-produced objects like Coca-Cola. Slavoj Žižek has remarked about the curious immateriality of a product like Coke, since, it is "surplus-enjoyment personified": "It is no surprise that Coke was first introduced as a medicine—its strange taste does not seem to provide any particular satisfaction; it is not directly pleasing and endearing; however, it is precisely as such, as transcending any immediate use-value . . . that Coke functions as a direct embodiment of 'it': of the pure surplus of enjoyment over standard satisfactions."[25] Žižek goes on to make this connection to materiality explicit: "when, some years ago, the advertising slogan for Coke

---

25. Slavoj Žižek, *The Fragile Absolute: Or, Why Is the Christian Legacy Worth Fighting For?* (London: Verso, 2000), 22.

was 'Coke is *it!*,' we should note its thorough ambiguity: 'that's it' precisely in so far as that's *never* actually *it*, precisely in so far as every satisfaction opens up a gap of 'I want *more!*'" (22). Warhol is similarly interested in the nature of the real within American social space. Warhol remarks, "What's great about this country is that America started the tradition where the richest consumers buy essentially the same things as the poorest. You can be watching TV and see Coca-Cola, and you can know that the President drinks Coke, Liz Taylor drinks Coke, and just think, you can drink Coke, too. A Coke is a Coke and no amount of money can get you a better Coke than the one the bum on the corner is drinking" (100–101). America is a place of uniformity, in which mass articles are identical. This uniformity produces a space that appears uncluttered.

In evoking such abstract, consumerist space, Warhol describes a landscape that will be familiar from Baudrillardian postmodernism.[26] Warhol's embrace of flat space is not a symptom so much as a response to the postmodern media environment. Warhol's fondness for television and his interest in the leftover seem to inoculate him against the "germs" of others' problems but in very different ways. Both work to ease the conflict between fantasy and social work or performance. In television, this resolution is a matter of simply anaesthetizing performance—allowing the media to distract us from the roles that we perform. Leftover art, conversely, foregrounds the conflict between work and fantasy. One of Warhol's goals both in *Philosophy* as well as in his painting and filmmaking is revealing what he calls the "machinery" of media. In thinking about his own death in the context of full and empty spaces, Warhol remarks, "The worst thing that could happen to you after the end of your time would be to be embalmed and laid up in a pyramid. I'm repulsed when I think about the Egyptians taking each organ and embalming it separately in its own receptacle. I want my machinery to disappear" (113). The disappearance of machinery is linked in Warhol's discussion to the reuse of leftover materials; thus, exploiting the unused clears space. Using leftover materials and clearing space works against the flat uniformity of contemporary media, but in the process it reveals at least for a time the very personal "machinery" of individual lives. Leftovers, in other words, for all that they aspire to empty space, threaten to entangle us back into the individual connections that contain the "germs" of others' problems.

26. Baudrillard opens *America* (trans. Chris Turner [London: Verso, 1988]), for example, by describing traveling across the American West: "Speed creates pure objects. . . . Triumph of forgetting over memory, an uncultivated, amnesic intoxication. The superficiality and reversibility of a pure object in the pure geometry of the desert. Driving like this produces a kind of invisibility, transparency, or transversality in things, simply by emptying them out" (6–7).

FOLK CULTURE, THE ARCHIVE, AND THE WORK OF THE IMAGINARY

There is a great deal of similarity between Warhol's appeal to the leftover and Walker's search for the archive. Both rely on disorganized and neglected materials for new artistic work, and both must reject standard artistic practices whose rules dictate that these materials should be ignored. The institutional neglect of these materials means that art based on the leftover will always seem to be a kind of misunderstanding, a mistake. A few pages after his discussion of the leftover Warhol claims that he likes to be misunderstood by the people he works with: "Something that I look for in an associate is a certain amount of misunderstanding of what I'm trying to do" (99). Warhol explains: "If people never misunderstand you, and if they do everything exactly the way you tell them to, they're just transmitters of your ideas, and you get bored with that. But when you work with people who misunderstand you, instead of getting *transmissions* you get *transmutations,* and that's much more interesting in the long run" (99). Warhol's language in this passage picks up on metaphors of media. A bad associate is one who functions essentially like a medium in much the same way that modern media allow individuals to take up more space than they could physically. In misunderstanding, however, this logic of space and the media is transformed; associates are not simply ways of allowing Warhol to extend himself in space. The use of the leftover, likewise, makes sense according to such a logic. While a traditional artist extends him- or herself into space by creating things that people don't want but that the artist thinks they should have, an artist of the leftover works with already existing materials. Such leftovers likewise seem to work by transmutation; as Warhol remarks, a buffoon of the original scene is the star of the outtake. Warhol is describing something similar to the way that Walker manipulates the situation to misrepresent herself to those that she visits, as when she allows the claim that "as far as I'm concerned, she *is* my aunt—and that of all black people as well" to be taken literally by the people that she meets. Both willfully ignore the original context of the statement—the way that Walker's audience will understand her claim to be Hurston's niece—and instead put it to some new use. These lies, we should note, are quite clearly the result of an intentional effort—work—on the part of both Walker and Warhol. Indeed, accidental misuse becomes possible for Warhol only in the context of artistic production, where he searches for material for new projects rather than in everyday viewing. Warhol is not interested in misunderstanding by those who view or buy his art as much as misunderstandings by those who are helping him to make it. Likewise, Walker's lies emerge in the course of her investigation as she adopts an identity that explains her task. The fanciful explanation that Hurston is the aunt "of all black people" is made possible only because the more literal (but untrue) explanation of her relationship is accepted by her interviewees to explain the job that she has undertaken.

These "accidental" interventions into an archive of neglected material occur on the boundary of artistic activity. Indeed, both Walker and Warhol self-consciously adopt a marginal position in relation to their subject matter and legitimate practices. In particular, Warhol's leftover art stands on the very edge of these institutions, marking the point at which we can see those institutions and their expectations at work. This is why a film like *Tub Girls* seems to be a misunderstanding of the conventions of the documentary. In the introduction I have suggested that the issue of fictionality reveals the functioning of disciplines and institutional boundaries. In Warhol's accidental lies we have the clearest articulation yet of the way that these fictions can point back to these boundaries, making them seem contingent and always susceptible to misunderstanding. Warhol's leftover art, in other words, is always on the cusp of entering into convention, much as Walker's discovered archive marks the point at which a field of study is being defined for the future. Both writers describe what we could call, to adopt a Deleuzian formulation, the *becoming-fictional* of the work, the point at which something mechanical begins to give way to a future where fiction can be used more directly.[27] The example in Warhol makes this point clearly: the mistake (the girl who didn't jump) simply tells a different story. It is only in the comparison between the legitimate and illegitimate forms of artistic work that we can see what he has done to these leftovers. Indeed, it is only in the gap between one narrative and the other that the archive is visible at all.

I would suggest that the focus on objects that I have noted in Warhol is already a step towards a theory of becoming-fictional, and that this understanding of fictionality is contained—although not really articulated by critics—in the concept of the social imaginary. This position of becoming-fictional means that fiction is just on the cusp of emerging into an acceptable

---

27. Although Deleuze and Guattari's description of "becoming" is well known and captures the sense of a threshold phenomenon, the instability that they associate with such becoming is not something that I want to emphasize here. Thus in *A Thousand Plateaus: Capitalism and Schizophrenia* (trans. Brian Massumi [Minneapolis: University of Minnesota Press, 1987]) Deleuze and Guattari describe interest in becoming as marking "the thresholds through which an idea passes, the journeys it takes that change its nature or object" (235) but also suggest that becoming involves a multiplicity whose transformation is ongoing: "Since its variations and dimensions are immanent to it, *it amounts to the same thing to say that each multiplicity is already composed of heterogeneous terms in symbiosis, and that a multiplicity is continually transforming itself into a sting of other multiplicities, according to its thresholds and doors*" (249). In the case of Warhol and Walker, however, I have described more an interest in one particular, fixed threshold, whose function as a transition point does specific institutional work rather than giving way to an endless series of new multiplicities.

discourse and that we can see the mechanical effort and tenuous boundaries that are exposed in the process. When Benedict Anderson refers to "imagined communities" in his influential book of the same name, he is obviously drawing on a notion of the fictional; in fact, many of his principal examples of the imagined community are provided by novels. For him, what makes a community "imagined" is that there are no objective reasons for the connections between individuals. Describing the modern newspaper, Anderson remarks, "Why are these events so juxtaposed? What connects them to each other? Not sheer caprice. Yet obviously most of them happen independently, without the actors being aware of each other or of what the others are up to. The arbitrariness of their inclusion and juxtaposition (a later edition will substitute a baseball triumph for Mitterrand) shows that the linkage between them is imagined."[28] The imagined connections that make up the nation transcend causal or strictly logical linkages; they are always on the cusp of capriciousness, and always retain a haze of appearing to be excessive, unnecessary, and on some level arbitrary. Some postcolonial critics have resisted Anderson's account of the modern nation as based on too neat and stable an understanding of a horizontal national space. Homi Bhabha's attention to crossing national borders and to national margins in "DissemiNation" is probably the best known of these critiques. In place of Anderson's image of the defined nation, Bhabha offers an image of constant and incomplete national writing in the concept of the performative:

> The performative intervenes in the sovereignty of the nation's *self-generation* by casting a shadow between the people as "image" and its signification as a differentiating sign of Self, distinct from the Other or the Outside. In place of the polarity of a prefigurative self-generating nation itself and extrinsic Other nations, the performative introduces a temporality of the "in-between" through the "gap" or "emptiness" of the signifier and that punctuates linguistic difference. The boundary that marks the nation's selfhood interrupts the self-generating time of national production with a space of representation that threatens binary division with its difference.[29]

Although Bhabha's emphasis on boundaries and self-division certainly is a change in tone from Anderson's account, even there we can see an emphasis on the rituals of daily citizenship embodied in the reading of the fictional

---

28. Benedict Anderson, *Imagined Communities: Reflections on the Origin and Spread of Nationalism*, rev. ed. (London: Verson, 1991), 33.

29. Homi K. Bhabha, "DissemiNation: Time, Narrative, and the Margins of the Modern Nation," in *Nation and Narration*, ed. Homi K. Bhabha (London: Routledge, 1990), 299.

newspaper. Bhabha's description of the performative clearly echoes Warhol's leftover art. Both appear to be excessive and unnecessary—accidental. The performative for Bhabha is precisely what is necessary to the nation but does not simply go without saying. It is on the boundary between social order and individual action. In this regard, it will remind us of Warhol's description of a social space that becomes personalized when we break from uniform media objects to emphasize the leftover. Both represent the activity of imagining on the boundary between the acceptable and the misunderstood; in other words, both are instances of becoming-fictional.

In treating the social imaginary as a fiction just on the cusp of emerging, then, Warhol is emphasizing the effort that goes into producing it; it is not a social structure so much as a constantly produced ontology. As Warhol has suggested, the stuff of American society is always the basis upon which the work of social performance is accomplished. Warhol's interest in the objects of the American imaginary in one sense simply exposes the institutional boundaries that define art and social conventions. But these objects also have a materiality that constantly reasserts itself. This is why the physical journey to Hurston's gravesite, and the very concrete act of erecting a gravestone, is central to her story of the discovery of a folkloric archive; this archive, she claims, will then make her own literary writing possible. Both are acts that direct us back to the raw "stuff" of this folklore. Such materiality is, it seems to me, the very basis of the archive, which always seems to be more physical than the disciplines that spring up around it. Recognizing this materiality helps us to understand why the lie that is the basis of the journey is so problematic for her essay. Her quest for the archival point is the attempt to create the condition of fiction. It is a point of becoming-fictional. That is, the archive is a point that balances between a space outside of the institutions of writing and the future, productive deploying of the fictional. We see much the same thing in Warhol, where the mechanical lie points back to the work of making art possible. Warhol's *Philosophy* is not an artistic theory built on institutional roles, nor is it a kind of Duchampian parody of the art world. It is, instead, an articulation of the way that conditions are opened up for artistic production.

Walker and Warhol capture the understanding of fictionality implicit but unspoken by the *Heath* and critics working under the banner of the construction of an archive of writing by those excluded from more traditional canons. This threshold position and gesture towards the future is one that recurs frequently in recent work on American culture. In the collection *The Futures of American Studies* (2002), Donald Pease and Robyn Wiegman foreground the issue of futurity by starting from a 1979 essay that foretells the future of American studies: "Insofar as the essays here deliver the future mutations of American studies from a past mode of representation in which it was incubating, they transform the defensive strategies expressive of Wise's future fears into the portals through which alternative futures will have entered American studies."[30] Walker, likewise, has shown us that creating an archive is a way of promising a future; such archives balance themselves on the cusp between origin and discipline. Derrida captures this balance when he describes the archive as a mechanical chore. The "impression" of the archive is technical, mechanical; it is, he says, "that re-producible, iterable, and conservative production of memory . . . that objectivizable storage called the archive."[31] If modern nations in some sense have always depended on this peculiar understanding of becoming-fictional, it is only as this model for fictionality has been adopted by both critics and writers that we can speak about it becoming one of the strands of contemporary fictionality.

30. Donald E. Pease and Robyn Wiegman, "Futures," in *The Futures of American Studies*, eds. Donald E. Pease and Robyn Wiegman (Durham, NC: Duke University Press, 2002), 4.
31. Derrida, *Archive Fever*, 26.

CHAPTER 3

Fiction, Fraud, and Fakes

Thus far I have suggested two distinct ways that fictionality is imagined and justified in contemporary American culture: as myth and as cultural archive. Both respond directly to literary institutions and represent attempts to redefine the relationship between a group of writers and literary traditions connected to those institutions. One difference between the two definitions is their relationship with the most traditional ways of thinking about literature's nature and value. While John Barth embraces a traditional understanding of literature as striving to transcend its moment, Alice Walker and Andy Warhol stand back from this traditional justification for literature and instead look for ways to reform our definition of art and literature.

In this chapter I would like to continue this movement away from traditional definitions of literature by considering a third definition that takes a position even more distinctly outside of literary institutions by defining writing as a variety of lying. In some sense, equating fiction and lies might be seen as typical of the poststructuralist-inspired postmodernism of the 1990s that I discussed briefly in the first chapter. There I noted that Barth's use of myth as a model for fictionality, with its roots in 1950s existentialist psychoanalysis, needed to be distinguished from later definitions of postmodernism based on the theories of Jacques Derrida and Jean-François Lyotard. To define writing as a form of lying would seem to reflect such later concerns, and indeed many of the writers most embraced by poststructuralist postmodernism—like Don DeLillo or Paul Auster—do seem to foreground misrepresentation or lying as a theme. Nonetheless, I will suggest that the equation of fiction and lying is considerably more complex and disparate than it might first appear. The use of the fictionality-as-lie justification for creative writing is significantly different from the first two definitions in that it is used by a variety of writers for a variety of different artistic and institutional purposes. More importantly, although we have seen many writers toy with the idea that fiction is just a matter of lying—indeed, both Walker and Warhol entertain the idea—all the writers that I have discussed so far eventually discard this idea for some other definition of fiction. To define fiction wholeheartedly as a lie and still to claim importance and legitimacy for it demands very careful rhetorical work.

It has become a cliché that postmodernism is fascinated with lying because we have lost confidence in traditional notions of the truth. The equation between fiction and lies has been deployed by critics as an easy explanation for postmodern texts. As I have done in other chapters, however, I will locate appeals to lying carefully within the context of changes in literary and publishing institutions. Why writers define their stories as lies has less to do with a deconstructionist suspicion about the truth, I will argue, and more to do with the position of writers within a public sphere defined by the marketplace of publishing houses, small magazines, and university criticism. These writers parody traditional literary and publishing institutions without the impetus for reform that we saw in the previous chapter, but their work is nonetheless clearly "literary" because these institutions continue to provide the context in which their stories must be read. This vestigial commitment to traditional literary values and definitions will continue to fade in subsequent chapters.

Nemerov's Fraud

We can glimpse the definition of fiction as a lie as it is beginning to develop in a contemporary context in Howard Nemerov's critical meditation, *Journal of the Fictive Life* (1965). Nemerov's "Reflexions of the Novelist Felix Ledger" circles around the issue of the referentiality of the novel and how it relates to the mind of its creator. These dynamics are evident on the very first page of the book:

> One thing "the novel" did, quietly, offhandedly, maybe by accident: It gave readers the possibility of believing in the past, in their own past, as substantially existing behind them (even though examination would have proved their memory of this past projected by means of novelistic fictions, hence absurdly at variance with what happened).
> "The novel," then, was a way of constructing a certain feeling of reality, rather than a reality, by means of formal presuppositions about life, especially the one which claimed that life was a story (with all the following propositions about purpose, identity, history, God).[1]

According to this passage, the past is invented, a kind of lie, because of the limitations of memory. We can see in this passage the anxiety we have noted in other contemporary writers about the need to define the validity of creative writing. This anxiety within Nemerov's book arises out of an understanding of psychoanalysis that defines the human mind as inevitably producing lies. Nemerov's claims about the fundamental working of guilt and deception in the writing of a novel are clear in the following passage:

> The game of the novel, that cruel initiation rite described earlier, isn't that exactly what I have been playing with myself? By means of slender filaments of association, remote and sometimes purely grammatical linkages, paranoiac assertions of a hidden guilt in the most obvious and trivial images of daily life, I have been building up certain structures; to what do these structures correspond? Do they, for example, have the nature of self-discovery? Or are they not, instead, discoveries of a fictive self corresponding—as in that game—to my fears about my own character rather than that character itself? (119)

As Nemerov describes it, writing does not represent the world, nor is it a vehicle for self-discovery. Instead, it is an attempt to construct a "fictive self" that feigns self-discovery, all the while really reflecting the writer's own fears and guilt. It is in this sense that Nemerov seems to use the term *fictive life* throughout his book—as a description of the way that individuals create selves that hide other facts of life.

---

1. Howard Nemerov, *Journal of the Fictive Life* (1965; Chicago: University of Chicago Press, 1981), 3.

As a literary theme, Nemerov's interest in the way that individuals fictionalize their lives and the past is an important component of contemporary American literature. Indeed, the gap between fantasy worlds and mundane reality has been an especially important issue in the post–World War II period. It is routine now to describe modern literature as concerned with the mind and perception; such an interest naturally leads many writers to be interested in the gaps between an interior fantasy world and reality. One thinks, for example, not only of tension between memories and clock time in the Quentin section of Faulkner's *Sound and the Fury* (1929) but also of more straightforward narratives of personal fantasy like James Thurber's "The Secret Life of Walter Mitty" (1939). As the period goes on, these individual fantasies more often become equated with the fictionalization of history and politics; it is in such cases that we most often characterize such fictionalization as postmodern. Thus, we might think of a conspiracy novel like Don DeLillo's *Libra* (1988) as an example of the migration of Nemerov's psychology of personal fraud to a larger political arena. A good example of the balance between personal delusion and historical rewriting is Walter Abish's *How German Is It?* (1980). Abish weaves together the personal and the political in his central character of Ulrich Hargenau, a writer whose own family history brings him up against the legacy of Nazi Germany. Hargenau himself constantly, if unconsciously, collects and reuses personal events for his own writerly purposes. Abish asks this question directly:

> I still love Paula Hargenau and I do not love Marie-Jean Filebra, he wrote in his notebook in Paris. That was the first entry he had made in his Paris notebook. Was he aware that he was taking notes for a future book? Was he aware that he would eventually return to Würtenburg and there, in a new apartment, quietly piece together his next novel, a novel based on his six months' stay in Paris, a novel based on his affair with Marie-Jean Filebra, a novel based on his desire to efface everything that had preceded his trip to Paris.[2]

Hargenau's struggles with his own creative rewriting of his past parallel the rewriting of the Nazi past that he experiences throughout Germany. In particular, he travels to Brumholdstein, a town built on the site of the former concentration camp Durst: "Durst was, so to speak, Brumholstein's antecedent. However, there are no books to be found on Durst. And Durst, accordingly, has no official history" (81). Here the fictionality of personal

---

2. Walter Abish, *How German Is It?* (New York: New Directions, 1980), 17.

effacement and fraud is extended to encompass the writing of history and social identity.

The example of Abish's *How German Is It?* makes clear, I think, that a very particular understanding of the lie is at the heart of much of our discussion of postmodernity. What differentiates "The Secret Life of Walter Mitty" from Abish's novel is precisely that the fantasies described are not allowed to remain personal and separate from the characters' interactions but are rather woven into the novel's social and political reality. The fictionality that develops around this way of thinking about fantasy depends on the movement beyond the individual into the social. It is in this regard that Fredric Jameson's definition of postmodernity as a loss of cognitive mapping makes particular sense. Jameson sees an interest in conspiracy as a reflection of our desperate need to makes sense of (or map) the larger geopolitical world. In a study of conspiracy films, Jameson writes about the climactic scene in *All the President's Men,*

> For it is the impossible vision of totality—here recovered in the moment in which the possibility of conspiracy confirms the possibility of the very unity of the social order itself—that is celebrated in this well-nigh paradisal moment. This is then the link between the phenomenal and the noumenal, or the ideological and the Utopian. This mounting image, underscored by the audible emergence, for the first time in the film, of the solemn music that so remarkably confirms the investigation's and the film's *telos,* in which the map of conspiracy itself, with its streets now radiating out through Washington from this ultimate center, unexpectedly suggests the possibility of cognitive mapping as a whole and stands as its substitute and yet its allegory all at once.[3]

According to Jameson, conspiracies are inherently postmodern because they mark our attempt to move beyond the individual perception to make sense of social space as a whole. In turn, fiction that is fascinated by fantasy becomes postmodern when that fantasy involves others.[4] Lying here is an act

---

3. Fredric Jameson, *The Geopolitical Aesthetic: Cinema and Space in the World System* (Bloomington: Indiana University Press, 1992), 79.

4. This definition of postmodernity is confirmed in an unlikely way by Brian McHale's influential early study, *Postmodernist Fiction* (New York: Methuen, 1987). McHale defines postmodernism as a shift from modernist interest in epistemology (how we know things) to ontology (our modes of being). His first, and key, example of this transition is Faulkner's *Absalom, Absalom!* which shifts from modernism to postmodernism at precisely the moment when fantasies are shared: "In Ch. 8, Quentin and Shreve reach the limit of their knowledge of the Sutpen murder-mystery; nevertheless they go on, beyond reconstruction to pure speculation. The

of shared deceptions. It should be no surprise that lies understood in this way dovetail naturally with the process of writing, since (as Nemerov suggests) the artist translates his or her own self-deceptions into the public sphere and asks others to share them.

In both Abish and Nemerov, then, we can see a great deal of anxiety about the fact that while fiction claims to mark a distance from the simply fictitious it actually ends up doing precisely the same thing. Nemerov points out this relation: "It may be altogether appropriate, though, that is, artful, that an attempt to find out why I cannot write fiction should turn into an attempt to tell the truth about myself, which in its turn is turning into a fiction about myself, the very self who a moment ago could not write fiction" (119). Writing fiction is predicated, first of all, on the principle of self-discovery and truthfulness, the process of which leads one to produce a fictive self. But that self-discovery arises not from the direct use of art to shape a represented world, since doing so, Nemerov implies, would entail an artificiality at odds with this process of self-discovery. Instead, fiction approaches truth only when it appears unwritable, thus forcing the author back into self-reflection. What this passage also suggests fairly explicitly, I think, is that just this same contradiction is at work within our everyday life, for the fictive selves that we inhabit everyday. Our movement through the world produces selves most strongly when we encounter guilt or fear, rather than the smooth operation within the everyday. So it is for him that all analysis is fictive, a lie: "perhaps even self-examination, analysis, all production of general ideas, thought itself, are in the end evasions of a story" (31). He brings these two ideas together most explicitly late in the book, where he directly describes storytelling as lying: "Of course! To write a work of fiction is essentially to tell a story. And to tell a story is to tell a lie, because a lie was a story. So there does exist a prohibition against telling stories, and this prohibition belongs to an early age" (173).

It is because both fiction and everyday life arise from a certain attempt to create fictive responses to the world that Nemerov associates the novel with fraud. Nemerov writes, "Hypothesis. The novel is about disclosure of secrets. The best secrets combine two secret realms: sex (generation) and money" (28). He more specifically links this interest in secrets to fraud: "Bill Troy

---

signs of the narrative act fall away, and with them all questions of authority and reliability.... The murder-mystery is 'solved,' however, not through epistemological processes of weighing evidence and making deductions, but through the imaginative projection of what *could*—and, the texts insists, *must*—have happened. 'Shall I project a world?' is Oedipa Maas' anguished cry when faced by the absolute limits of her knowledge in Pynchon's *The Crying of Lot 49* (1966). Quentin and Shreve project a world, apparently unanxiously" (10).

once wrote of Balzac that the novelist and the criminal are both interested in conspiracies, that is, plots" (31). The characterization of fiction as a kind of fraud seems to me to be especially important because it insists on the public nature of our private acts of fictional self-construction. When Nemerov characterizes the novelist and the criminal as plot makers, he is describing people who are able to impose a series of imagined events upon others. He is particularly explicit in associating this with the writing of fiction: "The first axiom of the novelist is: Nobody in the world knows how the world is. It follows that one guess is as good as another. You don't ask the reader's consent, you impose upon him with your phantasy" (35). Precisely this idea that one can impose one's fantasies on others is the basis of fraud.

The tension between the public and the private in fact runs through *Journal of the Fictive Life* and marks its concern with fictionality as distinctly contemporary. Nemerov's compositional style depends on attending to a series of associations that obey a psychological logic. Nemerov explains:

> If what I am doing here has any prospect of revealing a form, a species of narration less dull than I presently find fiction, yet more hugely architectural than lyric poetry, this form has also to be defined with reference to the things it isn't. The temptation, I observe, is to be drawn away into pure autobiography, on the one hand, the external and more or less chronological narrative of what happened; or, on the other hand, into random reflexions, not much inspected with reference to the center, something like a notebook. Neither is anything but a parody of what I intend, or a failure to accomplish what I intend. The principle that everything is relevant, simply because it comes into my mind, remains the principle of this work, but a principle which must get its justification daily so far as this is possible. It would appear, for example, that my dream-life is pretending to cooperate in the adventure by supplying an abundance of materials, but really trying to put a stop to it by giving me more than I can handle in a working day. (100–101)

Throughout *Journal of the Fictive Life* Nemerov remains interested in the movement between the private associations and reflections that make up his daily life and the poetic structures that arise out of those associations (the "revealed" form that Nemerov mentions), and which seem to be essential to making them into what we would call fiction. It is just such ambiguously public fantasies that have the most important role within the book. At one point, for example, Nemerov invents several dreams as examples of his discussion of associations, and remarks, "Now I 'made these up.' Or they 'came to me.' And they are not dreams, but daytime fictions. Still, according to the theory of this book they should be interpretable. And according to Freud they should turn out to be two versions of the same thought" (121). Nemerov suggests, then, that poetic or rhetorical invention obeys the same rules and psychological principles as dreams. If this is the case, the texts that are offered to the public by the novelist problematically straddle the line between the private and the public. This is an issue that Nemerov evokes explicitly a few pages later: "But what criticism doesn't care about is exactly what I do care about: the delineation of readings—of anything, lives, dreams, poems, newspaper items—that shall satisfy these requirements: They are private, not public, and can be arrived at only by the individual on the basis of his own life, hence they differ from (and are crazy with reference to) the readings of public, objectively minded criticism" (129).

Nemerov represents, I think, a forthright response to the compositional issues raised by Freudian thinking about the unconscious and the necessarily dishonest motivation of dreamwork. Chapter 1 has shown that Freud is an important background for the equation of fiction and myth. It is clear that Nemerov's interest in fraud is a different response to the same general intellectual backdrop of mid-century America, and thus represents the origins of a separate strand of fictionality based on concerns about the nature of public space and how individual inventions and associations can claim a place within that space. As writers reflect further on the way that they can justify their writing as a kind of lie and how they can position themselves against traditional definitions of literature, the nature and effect of linking fiction and lying will become more complex and aesthetically rich.

Sorrentino's Walk-On Characters

Gilbert Sorrentino's *Imaginative Qualities of Actual Things* (1971) reflects much the same intellectual backdrop as Nemerov's *Journal of the Fictive Life*. Both are fictions written by writers known for their poetry and take as their subject the struggle to write a story. The fact that both Nemerov and Sorrentino are better known as poets is not incidental. Both approach the question of fictionality from the distinction between public and private space that has been more important within twentieth-century theories of poetry, although we will see that Sorrentino more directly uses this definition as a way to critique these theories.[5]

5. I discuss the feeling among American writers of the 1960s and '70s that poetry had

Imaginative Qualities describes the New York literary scene of the 1950s and '60s, frequently creating characters that allow Sorrentino to criticize what he takes to be the mythologized lives of poets. As Sorrentino remarks about a minor character, Duke: "Duke was always a deadbeat as far as I'm concerned. Third-rate musician. Dull. He used to talk about Dostoevski and Hesse a lot, and smoked pot all the time. What a pleasure to make him up, so that I can put him down."[6] As Sorrentino develops his satire of the often small-minded characters who inhabit this literary world, it is clear that much of his thinking about poetic form—and thus the basis for his critique of his own fictional characters—depends on a broadly New Critical understanding of poetry as a kind of machine. New Criticism is, of course, a dominant force in the American academy throughout the period that I am investigating in this book. It makes its presence felt with particular power in Sorrentino's and Nemerov's books, however, because they arise out of the poetic traditions in which New Criticism exerts the strongest influence. Sorrentino's satire on the shallow members of the literary scene who aspire to the life of the poet without taking seriously the task of composition, defines the poem as a verbal whole whose elements transcend everyday language. We might recall Wimsatt and Beardsley's influential assertion in "The Intentional Fallacy" that "[t]he poem is not the critic's own and not the author's (it is detached from the author at birth and goes about the world beyond his power to intend about it or control it). The poem belongs to the public. It is embodied in language, the peculiar possession of the public, and it is about the human being, an object of public knowledge."[7] We might generalize and say that the writing-as-lying definition of fictionality arises initially out of an anxiety about reference that is more strongly felt in poetry than in prose. This connection is quite obvious in *Imaginary Qualities*. A good deal of Sorrentino's satire is summarized in a passing critique of an aspiring poet: "This was a very hip publisher, who spent every waking moment convincing the world at large that he was a poet. There were days when he would spend hours trying to decide how a poet should look on such a day . . . should he wear his smoke shakes or his blue ones? Anton listened to him, and Yea, he understood. Published a lot of poems in his magazine, starting in about 1967 or so. Free! Free! Irremediably poor. Such work is irremediable because it

---

developed a more satisfying aesthetic than fiction in chapter 3 of *Narrative after Deconstruction* (Albany: State University of New York Press, 2003).

    6. Gilbert Sorrentino, *Imaginative Qualities of Actual Things* (1971; Normal, IL: Dalkey Archive, 1991), 141.

    7. W. K. Wimsatt, *The Verbal Icon: Studies in the Meaning of Poetry* (Lexington: The University Press of Kentucky, 1954), 5.

has no working parts" (179; Sorrentino's ellipsis). Sorrentino goes on explain that such pretenders to poetry rely on clichés like "to be alive, to be in life, is more important than any poem" (179). What seems to be the principal failure of these poets is their inability to see the real seriousness of the task of constructing a poem. When they make claims about the importance of life, "they are apologizing—in an aggressive way—for the mediocrity of their productions. Smug people, dear God. Can you imagine Anton Harley believing that 'metaphor is real,' and so on? He may, of course, think that it's edible. Good Metaphor, slurp, slurp!" (179–80). Sorrentino describes a naïve understanding of what one does with poetry—naïve in the sense that it relies on clichés dressed up as new discoveries, but also naïve in that it depends on a fundamentally simplistic understanding of language and the poem. A metaphor, for Anton, is a thing to be eaten but not something to be constructed in a way that makes real demands on the writer—in a way that involves real "working parts."

As part of its definition of fictionality, *Imaginative Qualities* distinguishes between mundane and literary uses of language. Indeed, at one point late in the book, as he criticizes his own failure to construct an engaging plot for this novel, Sorrentino suggests that unlike nonfiction writing, both poetry and fiction depend on their language rather than any referentiality to things in the world: "Nonfiction is a kind of magic-lantern show to captivate the minds of those who think it describes or reveals reality; a sort of sweet narcotic to take you to some other world. While there, you think you're perceptive of everything. But, worse, you think that you can use this when you get back home to the Rock. Did I hear you say poetry? Poetry is fiction, in my specialized definition" (168–69). Sorrentino's most explicit and, I think, helpful statement about fiction occurs as he describes the ending of a scene between two primary characters, Leo and Anne:

> This did not really happen, but the story made its point. It's not a bad story at all, except for the fact that it ended, and stories that are replete with sadness and despair never end at all: they stop. The way this day ended was with Leo going home, sodden, to Anne and his daughters. She said nothing and he fell asleep on the broken-down couch. You can't solve any of these things by fiction. Or, let me say that you make sense of them, and even solve them, if what you mean by fiction is prose. Prose. If you pay enough attention to the way the sentences fall, and if the events are presented in only the clearest contours—what is salient—you will have a perfect fiction: reality. (114)

In denying that fiction can really solve anything, Sorrentino seems to be rejecting the idea of the usefulness of the literary work; it is, as he says, never a tool to accomplish some end. To turn a situation into prose seems to mean to attend to its construction in language and to the strict concern with the salient, a focus that allows the work genuinely to reach conclusions and achieve a sense of form. This is how I interpret the final line of this passage, as a perfectly constructed text comes to take on its own reality. In this regard, he tells himself later in the book not to worry about the reality of his characters ("He's certainly not a flesh-and-blood character who shows signs of walking off the page") and instead to concentrate on their linguistic construction: "*Prose* these figures! Prose them right into the paper and the shape of the letters" (168).

Like the New Critical tradition from which he draws his poetic theory, Sorrentino is interested in the tension between the public and the private qualities of his text and its origins in a space beyond his control, but ultimately ends up seeing in this distinction implications corrosive to the traditional understanding of the literary work as self-sufficient. Indeed, one of the most remarkable elements of *Imaginative Qualities*—the one that connects this novel to the lying definition of fictionality that is my topic in this chapter—is the way that it toys with the idea that Sorrentino's characters are not literary creations but actual people. Early in the novel, for example, Sorrentino describes Lou in terms that maddeningly defy easy definition as either invented or found:

> Best to let Lou run down—and out—as he will. Peter out as the book ends, or stops. Maybe I'll meet him someday—he's not that rare. If someone like, let's say, Larry Poons is endlessly reproducible, then certainly Lou Henry is. I'll say to him that I think I've met him before, no? I think I've met your wife—Sheila? That will not be his wife's name, of course. We'll have a Robbe-Grillet conversation, infinite boredom. He'll have read this book, and will not have recognized himself. (48)

In part Sorrentino here seems simply to suggest that he is working with types—that his novel borrows its characters from the real world because it represents common sorts of people who circulate around the literary world. In other places, however, characters seem more ambiguously tied to the real word. A footnote remarks of another character, "I wrote under this name in my youth, when Guy was someone else" (82). If Guy is a type, it seems oddly roundabout to suggest that he was once "someone else." These histories of characters become even more important as the novel goes on. Later he admits that "I'm getting into trouble with these people, as soon as I stop watching them, they start moving around on me, and acting in an utterly uncharacteristic way" (102). The types that he seems so eager to associate with his characters are problematized by the actual writing of the novel. He concludes this discussion by reference to another character: "At this very moment Sheila may be in Miami Beach, watching the dog races. But that's Sheila outside my concerns; the only real Sheila is in Chapter One" (102).

The borrowed origin of the characters becomes an important thematic element of *Imaginative Qualities,* and the grounds on which he ends up critiquing the New Critical understanding of the autonomy of the work. Later in his description of Leo, Sorrentino seems to undercut much of what he has said about the typical quality of this character: "I'd rather he were simply defeated, that his sweet line lost its charge and power. What do *you* know about my life? I hear him say. The poor bastard doesn't know that I invented him, he thinks he's real" (129). To treat the task of the novelist as a matter of giving shape and order to the character types of contemporary America is one thing; to speak of a character as invented is quite another. This blurring of the common and the individual, the public and the private, is essential to Sorrentino's characterization. A typical if especially rich example is Sorrentino's discussion of the unreality of Anton Harley: "One of my great problems with Anton Harley is that I can't make up enough terrible stories about him to make him totally unreal, absolutely fleshless and one-dimensional, lifeless, as my other characters are. I'm afraid that the reader may get the idea that some monster like this actually walks the earth" (160). He goes on then to create a story about when "I saw him on Second Avenue the other day" to accomplish just this: "It was seeing him that made me realize that I had to really stir this prose around to make sure that he doesn't walk around in this book with any degree of reality. That is, *his* reality. I want him to walk around in this book with my reality. Fiction" (160). Sorrentino seems to shift between two contradictory ways of thinking about fictional characters: one in which characters are found in everyday life (either as actual people or as types to be shared among many writers), and one in which characters are created by and subject to the whims of authors. It is this conflict that creates the seemingly incoherent statement that having seen Anton on Second Avenue; Sorrentino becomes convinced of the need to make sure that no reader thinks that such a monster "actually walks the earth."

It is this conflict between public and private, and between the found and the invented, that allows Sorrentino's description of fiction as a kind of lie to critique the traditional insistence on the autonomy of the poet and his or her disengagement from everyday commercial life. Like Nemerov, Sorrentino is not shy about admitting that fiction is a lie. He remarks early in the book, "I'm going to make up, based on my own experience (plus inventions and lies), an early rendezvous between" two principal characters (43). The description of fiction as a lie seems to me to arise from the contradictory ways in which he defines the origins of his characters. As both public and private, inherited and invented, Sorrentino's characters are always on the verge of plagiarism instead of the being pure products of a creative mind or accurate representations of types found in everyday life. In both senses, then, Sorrentino can be seen as misusing representation—as lying. How Sorrentino defines his fiction as a lie improves on Nemerov because he describes lying in terms that move beyond the ironies of subjectivity in very broad terms to locate the tensions of fiction in the nature of the construction of texts themselves.[8] More importantly, Sorrentino locates his walk-on characters within a critique of publishing institutions. It is clear over the course of this novel that Sorrentino's turn to metafiction and embrace of lying as a definition of his own fiction offers a thorough critique of the clichés of poetry as autonomous from the political and economic world. Self-consciously lying becomes a way of adopting a position outside of these publishing institutions. In contrast to Barth's genial celebration of literary occasions or even Walker's attempt to reform the literary canon, Sorrentino's claim that he is lying as he writes represents a much more thorough rejection of literature as an institution by showing that it is self-deluded about its own involvement in the commercial world. As we delve further into the lying model of fictionality, we will see that changes in the nature of publishing complicate what we normally think of as the avant-garde nature of literary writing.

Lies and the Space of the Page

I have suggested, then, that *Imaginative Qualities of Actual* things moves beyond *Journal of the Fictive Life* in its definition of fictionality as a lie by using this definition to produce specific narrative features. These features

---

8. Clarence Major, too, has written about the need to transform Freud's influence into something aesthetically useful. In *Necessary Distance: Essays and Criticism* (Minneapolis: Coffee House Press, 2001), he remarks, "I did notice ... how writers of fiction, and poets too, from around the turn of the century on, were using the principles of psychoanalysis as a tool for exploring behavior in fiction and poetry. So I gave it a shot. But the real challenge, I soon learned, was to find a way to absorb some of this stuff and at the same time keep the evidence of it out of my own writing" (27).

will come to be the hallmark of American metafiction of the late 1960s and 1970s as a distinct narrative style develops around this definition. Much of the critical interest in writing of this period has focused on the issue of the representation of history, which frequently involves the mixing of historical and fictional entities. Indeed, ever since Linda Hutcheon distinguished "historiographic metafiction" practiced by writers like E. L. Doctorow, Salman Rushdie, and Toni Morrison from relatively ahistorical writing by Ronald Sukenick, Raymond Federman, and (we can suppose) Sorrentino, the peculiar nature of historical fact in the postmodern novel has been one of the central sites in which the nature of contemporary fictionality has been debated.[9] As Naomi Jacobs says, "The writers of these pseudohistorical and antihistorical fictions have been directly and indirectly influenced by theories of history, character, and language that question the existence and even the desirability of factual truth, unified identity, and aesthetic perfection. Freed from the constraints that had limited the use of historical figures under the reign of realism, contemporary writers are using such figures with increasing frequency to serve a variety of fictional aims."[10] The trend in the best recent work on postmodern historical fiction is to move away from Hutcheon's distinction between two fundamental types of postmodernism and to insist, instead, that this historical fiction be read in a narrow context. Amy Elias argues, "it is most useful to resituate postmodern historical fiction in literary history as an evolutionary form of the classic historical romance."[11] What I have suggested, however, is that the particular features of this writing depend on more fundamental shifts in thinking about publishing and its relation to the public sphere; these shifts will manifest themselves both in historical novels and in works, like the novels of Sorrentino and Nemerov, that may initially appear historically disengaged. In this regard I agree with Marcel Cornis-Pope, who has argued that we need to take into account "the 'extraliterary' causes of narrative self-reflection" and to see even playful narrative styles as an attempt to tackle the serious issue of literature's place in the American political and economic landscape.[12]

    9. Linda Hutcheon, *A Poetics of Postmodernism: History, Theory, Fiction* (New York: Routledge, 1988).
    10. Naomi Jacobs, *The Character of Truth: Historical Figures in Contemporary Fiction* (Carbondale: Southern Illinois University Press, 1990), xiv.
    11. Amy J. Elias, *Sublime Desire: History and Post-1960s Fiction* (Baltimore: Johns Hopkins University Press, 2001), 89.
    12. Marcel Cornis-Pope, *Narrative Innovation and Cultural Rewriting in the Cold War and After* (New York: Palgrave, 2001), 5. Cornis-Pope draws the term *extraliterary* from Jerome Klinkowitz, "The Extra-Literary in Contemporary American Fiction," in *Contemporary American Fiction*, eds. Malcolm Bradbury and Sigmund Ro (London: Edward Arnold, 1987), 19–38.

These shifts in the position of the writer in relation to both literary and popular publishing demand that we very carefully tease apart differences between modernist and postmodernist writing. The fine line between these two forms of writing is especially important in those writers who use the space of the page as a unit of poetic meaning. At first glance, in fact, attention to typography and page design seems to have little to do with thinking about fiction as a lie. And yet, when we think of many of the novels we most associate with American metafiction, they frequently involve innovative use of type and page space. This relationship suggests how subtly definitions of fictionality influence the way that we tell and read stories. Page design and typography as an aesthetic element of the literary text is, of course, a classic modernist concern. Jerome McGann has described the "visible language of modernism" as a kind of "renaissance of printing" that can be traced back to William Morris:

> Morris worked to integrate the poem and its performative medium not by seeking a return to oral traditions of production, but by acknowledging the compositional environment as a necessary condition for the creation of modern poetry. Of course part of his acknowledgement called for acts of resistance against current printing and publishing practices. But as with Dickenson and Blake, those resistances were carried out as part of a broad-scale effort to exploit as completely as possible all the resources of the physical media that were the vehicular forms of his writing.[13]

McGann observes a link that will be easy to recognize in contemporary writing—the relationship between typography and a critique of commercial forms of literary production and dissemination. Indeed, attention to the materiality of the page in work by concrete or visual poetry seems to be a point at which almost no difference exists between modernist and postmodernist writing. Both turn to the page as a way to draw our attention back to neglected aspects of publishing, in the process critiquing literary institutions. McGann sees modernist typography as a writing in touch with its material conditions, and thus less alienated (42). We might recall the title of Wimsatt's *Verbal Icon* as a model for what many of these writers of fiction will discover: that once we suspend the normal reference of language, once we allow it to turn back and "lie" to us, the writing itself becomes a kind of artifact that can be treated as a language sculpture.[14] McGann carries over his analysis of

---

13. Jerome McGann, *Black Riders: The Visual Language of Modernism* (Princeton, NJ: Princeton University Press, 1993), 46

14. Wimsatt writes, "Poetry achieves concreteness, particularity, and something like

material poetics into postmodern poetry, emphasizing in language poetry an interest in the activity of reading: "Far from being asked simply to 'overhear' the sublime reflections of the poet, the reader is forced to assume a position of active consciousness in face of her work" (134).

On this point, however, I think that McGann is mistaken. Understanding the differences between what typography stands for institutionally to the modernist and the postmodernist writer will go a long way towards explaining how contemporary writers use page space as a component of the lying model of fiction. It is, of course, a classic definition of modernism that it distinguishes itself from mass tastes. Margaret Anderson's famous dictum for the *Little Review* (1914), "no compromise with the public taste," is perhaps the best example of this attitude. Harriet Monroe's justification for *Poetry* in 1912 is more expansive: "The present venture is a modest effort to give to poetry her own place, her own voice. The popular magazines can afford her but scant courtesy—a Cinderella corner in the ashes—because they seek a large public which is not hers, a public which buys them not for their verse but for their stories, pictures, journalism, rarely for their literature, even in prose."[15] When "serious" publication is contrasted to mass-marketed magazines and associated with an educated elite that sees through conventional pieties, it will seem natural that literary texts will exist to critique our conventional ways of reading. Indeed, the assumption behind magazines like *Little Review* and *Poetry* is that they will serve to educate the general public; Monroe writes, "We believe that there is a public for poetry, that it will grow, and that as it becomes more numerous and appreciative the work produced in this art will grow in power, in beauty, in significance" (369). The hope of linking writing and its material (typographic) object described by McGann clearly reflects the elite publishing position of this type of writing in relation to the mass-produced and "compromised" nature of mainstream writing.[16]

The distinction in America between serious and mass publishing that provides the aesthetic principle for literary modernism changes funda-

---

sensuous shape not by irrelevance of local texture, in its meter or in its images . . . but by extra relevance or hyperrelevance, the interrelational density of words taken in their fullest, most inclusive and symbolic character. A verbal composition, through being supercharged with significance, takes on something like the character of a stone statue or a porcelain vase. Through its meaning or meanings the poem *is*. It has an iconic solidity" (231).

15. Harriet Monroe, "The Motive of the Magazine," in *Perspectives on American Book History: Artifacts and Commentary*, eds. Scott E. Casper, Joanne D. Chaison, and Jeffrey D. Groves (Amherst: University of Massachusetts Press, 2002), 369.

16. In *Institutions of Modernism: Literary Elites and Public Culture* (New Haven, CT: Yale University Press, 1998), Lawrence Rainey describes literary modernism as an attempt to recreate a kind of patronage system, especially through selling extravagantly produced, limited-run editions of novels like *Ulysses* (44–45).

mentally as we move into the post–World War II period. As writers routinely complained throughout the 1960s and '70s, serious publishing houses increasingly became more commercially oriented. John Tebbel concludes his history of American book publishing, *Between Covers* (1987), by arguing that "the greatest change" in publishing since the 1950s is "the imposition of the corporate mentality on a business diametrically opposed to it in the past."[17] As old publishing houses like Knopf, Macmillan, and Harper were bought by or adopted the philosophy of larger corporations, "much of the fun has gone out of publishing" (462), and decisions have been made more and more by people recruited "from the ranks of nonbook businesses" (464). This shift towards corporate publishing produces not the urge to create a literary alternative to such mass production but rather a splintering of literary institutions and audiences through these corporations into a variety of separate if not hostile groups and publishing outlets. Charles Robinson remarks, "Where once there was a unified force of little magazines and supporters fighting for recognition against popular tastes, today the forces have split. The independents feel that not only have the popular magazines sold out, but that the university magazines have followed suit—that, although the latter may not appeal to popular tastes, they have adopted a peculiar academicism as sterile as the policy of popular magazines turning out formula pieces."[18]

The splintering of groups who define themselves as serious, literary, and even avant-garde worked to foster the particular publishing atmosphere that developed during the 1960s and remains with us today. As writers have lost faith in a particular journal or magazine that will function as a corrective to mass tastes, and as development of mimeograph and offset publishing has made small-run, self-produced literary magazines possible, writers have found themselves in a world of multiple serious but often subtly compromised publishing options. Indeed, Sorrentino in particular was directly involved with the small magazine *Kulchur* and has spoken quite directly about how his understanding of contemporary poetry was shaped by his experience with these alternative publishing media: "The magazines I speak of were not academic or scholarly, and had little to do with what are called quarterlies; nor were they open to anything at all, refuges for writers who wished to 'express' themselves—in other words, they were not what might be termed bohemian publications. On the contrary, they had a definite bone to pick, and they set themselves up not as a mere *alternative* press but as a press that considered

---

17. John Tebbel, *Between Covers: The Rise and Transformation of Book Publishing in America* (New York: Oxford University Press, 1987), 464.

18. Charles Robinson, "Academia and the Little Magazine," *TriQuarterly* 43 (Fall 1978): 31.

its criteria to be correct."[19] Sorrentino's sense of literary aesthetics is deeply woven with the outlet provided by these little magazines. The very means by which this writing is produced, edited, and disseminated becomes a matter of poetic theory in a much stronger way than we see in Morris's concern for the visual quality of the work. Surveying the politics of contemporary publication, Ronald Sukenick concludes that "in America writers are one another's enemies" based in part on the competing definitions of literary value that different groups adopt.[20] Although such conflicts will be a part of publishing in almost any milieu, they have become so central to publishing in America since 1950 that they define for writers what it means to write fiction today.

We might recall Robert Coover's observation about the isolation of American writers, which I quoted in the first chapter: "We felt that we were all alone. No one was reading us, nor was anyone writing anything remotely like the sort of writing we were doing until, in the little magazines, we began slowly to discover one another. Few of us knew one another at the time we began writing. There was no manifesto, no group, or no school."[21] As much as critics like to compare American metafiction with the aesthetic programs of Dada and Oulipo, Coover makes clear that these writers found kindred spirits only gradually through publication. In other words, experimentation with page space is less the result of an aesthetic principle and more a site where these sorts of aesthetic principles are developed. It is for this reason that the one true literary group that American postmodernism can boast is not a matter of shared aesthetic principles but rather of publishing opportunities—the Fiction Collective, founded in 1974, which places editorial decisions not in the hands of editors who might be influenced by market concerns, but in the hands of other writers who have published there.[22] The Fiction Collective embodies the problems of avant-gardism in the contemporary American literary scene and makes clear that page space is not only a component of a finished literary product but also a place where writers define themselves and position their work in relation to other literary spheres and publishing outlets.

19. Gilbert Sorrentino, "Neon, Kulchur, etc.," *TriQuarterly* 43 (Fall 1978): 300.
20. Ronald Sukenick, *In Form: Digressions on the Act of Fiction* (Carbondale: Southern Illinois University Press, 1985), 57, 61.
21. Robert Coover, "'Nothing but Darkness and Talk?': Writers' Symposium on Traditional Values and Iconoclastic Fiction," *Critique* 31 (1990): 233.
22. For a history of the Fiction Collective, see Jonathan Baumbach, "Who Do They Think They Are? A Personal History of the Fiction Collective," *TriQuarterly* 43 (Fall 1978): 625–34, and Gene Lyons, "Report on the Fiction Collective," *TriQuarterly* 43 (Fall 1978): 635–47. Ronald Sukenick makes a more extensive argument for the importance of the Collective in *In Form*, 49–65.

Postmodernist page design therefore seems to be especially interested in the conditions under which a work is created. Gérard-Georges Lemaire notes the limits of readability in William Burroughs and Brion Gysin's "cut up" technique—pages created by slicing two unrelated pages together and retyping the apparently random result. Lemaire writes, "The main intention of Brion Burroughs and William Gysin [sic] has been to free the text from the page, to free the word from the surrounding matrix. Not actually, but by placing the text and graphics at the extreme limit of readability. Not so that these elements are unreadable in an absolute sense—in other words, so that they escape comprehension—but that, within the confines of the printed book, they reach a point indicative of unreadability."[23] Lemaire's claim that the cut-up points to unreadability without itself actually being unreadable captures the complex position of this type of writing in relation to the page and the institutions that police it. This randomness is not just a surrealistic interest in moving beyond the conscious mind, nor a Duchampian critique of artistic boundaries.[24] It is, instead, an interest in what it means to act as a writer. In separate essays, both Burroughs and Gysin emphasize that the cut-up is in its essence a form of action that cannot merely be imagined: "You cannot cut up in your head any more than I can paint in my head. Whatever you do in your head bears the prerecorded pattern of your head."[25] Much more than the modernist iconic page that McGann describes, Gysin draws our attention to the writer's position both on and beyond the page. The literary work, as a result, appears more as an *index* than an *icon*, more a gesture towards some cause than a fully formed verbal sculpture.[26] As a general

---

23. Gérard-Georges Lemaire, "23 Stitches Taken," in *The Third Mind*, by William S. Burroughs and Brion Gysin (New York: The Viking Press, 1978), 20.

24. This is not to say, however, that Burroughs and Gysin do not appeal to Dada and Duchamp as their precursors. Indeed, *The Third Mind* is littered with references to Dada and to visual art in general. Close attention to the particular way that Burroughs and Gysin describe their practice, however, makes me believe that they have in mind something quite different from either earlier movement. I would cite the distinction that Arthur Danto draws in *Philosophizing Art: Selected Essays* (Berkeley: University of California Press, 1999) between Duchamp's *Fountain* and Warhol's *Brillo Box*. While superficially similar, Danto argues, Warhol's work is much more concerned with broadly philosophical questions: Duchamp "did not, however, raise the other part of the question, namely: Why were all other urinals not works of art? But that was Warhol's marvelous question: Why was *Brillo Box* a work of art when the ordinary boxes of Brillo were merely boxes of Brillo?" (73). Although my reading of Warhol in chapter 2 is different from Danto's emphasis on the critique of institutions, his larger point is worth noting: apparent similarities between postmodernism and Dada can hide complex differences in how they understand their relationship to artistic institutions.

25. Brion Gysin, "Cut-ups: A Project for Disasterious Success," *The Third Mind*, 44.

26. It is also no doubt the case that the attempt to write *fiction* while talking about of page space encourages writers to think more indexically, since they need to take account not of a single space, but of a series of page spaces that make up the book. It is a relatively unremarked

principle, an indexical approach to page space and typography is interested not in the object on the page so much as the conditions by which it has been produced. Sorrentino himself, writing about the process of composition, has described the poetic text as an artifact: "I don't think that it has been fully acknowledged, or even admitted, that the writer's finished product, the artifact, is not as important to its maker as it has been made out to be by critics and scholars." He goes further and asserts, "when the act is completed its product is, in truth, but a by-product."[27] Sorrentino is describing the process of writing poetry, but I think that his comments apply even more strongly to postmodernist fiction: the composition of the work struggles against the artifact created. This artifact, in turn, has its strongest formulation in the space of the page.

There is, of course, a whole history of typography in experimental writing during the twentieth century that I am treating in only the broadest terms; my interest in this experimentation, however, is limited to the way that it supports the equation of fiction and lying. I would like to show this support by turning to a somewhat more obscure example of American metafiction, Steve Katz's *The Exagggerations of Peter Prince* (1968). Katz's heavily metafictional story is loosely organized around the character of Peter Prince but lacks the coherent setting of Sorrentino's novel. Instead, *Exagggerations* tells stories about its principal character that seem to have little in common with each other and that obey only the loosest sense of plot coherence. Indeed, late in the novel one character remarks to Peter Prince, in response to his simple question of why he is threatening him with a gun, "The way this bloody book is put together do you expect that we know?"[28] This sense of incoherence seems to arise from the pure invention of the novel. Just three pages into the novel, Katz abruptly stops the narrative action and intervenes, apparently criticizing himself: "Enough! Katz, you're making this all up. It doesn't make a bit of sense. It's not a promising beginning. Why can't you follow the instructions? You can't write whatever you want: Peter Prince Peter Prince Peter Prince. Where's the story?" (3). In this passage, the sense that this novel is all a lie, all pure invention, is connected to the inability of Katz to rein in imagination and subordinate his own whims to the demands of

---

element of contemporary fiction that the best known examples of innovative page and book design in contemporary writing attend to the movement through the book, rather than the self-contained object on the page. For a discussion of the importance of movement and improvisation in contemporary writing, see Sukenick's *In Form* (especially 3–15).

27. Gilbert Sorrentino, *Something Said: Prefaces by the Author* (Normal, IL: Dalkey Archive, 2001), 3, 4.

28. Steve Katz, *The Exagggerations of Peter Prince* (New York: Holt, Rinehart and Winston, 1968), 257.

the writing of the novel. This seems to be a corollary to the feeling that Sorrentino expresses that his characters get away from him; in both cases, the novels seem to become incoherent because the authors are unable or unwilling to exert sufficient control over their material. Near the end of the novel, Katz realizes that some events are happening to Peter Prince without his awareness: "This makes things a little spooky for me, because if Peter Prince just got there by himself to that bench then this novel can easily end by itself, behind my back; I could turn my back for an instant to gather up the summation and the climax I had planned, and by the time I spin back it could be done, bound and sealed" (272–73).

There are a number of traditional ways in which critics understand statements by metafictional authors admitting that they do not have control over their stories. Most assume some broad thematic connection between such loss of control and the nature of language and representation. Patricia Waugh, in an influential early discussion of metafiction, describes the loss of control modeled on role playing: "The concern with freedom in both cases is, however, a consequence of the perceived analogy between plot in fiction and the 'plot' of God's creation, ideology or fate. It is a concern with the idea of being trapped within someone else's order. At the furthest metafictional extreme, this is to be trapped within language itself, within an arbitrary system of signification which appears to offer no means of escape."[29] Such generalizations fail, however, to recognize the specific way in which control and lying are linked by different authors as part of a definition of fictionality itself. *Exagggerations* is better than many postmodern novels in helping us to understand how defining writing as pure invention leads authors to feel that they have lost control of their material.[30] Initially this link may seem counterintuitive, since novels freed from the demands of representation should be able to spin worlds and stories with more rather than less control.[31] But

---

29. Patricia Waugh, *Metafiction: The Theory and Practice of Self-Conscious Fiction* (London: Routledge, 1984), 119–20.

30. It is for this reason that a writer like Guy Davenport, whose metafictional verbal collages are clearly the product of great authorial control, has always been a problematic figure within the postmodern canon. For examples of Davenport's stories, see "The Richard Nixon Freishütz Rag" or "Au Tombeau de Charles Fourier" in *Da Vinci's Bicycle: Ten Stories* (Baltimore: Johns Hopkins University Press, 1979). For his claims about artistic control, see his discussion of the "grammar of symbols" in *The Geography of Imagination: Forty Essays* (New York: Pantheon, 1981), 8.

31. The implication that historically informed postmodernism somehow gives the author less leeway than more self-reflexive metafiction is implicit within Linda Hutcheon's characterization of historiographic metafiction: "What I want to call postmodernism in fiction paradoxically uses and abuses the conventions of both realism and modernism, and does so in order to challenge their transparency, in order to prevent glossing over the contradictions that make the postmodern what it is: historical and metafictional, contextual and self-reflexive, ever aware of

this loss of control goes to the heart of fictionality, since it reminds us how much work goes into deciding what is appropriate to invent and how those inventions can be made useful and meaningful. Indeed, the issue of authorial control makes clear how important a particular definition of fictionality is to our understanding of postmodernism in general and postmodern historiography in particular, since Katz makes quite clear that merely being *permitted* to invent a story does not explain the conditions that will make those inventions meaningful.

Like Sorrentino, Katz shows that his control over the story is limited by using walk-on characters. More explicitly and humorously than Sorrentino, Katz's borrowed characters are not described as types but rather as characters *hired* for the novel. In particular, Katz describes Linda Lawrence and Philip Farrel as hired: "As for Philip Farrel and Linda Lawrence, most of you understand by now that they aren't per se characters in this book, but hired hands, like mercenary muses, working under pseudonyms, whose real names I can't divulge, but who have agreed to work at a low salary that I can afford, and a small percentage of the take, if any. They show up whenever they're needed, sometimes causing a little ruckus, but usually on the job, as you will see in the following passages" (113). Both novels dramatize the gap between the author's materials and the use that he makes of them, raising questions about how much these characters are inherited artifacts and how much they are the product of pure invention. Katz's emphasis on the hired character, however, frames these questions by appealing more strongly to the struggles of the author himself. In *Imaginative Qualities*, Sorrentino's types come and go but cause little anxiety for the author; in *Exagggerations*, Katz claims to turn to hired characters precisely because of his inability to control his story. Ironically, of course, appealing to such hired characters seems further to erode his control, as characters have divided loyalties. Late in the novel both Philip Farrel and Linda Lawrence are brought before a mysterious board of directors: Farrel is "being talked to by one of the board members, a principal stockholder, and a man of influence in that community, with a daughter at a leading eastern university, and a son in Naval O.C.S." (176). This board member seems to know more about the novel than Katz himself: "It sent a chill up my backbone to think that someone could be looking on like that at what I'm doing, a constant surveillance. Nothing makes me shake as much as spying. Even I wasn't sure. Maybe he did know something I didn't know, something my characters were going to do. Don't think that it doesn't scare

---

its status as discourse, as a human construct" (*Poetics of Postmodernism*, 53). By implication, the less historical writing of Sorrentino or Katz is willing to "gloss over" these contradictions, to easily accept transparency.

me" (180). This corporate board confidently claims to know a great deal about the novel and how it will develop, and in doing so embodies the control that Katz lacks.

The corporate board that confidently understands the direction of the novel is clearly a stand-in for the commercial publishing pressures that hover around Katz's unconventional novel. In dramatizing his struggle against the board and those who claim authority over how to produce a novel, Katz mounts a critique of publishing institutions that treat the work as a product, and instead draws our attention back to the imperfect agency of the writer. Indeed, writing for him is a struggle against the page itself. In *Exagggerations*, the space of the page stands in for this struggle. Indeed, the dust jacket for the novel is comprised of four pointing fingers (☞), dingbats frequently used for typesetting items in a list, pointing outward in four different directions from the center of the book.

The way the text uses such references across the space of the page is most directly handled in the novel when the story breaks into two, and then three, page columns, each telling a different story at the same time (22–60). At one point, Peter Prince appears in the second (right-most column) represented only as this symbol, ☞. Initially confusing, the meaning of this symbol becomes clear when Prince announces his name using this symbol: he is simply "pointing" to his name in the other column. Nonetheless, the characters whom Prince meets in this story do not find this form of reference satisfying: "Aren't you the playful one. I just don't feel like playing silly games with you, if you please" (33), remarks one character. Prince is surprised at one point to find his name in a story written by one of the characters (31), and responds with frustration and confusion when other characters accuse him of stealing the name from the other column: "Peter Prince is a figment. Heck invented it in his charming way. I'm going to have to call you Bruce in the meanwhile. You decided on Peter Prince because you saw it on the page, and liked it" (37). Katz's fictional invention is shaped by the page space on which it appears, and indexical references across page space embody the way that his composition is conditioned by the space and circumstances in which it is created.

Fictionality that is self-consciously defined by the space of the page helps to explain why so much of this contemporary self-reflexive fiction is scenic in structure. What I mean by this is that these novels tend to organize the narrative into individual scenes that then take on a life of their own, frequently going off in directions that the author appears not to anticipate. We might think in particular of the way that Robert Coover uses scenes in short stories like "Charlie in the House of Rue," where characters frequently find themselves trapped in situations over which they have no control and which develop according to a logic that neither they nor the reader immediately grasps. This story, like Coover's description of a magic act in "The Hat Act," places its central character on a dramatic set that first promises performance and entertainment but quickly degenerates into tragedy as the central character loses control of events.[32] Allan Wilde describes such scenes in Coover's fiction: "Pushed to produce greater and greater marvels until he at last commits murder, the magician of the tale figures the artist as overreacher and dramatizes Coover's critique of an aesthethicism seeking to dominate a reality (the magician's assistant) that will be subjugated only so far."[33] Of special importance is the fact that such scenes are framed as easily recognizable institutional spaces (the theater stage), making the performance of Coover's characters not merely a private act but a struggle between individual and public conditions. The construction of independent scenes with a logic of their own, whose place within the larger narrative is more tenuous, seems to be a common element of a great deal of postmodernist fiction and a corollary to the page-space invention we see in *Exagggerations of Peter Prince*.

As the building blocks for such metafictional narratives, these scenes seem to me to do two things. First, they place a great deal of emphasis on a single central character whose particular reactions organize the story and which give us our perspective on the logic of the scene. Second, they emphasize the spatiality of the narrative that is developing, frequently by invoking theatrical language. An especially good example of how these two issues are combined is Marianne Hauser's novel, *The Talking Room* (1976). Hauser's novel describes the possibly hypothetical life of a young girl, mostly through overheard conversations. Indeed, the novel opens with the young girl (B) listening to her mother (J) and her lesbian lover (V) argue over B's conception: "Again I can hear their voices coming nonstop from the talking room downstairs. I hear them through the rumble of the trucks in the night rain as I lie on my back between moist sheets, listening. And I know they are talking about me. But they call me an idea."[34] The hypothetical, overheard conversation that seems to call B into existence becomes the central theme and style of the novel. At the outset J accuses V: "Our names got lost in the

---

32. Robert Coover, "Charlie in the House of Rue," *A Night at the Movies: Or, You Must Remember This* (New York: Collier, 1988), 87–111; Robert Coover, "The Hat Act," *Pricksongs & Descants* (New York: Plume, 1969), 240–56.

33. Alan Wilde, *Horizons of Assent: Modernism, Postmodernism, and the Ironic Imagination* (Philadelphia: University of Pennsylvania Press, 1987), 151.

34. Marianne Hauser, *The Talking Room: A Novel* (New York: The Fiction Collective, 1976), 1.

rumpled sheets, and what, my love, my dove, will they write on our communal headstone? Two capital letters? One capital lie? Here lies the lie, the fly, initial parents of one baby B" (1). This cancelled narration locates a single consciousness in a very particular place and implies that the narrative is caused by that space. In the end, Hauser has created a "talking room" of a book. Here space and a focusing consciousness come together to emphasize the fictional artifact that has been created. Such scenic narratives are certainly not as radical as Katz's typographical experiments, but both link the process of composition to the space upon which it acts.

This indexical reference across and beyond the space of the page comes to embody the problems of narrative coherence in *Exagggerations* as a whole. References to some other point in the book are handled spatially—they are somewhere else on the page—and thus the metafictional reference to characters and their stories is translated into a movement through a spatial artifact. At one point Philip Farrel and Linda Lawrence are arguing:

> "You know I have to wake him up. I mean it doesn't make any difference to me or anything, but . . . " and he points off the page to where I am sitting. "I just have no choice." This embarrasses me no end, because I sit here picking wax out of my ear with a paper clip, and expect to hear Linda Lawrence say at any moment, "Nothing bigger than your elbow, sweetie" (167; Katz's ellipsis)

At another point Farrell "turned around to gaze back through the pages he'd come" (96). Later Katz is confronted by Prince himself:

> Then he spots me. He leans toward me over the table. "There you are. So. Well. There you are." He lets out a creepy little muttering giggle. "I've got you pegged, you know. I've got you just about doped out." His body sways back and forth on his stiff arms. "I know what you're about." (162)

Katz contrasts the freedom of movement that he associates with his characters to the stasis that seems to make him an object of their scorn. Noting that Prince is "always skimming. He never leaves a wake" (166), Katz goes on to contrast this to his own circumstances: "Peter Prince in motion. I sit still and try to get the book launched. My sedentary commitment. Where would Peter Prince be without that? The more I sit on my ass the better he moves. I hear it's that way all over: oppositions, actions, reactions—the forward motion, the canceled thrust; matter and its anti-. Ha. Love and hate they say in me is intermixed. And I saw, and listen to me, I say that no one knows what's going to happen next" (166). This contrast between the static Katz and the mobile Prince seems to me to say a great deal about the nature of representation in *Exagggerations*. Katz remains a static reference point for the book, and his "creation" of characters means moving them—or observing their movements—around the space of the page. The only thing that gives this movement a focus is Katz himself. His struggles, in other words, frame and define the play of story and language that is the novel's topic.

In making Katz the centering point for the novel and defining the dynamic tension of the work in the movement of characters across the space of the book itself, *Exagggerations* refines the definition of fictionality as a lie that we see used in Nemerov and Sorrentino, and extends the satirical uses to which it can be put. Here the artifact of the book itself emerges as an essential component of the novel's fictionality. The artist's struggle with the page serves as a critique of publishing institutions and the conditions they have imposed on the novel. This fictionality is based not on the book's inadequacy to reality, or even on the inherent ambiguity of language—both ways that incoherences in postmodern novels are often explained—but on the indexical references within the space of the book.[35] We might recall Hauser's remark, "Here lies the lie"—a pun that appears frequently in postmodern fiction.[36] Although they may at first seem more concrete than traditional language use, such references are inherently connected to the lying that is the theme of so many of these books. After all, to point to something is also to defer to it, to displace the narrative from one point to another. Such ironies frequently have a more subtle corollary in the playful metafiction that plays the active and the representative functions of novelistic language against each other. In Clarence Major's *Reflex and Bone Structure* (1975), for example, words become things: "Body is a word nobody notices. The word naked is naked. I cover it with

---

35. Writing of Peirce's distinction between the icon, the index, and symbol as it applies to page design, Mary Keeler has noted that the three concepts work together, and that the movement between them is one of the conditions of creativity: "These presymbolic conditions of meaning are the 'grounds' for any effective symbolic meaning to occur. We can use the concepts 'iconic' and 'indexical' to examine the sign potential of any medium to make effective reference, but we must remember that its symbolic potential is not simply determined by these presymbolic grounds but must be created by the habitual or conventional response that occurs in someone's interpreting. No one can say *as a matter of fact* that something is a sign of something else for you or me or anyone else. 'Sign' is the tri-relative concept of *potential representation* and, as such, theoretically reminds us that meaning *is always growing*" ("Iconic Indeterminacy and Human Creativity in C. S. Peirce's Manuscripts," in *The Iconic Page in Manuscript, Print, and Digital Culture*, eds. George Bornstein and Theresa Tinkle [Ann Arbor: The University of Michigan Press, 1998], 176–77). What Keeler suggests is that signifying conventions depend on and can hark back to its iconic and indexical conditions.

36. For example, in *The Madame Realism Complex* (New York: Semiotext(e) 1992), Lynne Tillman puns, "The words lie there and they may be lies. They lie on the page" (22).

the word cover. I'm still writing."[37] In *Up* (1968), Ronald Sukenick talks with a character about a scene and is asked, "Why don't you put that in actually?" and responds, "I just did."[38] In such scenes, the language of the novel functions in two ways: as a component of the dialogue and as a component of the novel itself.

Linking the space of the page to the act of lying is a way of asserting the agency of the writer within the particularly contentious publishing environment of contemporary America. This agency in turn becomes a way of claiming legitimacy for writing that can obey no universal principle for literary value since—as Sukenick has suggested—none is shared across the many groups that make up the contemporary literary scene. Raymond Federman has been particularly energetic in articulating how the lie can (paradoxically) be used to assert the legitimacy of this writing. In his essays Federman has been quite explicit in embracing the definition of fiction as a lie: "The New Fiction affirms its own autonomy by exposing its own lies: it tells stories that openly claim to be invented, to be false, inauthentic."[39] Like Katz, Federman's use of page space emphasizes the creating subject within the text. He introduces *Take It or Leave It* (1976), for example, with the following "recommendations":

RECOMMENDATIONS FOR THOSE WHO ARE NOT DIRECTLY
INVOLVED IN THIS TALE

Writing is not [I INSIST] *the living repetition of life.*
The author is [PERHAPS?] *that which gives the disquieting language of fiction its unities, its knots of coherence, its insertion into the real.*
All fiction is [I THINK] *a digression. It always deviates from its true purpose.*
All reading is [IN MY OPTION] *done haphazardly.*
THEREFORE
One must never tumble down into the psychology of the self.
CONSEQUENTLY
All events in this tale are distorted [AS MUCH AS POSSIBLE] *from reality.*
All the characters in this tale are given [OF COURSE] *false names.*
All places have their true names but could [INDEED] *be given other names.*[40]

    37. Clarence Major, *Reflex and Bone Structure* (New York: Fiction Collective, 1975), 69.
    38. Ronald Sukenick, *Up* (New York: Dial Press, 1968), 225.
    39. Raymond Federman, *Critifiction: Postmodern Essays* (Albany: State University of New York Press, 1993), 9.
    40. Raymond Federman, *Take it or Leave It* (New York: Fiction Collective, 1976), n.pag.

Like Katz and Sorrentino, Federman's interest in fictional lies arises out of a belief in personal associations that are part of a broadly Freudian backdrop for post–World War II fiction. Federman likewise turns to the lie to assert the agency of the writer on the page, even through the aesthetics that he develops seems miles away from Sorrentino's understanding of the poem as a machine. Federman's rather romantic notion of creativity is also a stark contrast to Katz's angst, but likewise serves to critique those economic and institutional forces that work to limit literary writing. He describes the acceptance of everything in the text a few pages earlier:

> A dangerous game
> because everything here has a positive value:
>   nothing is cancelled
>   nothing is erased
>   lost—no possibility of sad erasures!
>
> [Or else everything is cancelled erased lost
> when the writer begins his battle against the linearity of syntax]
> with wild strokes all strokes are recorded a word carries another]
> word the writer can always add another cross it out repeat it and]
> thus multiply the network but the rule of the game forbids him to]
> come back upon what has already been done a return to zero is not]
> possible is in fact excluded from the start the played stroke has]
> to remained played]

Federman's writing promises to accept everything written without concern for coherence, but in the process loses the ability to return to a start and to claim closure and control of the past. The anxiety of the narrative in this sense reflects a wholehearted embrace of the lying basis of fictionality, a basis that allows the text to include everything in a relentless, onward movement. The space of the page becomes something outside of the control of the author and is the point at which he can be caught unawares by characters (as in Katz's novel) or where digressions and distortions can be recognized. In Sorrentino's novel, incoherences are made possible by the way that characters are imported from the outside world; in these latter two novels the movement between real-world and fictional text becomes less important because the space of the page becomes a site that reveals the author's act of invention.

    Attention to the space of the page allows these writers to achieve a kind of hyper-correctness, a conspicuous literariness and writerly agency that works to legitimate their writing. It seems to me that it is precisely this anxiety about how a story gains literary value that is evident in Federman's use of page space. In *Take It or Leave It,* Federman writes in response to the question of whether the story of his trip "[w]ould . . . be literature" told in a straightforward way: "Whereas by sprinkling smart quotations here and there in the recitation it gains a denseness in thickness also what it loses in speed and straightforwardness and in so doing appears to be literature. In other words it is by a system of double-talk that the story rises from its banality to what can be called a level of surfiction for were it not for the digressions and diversions inserted into the story as it goes along . . . it would be at best of minor interest." Federman accepts that an event is changed and legitimated by appearing on the page and uses the marking of pages in the process of writing to stand in for all those conventions that legitimate some forms of experience instead of others. Federman concludes, "And that is why one must talk (and sometimes double-talk) at ease and without much concern for logic or for credibility about life life and death death and laughter laughter as literature literature as politics (eventually) for then and only (am I anticipating too much?) then can one approach the realm of literature. For what are we barbarians? What are we here for? If not to improve reality so that it may someday become fiction or literature" (n. pag.). Like Katz and Sorrentino, Federman sees page space as a stand-in for literary authority and the institutions that condone a certain type of writing. I see this as a response to Katz's sinister corporate board: appealing to page space is a way of both gaining legitimacy and forfeiting of control. In emphasizing the agency of the writer upon the page, Federman is drawing our attention to his strict and literal acceptance of the rules of literary writing. We could say that these writers are producing something akin to Wimsatt's "hyper-verbal" poetic objects—but with a difference. Instead of works that are hyper-verbal, obsessively concerned with their own language, these works are hyper-institutional, obsessively concerned with their own printing and page layout.[41] Like Sorrentino and Katz, Federman signals constantly that he

---

41. In *The Novel Art: Elevations of American Fiction after Henry James* (Princeton, NJ: Princeton University Press, 2001), Mark McGurl describes metafiction of the 1960s as a hyper-institutionalized form of modernism: "fiction, as metafiction, has become rhetorically indistinguishable from literary criticism, one is tempted to say that the programmatic 'technicality' of the metafictional experiments of American professor-writers such as Barth and Barthelme and Coover should be read, in a sense, as *instances* of the bureaucratic-technical discourse produced in the postwar American university" (179). McGurl attributes this to the special institutional position claimed by metafictional writers: "we have something [in metafiction] like an image of what happens when modernism gets what it wants: a heightened (never total) autonomy from an all-engulfing mass market, and from its traffic in realist representations" (181).

is doing what he is supposed to do, using the tools and materials of conventional writing in quite explicit ways. Indeed, in a work like *The Voice in the Closet* (1979), Federman pushes this acceptance of the rules of writing to an almost absurd point as he constructs his narrative by counting the number of letters in each line and selecting words that will make each line work out to same total: 68.[42] Such a work blatantly accepts the conditions of traditional writing—the need to confine a work to forms that can easily be typeset, the need to edit works to keep them within clear material boundaries. It is hard not to marvel at the agency here. Such a work at first seems to be a modernist icon but actually continually reminds us of the effort of following the rules of typography. It thus points indexically to the obsessive adherence to the rules for publication.

Fake Books

The definition of fiction as a lie, we have seen, works to transform the nature of reference upon the institutionally conditioned space of the page. There is, however, a significant strand of contemporary fiction in America that presents a definition of fiction as a lie in a way that is not so self-erasing and that thinks about the book as an artifact in a different way. To understand the page as a space where indexical reference plays out is in some sense to take this space as a kind of artistic object. Anyone looking at Federman's novel, for example, must be struck by how much it appears to be an artwork on a purely visual level. There is another way to think about the book as an artistic artifact that is perhaps somewhat more subtle: as first and foremost a *book*. Thinking about a fictional narrative as a book seems to be an important if somewhat subtle corollary to the page-space aesthetics that I have been describing.

In some sense, the tradition of the book-as-artifact has its early and most forceful articulation in the nonfiction novel, or in the new journalism as it was sometimes called. Writing that describes real events using fictional devices is, of course, a special challenge for a theory of fictionality since it so obviously crosses boundaries between the real and invented. Nonfiction novels like those of Tom Wolfe, Norman Mailer, and Truman Capote clearly offer themselves to us as scandalously imaginative handlings of materials usually considered appropriate only for the historian. The justification for this hybrid form of fictionalizing seems to draw quite directly upon the

---

42. Raymond Federman, *The Voice in the Closet* (Madison, WI: Station Hill Press, 1979).

appeal to lying. Mailer's *Armies of the Night* (1968) is written as a corrective to the misperceptions of the March on the Pentagon that had circulated through the media. Mailer writes, "The mass media which surrounded the March on the Pentagon created a forest of inaccuracy which would blind the efforts of an historian; our novel has provided us with the possibility, no, even the instrument to view our facts and conceivably study them in that field of light a labor of lens-grinding has produced."[43] Mailer describes his own novelistic account of the events as a tool for allowing the historian to move beyond these misperceptions: "As a working craftsman, a journey-man artist, he is not without his guile; he has come to decide that if you would see the horizon from a forest, you must build a tower" (219). Mailer asserts that the creative license that he has taken with his account of the events is not fundamentally different than what any historian would do. Indeed, he suggests that, since all writing is flawed in some ways, describing the conditions under which this novelistic account is offered make it superior to seemingly objective accounts of history: "Of course, the tower is crooked, and the telescopes warped, but the instruments of all sciences—history so much as physics—are always constructed in small or large error; what supports the use of them now is that our intimacy with the master builder of the tower, and the lens grinder of the telescopes . . . has given some advantage for correcting the error of the instruments and the imbalance of his tower" (219). Fiction is a lie, but one that corrects other falsehoods. Such a claim is not Mailer's alone. Capote opens *In Cold Blood* (1965) by inviting readers into the village of Holcomb, describing the people who will figure in the real-life murder that he is investigating as characters in order to understand what others would ignore. "Until one morning in mid-November of 1959, few Americans—in fact, few Kansans—had ever heard of Holcomb. Like the waters of the river, like the motorists on the highway, and like the yellow trains streaking down the Santa Fe tracks, drama, in the shape of exceptional happenings, had never stopped there."[44] Capote makes it his job to understand the village as outsiders do not and, indeed, as members of the village themselves are no longer able: "But afterward the townspeople, theretofore sufficiently unfearful of each other to seldom trouble to lock their doors, found fantasy re-creating them over and again—those somber explosions that stimulated fires of mistrust in the glare of which many old neighbors viewed each other strangely, and as strangers" (5). Like Mailer, Capote embraces the fictional in order to inoculate himself

43. Norman Mailer, *Armies of the Night: History as a Novel, the Novel as History* (New York: New American Library, 1968), 219.
44. Truman Capote, *In Cold Blood: A True Account of a Multiple Murder and Its Consequences* (New York: Random House, 1965), 5.

against the "fantasy" that has wrongly "re-created" this town. To lie as an author in this case is to be hyperactive, to be an agent in the writing process in a much stronger sense than the traditional historian or reporter.

What is striking about this subgenre of contemporary writing is less its participation in a debate about truth and more the way that the embrace of lying is linked to specifically institutional challenges. In reading debates and manifestos about the nonfiction novel, one is struck above all not by claims about truthfulness but more by the jockeying between several different genres of writing and their competing claims to represent social reality. In his introduction to *The New Journalism,* Tom Wolfe is quite explicit in framing the history of the nonfiction novel in these terms: "The panic hit the men of letters first. If the lumpenproles won their point, if their new form achieved any sort of literary respectability, if it were somehow accepted as 'creative,' the men of letters stood to lose even their position as the reigning practitioners of nonfiction. They would get bumped down to Lower Middle Class."[45] The quite Bourdieu-like language of institutional conflict is explicit through most of the debate about the nonfiction novel, and I would suggest that claims about truth and our access to history should be understood as first and foremost an attempt to sort out these institutional relations. Much as we have seen throughout this chapter, arguing about writing as a form of lie is a way to define agency against an institutional backdrop. The nonfictional novel picks up on the agency of the writer producing a *thing*, which then stands for those institutional relations.

Appeals to the actual artifact of the book function in this way across a wide spectrum of commentary. Conservative responses to electronic writing, for example, frequently eulogize the book itself as an object whose disappearance is a kind of allegory for larger changes in culture.[46] In *The Death of Literature* (1990), for example, Alvin Kernan uses the image of books printed on paper containing acid disintegrating on library shelves, or "[u]nsold books [that] go quickly to that sad limbo of the book, the remainder house, or to the shredding machine to save warehousing costs and taxes on inventory" as a way to talk about a postmodern world in which "knowledge would become first difficult and then impossible."[47] The book here is a kind of allegorical object that stands in for all of the traditional and institutionally legitimated

---

45. Tom Wolfe, "The New Journalism," in *The New Journalism*, eds. Tom Wolfe and E. W. Johnson (New York: Harper & Row, 1973), 25–26.

46. The best-known and more explicit such book is Sven Birkerts's *The Gutenberg Elegies: The Fate of Reading in an Electronic Age* (New York: Fawcett Columbine, 1994).

47. Alvin Kernan, *The Death of Literature* (New Haven, CT: Yale University Press, 1990), 137–38.

forms of reading and writing. The same is true of Mailer, although his interest in invoking the traditional book is quite the opposite: not to eulogize the loss of reading but to assert and legitimate a form of writing not otherwise respected.

Mailer, Wolfe, and even Kernan use the physical book as an institutional site where authors act; they therefore recreate the fictionality of page space at the level of the whole book. The self-consciously "fake" books of Mailer and Capote seem to exemplify a distinct variation on the fiction-as-lie definition that I have been describing in this chapter. When Maxine Hong Kingston writes *Tripmaster Monkey* (1989), she subtitles it *His Fake Book* to suggest a degree of improvisation and exaggeration that will remind us of the fiction of Katz and Federman. Nonetheless, Kingston's metafictional comments within the novel are much better described simply as reflecting an oral style. She ends the first chapter, for example, by exhorting the reader to follow along to the second: "Our Wittman is going to work on his play for the rest of the night. If you want to see whether he will get that play up, and how a poor monkey makes a living so he can afford to spend the weekday afternoon drinking coffee and hanging out, go on to the next chapter."[48] Exaggeration within this novel is associated with the character of Wittman himself, who intentionally adopts the role of a trickster inventing stories to bring together his community and to reveal racist stereotypes about the Chinese within America. Kingston describes the "one-man show" that Wittman puts on at the end of the novel: "Our monkey, master of change, staged a fake war, which might very well be displacing some real war. Wittman was learning that one big bang-up show has to be followed up with a second show, a third show, shows until something takes hold. He was defining a community, which will meet every night for a season. Community is not built once-and-for-all; people have to imagine, practice, and re-create it" (306). Imaginative playfulness is described here as a natural part of the creation of a community. In the context of my discussion of fake books, it seems clear that Wittman's faked history is a kind of lie that asserts his agency and creates new institutions through which the community can coalesce.

Kingston's own narrative style tends to reflect the exaggerated and playful style of Wittman but in more muted ways. She is quite explicit about distinguishing between real acts of lying and the pretended and institutionally sanctioned acts of Wittman's play: "Of course, Wittman Ah Sing didn't really burn down the Association house and the theatre. It was an illusion of fire.

---

48. Maxine Hong Kingston, *Tripmaster Monkey: His Fake Book* (New York: Knopf, 1989), 35.

Good monkey. He kept control of the explosives, and of his arsonist's delight of flames. He wasn't crazy; he was a monkey" (305). The concept of a fake book in this regard allows her to define an institutionally recognized space for improvisation. In musical terms, a fake book is simply a rough musical guide to playing a song, usually stripped down to its basic melody. There are examples of actual musical fake books in contemporary fiction. At one point in *Vineland* (1990), for example, Thomas Pynchon narrates a scene in which Billy Barf and the Vomitones are booked to play an Italian wedding, even though they know none of the traditional wedding favorites that the guests expect. Help comes when they discover a useful book at the house: "Fortunately, Ralph Wayvone's library happened to include a copy of the indispensable *Italian Wedding Fake Book,* by Deleuze & Guattari, which Gelsomina, the bride, to protect her wedding from such possible unlucky omens as blood on the wedding cake, had the presence of mind to slip indoors and bring back out to Billy Barf's attention."[49] The title of this volume is bizarre and its purpose within the novel is obscure; nonetheless, precisely this sort of method of "faking it" runs throughout Pynchon's novels, as characters routinely find themselves in situations for which they are ill-prepared and are expected to act out roles in disguise often with severe penalties for failure. Indeed, the fake book is a kind of corollary to the scene, a guide that sets conditions on performance while often leaving open the possibility of surprising freedom.

 A fake book is a kind of a lie that works to legitimate performances by making it possible to follow broad rules that leave room for tangents and variations. While we can see this as a traditional postmodern emphasis on improvisation, I would point to the other side of these fakes—the way their conventional form gives them legitimacy and creates a space like the page or scene space I discussed in the previous section. In such a context, the traditional book comes to stand in for the status quo, and narratives faked on its basis acquire a kind of borrowed legitimacy. Typical in this regard is Robert Coover's well-known *The Public Burning* (1977), a novel that invokes numerous types of writing while offering up a radically unconventional look at the 1951 Rosenberg trial. Like Kingston, Coover is interested in the ways that lies allow communities to define themselves. Early in the novel Uncle Sam admonishes Richard Nixon not to worry about whether the prosecution of the Rosenbergs was rigged: "Hell, *all* courtroom testimony about the past is ipso facto and teetotaciously a baldface lie, ain't that so? Moonshine! Chicanery! The hole gum game! Like history itself—all more or less bunk, as

---

 49. Thomas Pynchon, *Vineland* (Boston: Little, Brown, 1990), 97.

Henry Ford liked to say, as saintly and wise a pup as this nation's seen since the Gold Rush—the fatal slantidicular futility of Fact! Appearances, my boy, appearances! Practical politics consists in ignorin' facts! *Opinion* ultimately governs the world!"[50] As he investigates the trial, however, Nixon works at filling in the story of the Rosenbergs—inventing and guessing events in different places (117), all the while coming to identify with Ethel in particular.

Like all fake books, Coover's novel is about agency and the indirect routes of legitimacy. *The Public Burning* is not just a novel that investigates the need for national stories; it also is interested in the way that Nixon himself becomes an agent in these events. Challenged by Uncle Sam to investigate the trial, Nixon comes to a realization: "*That* was what Uncle Sam was expecting of me! That was what language was for: to transcend the confusions, restore the spirit, recreate the society! Ahead of me, I knew, was a day of almost superhuman effort" (247). And it is in these efforts that Nixon becomes part of the national spirit and, eventually, a vehicle for Uncle Sam's actions: "*A nation, like a person, has got something' deeper, somethin' more permanent and pestiferous, somethin' larger than the scum of its parts, and what this nation's got is ME!*" (524). Even though everyone in the nation participates in some way, Nixon's role at the center of the events—at the end of the novel he is on the very stage of the execution in Times Square—marks him as special: "It ain't easy holdin' a community together, order ain't what comes natural, you know that, boy, and a lotta people gotta get killt tryin't to pretend it is, that's how the game is played—but not many of 'em gets a chance to have it done to 'em in Times Square!" (559). The agency that emerges in this work is defined against the backdrop of institutional spaces (like the courtroom) that are mirrored in the object of the book itself. Indeed, while much of the novel is organized by a simple three-day chronological structure, Coover inserts several dramatic "intermezzo" scenes that are presented as stage dialogue or even light opera: "Human Dignity Is Not for Sale: A Last-Act Sing Sing Opera by Julius and Ethel Rosenberg." Nixon emerges as an agent by borrowing institutional spaces: the courtroom, the opera stage, and the book itself.

We can see the complexity of agency in relation to the physical object of the book in what is probably the best-known fake book of postmodern American literature, Ishmael Reed's *Mumbo Jumbo* (1972). Reed's novel offers a radical reinterpretation of Western civilization and its understanding of race and power. Like Coover, Reed combines historical figures and fictional creations, frequently mixing novelistic narrative with invented news reports and recontextualized diagrams and photographs. As W. Lawrence Hogue

---

50. Robert Coover, *The Public Burning* (New York: Viking, 1977), 90.

describes it, "The text, a pseudoacademic system of quotes, footnotes, and even a bibliography, is a mixture of the fictive, or mythical, with the historical."[51] Like Coover's *Public Burning*, *Mumbo Jumbo* quite explicitly presents itself as a book, as a particular textual artifact. Indeed, one of the themes of the novel is the need for a text to give shape and cohesion to the African spiritual traditions that the novel unpacks within Western civilization. Reed's central character, PaPa LaBas, explains that Jes Grew, the African musical/spiritual/visionary plague that threatens white America, is seeking a text that will become its reference point: "It's up to its Text. For some, it's a disease, a plague, but in fact it's an anti-plague.... Being an anti-plague I figure that it's yearning for The Work of its Word or else it will peter out as in the 1890s, when it wasn't ready and had no idea where to search. It must find its Speaking or strangle upon its own ineloquence."[52] It is quite clear within the novel that *Mumbo Jumbo* represents just such a text. Not only does Reed include such typically bookish elements as a "partial bibliography" but he also takes the unusual step of beginning the novel before its title page. Reed presents a whole chapter setting up the narrative background for his novel, and only then offers the novel proper—as if this book, Reed's book, were already part of some larger narrative that he is presenting. In doing so, Reed makes clear the continuum between fake books and those that use page space indexically. In both, the author's work gestures outside to the larger publishing context that gives those actions meaning.

Like *The Public Burning*, Reed's faked history contains the story of character performance that in turn challenges the institutions that define the book. Indeed, the last sixty pages of the novel present a history culled by LaBas from his research and insight presented to an eager audience in a revelation scene familiar from murder mysteries. "Well, if you must know, it all began 1000s of years ago in Egypt, according to a high up member in the Haitian aristocracy," begins a sweeping rewriting of Western civilization (160). LaBas's performance is greeted with suspicion by some of his audience: "I don't believe a word of it. You made the whole thing up" (191). This reception is quite in contrast to what Nixon finds at the end of *The Public Burning*: one character stands outside of the power structures and finds his invention rejected, and the other is swept up into American society and its traditional power centers. As readers, however, we see what LaBas's audience cannot: the form of the fake book, which grants Reed's narrative a borrowed

51. W. Lawrence Hogue, "Historiographic Metafiction and the Celebration of Differences: Ishmael Reed's *Mumbo Jumbo*," in *Productive Postmodernism: Consuming Histories and Cultural Studies*, ed. John N. Duvall (Albany: State University of New York Press, 2002), 95.

52. Ishmael Reed, *Mumbo Jumbo* (1972; New York: Scribner, 1996), 33–34.

legitimacy. Indeed, Reed's work brilliantly reveals the central role of the book itself in shaping the fiction-as-lie definition of fictionality. We have in our hands the text that Reed's characters are seeking, and our response is fundamentally different because of the legitimacy granted to that physical object.

In the fake books of Reed, Coover, and Kingston we see a gesture towards institutionally recognized forms of writing that become allegorically applied to these books. The fake book, like the space of the page in Federman's and Katz's novels, reflects the feeling that there is no "elite" publishing venue that simply corrects mass taste. Rather, all publication occurs in spaces defined by competing institutional forces. When critics claim that postmodern novels refer to themselves as lies because of some deconstructive understanding of language and reference, they fail to take account of the context into which these writers are intervening. By gesturing beyond the page or the book artifact to the conditions under which it was produced, these writers work to establish legitimacy for their fiction in a time of conflicting critical standards and an often splintered literary public sphere.

CHAPTER 4

Style and Symptom in Postmodern Science Fiction

Thus far, I have described three different definitions of fictionality circulating within contemporary American culture that represent different degrees of acceptance of the traditional understanding of literature as serious, timeless, economically disinterested, and valuable for self-understanding. John Barth represents the closest embrace of these traditional values, while Alice Walker and Andy Warhol critique current institutions, and thus attempt to rethink such traditional models for the literary. Writers like Gilbert Sorrentino and Steve Katz move even further away from these institutions, since their understanding of writing as a lie undermines the traditional ground on which literature is valued. I shift now towards those definitions of fictionality that do not begin from literature but instead draw from other audiences and contexts. When these definitions address the issue of literature's place within American culture—if they do at all—it is as outsiders. The next definition of fictionality circulating within American culture that I would like to discuss arises out of contemporary science fiction.

The position of science fiction within contemporary definitions of fictionality is paradoxical. Science fiction is deeply entwined with one of the most powerful definitions of fictionality, which emerges in the eighteenth century but reaches its literary apex in the late nineteenth century. Like fiction in its classic definition, science fiction is essentially a vehicle for investigation and decision making. Critics have almost universally defined science fiction as inherently connected to the act of creating and exploring worlds that function as logical alternatives to our own reality. As Darko Suvin asserts, "*SF is, then, a literary genre whose necessary and sufficient conditions are the presence and interaction of estrangement and cognition, and whose main formal device is an imaginative framework alternative to the author's empirical environment.*"[1] He concludes his introduction by insisting that this cognitive shift is the essence of our interest and enjoyment of science fiction: "Once the elastic criteria of literary structuring have been met, *a cognitive—in most cases strictly scientific—element becomes the measure of aesthetic quality, of the specific pleasure to be sought in SF.* In other words, the cognitive nucleus of the plot codetermines the fictional estrangement itself" (15).[2]

In one sense, postmodern culture seems to have taken this sort of modeling to heart. In 1990 James Der Derian described the growing dependence of the military on computerized war games for strategy as "the *continuation of war by means of verisimilitude.*"[3] Likewise, we might think of the proliferation of focus groups used for deciding everything from which movies Hollywood makes to which tax proposals the president will take to Congress as a form of modeling. The widespread acceptance of this sort of modeling is likewise reflected in the explosive popularity of computer and video games that ask players to participate in simulations. One of the best-selling computer games of all time is *The Sims,* in which players manipulate virtual characters to shepherd them through career choices, furniture purchases, and social networking. At the same time, however, confidence in our ability to predict and logically plan for the future is at a low point. Frederic Jameson is, of course, best known for asserting that the increasing complexity of multinational

---

1. Darko Suvin, *Metamorphoses of Science Fiction: On the Poetics and History of a Literary Genre* (New Haven, CT: Yale University Press, 1979), 7–8.

2. In this regard, we might recall Tzvetan Todorov's claim in *The Fantastic: A Structural Approach to a Literary Genre,* trans. Richard Howard (Ithaca, NY: Cornell University Press, 1975) that in order for something to remain "fantastic" it cannot be allowed to slide into allegory (32). The same literalism is true of science fiction as well; this is what I take Suvin to mean when he says that the aesthetics of science fiction depend on investigating an alternative imaginative framework.

3. James Der Derian, "The Simulation Syndrome: From War Games to Game Wars," *Social Text* 8, no. 2 (1990): 189.

corporations has made it impossible for people to "cognitively map" their everyday reality: "this latest mutation in space—postmodern hyperspace—has finally succeeded in transcending the capacities of the individual human body to locate itself, to organize its immediate surroundings perceptually, and to map cognitively its position in a mappable external world."[4]

As a result of this loss of confidence in cognitive mapping, the concept of the future itself has become radically complicated. We live in an age characterized by Jerome Klinkowitz as "post-contemporary."[5] Likewise a recent collection of essays on "postmodern times and places" is titled *After the Future*.[6] In a recent volume on Derrida's writing, the issue of furturity itself is foregrounded as inherent to the deconstructive understanding of philosophy itself: "Philosophy is a discourse that knows all about the future, or at least about *its* future. It knows, and has always known, that it has no future. Philosophy knows that the future is death. Philosophy is always going to die. Always has been going to die. Always will have been going to die. From the beginning, its future will have been its end: and from this end, its future will have been always to begin its ending again."[7] The tendency to describe contemporary culture in apocalyptic terms is at least as old as the concept of postmodernism itself. Ihab Hassan speaks to the conflicted feelings about the future that define postmodern literature in the 1970s in his well-known essay, "POSTmodernISM": "I am possessed by the feeling that in the next few decades, certainly within half a century, the earth and all that inhabits it may be wholly other, perhaps ravaged, perhaps on the way to some strange utopia indistinguishable from nightmare. I have no language to articulate this feeling with conviction, nor imagination to conceive this special destiny. To live from hour to hour seems as maudlin as to invoke every hour the Last Things."[8] Postmodernism as a critical concept comes into existence at this balance point between apocalypse and open-ended futurity. A number of critics have noted that one of the reasons why history has been treated so problematically in postmodern novels is because of precisely this uncertainty

---

4. Fredric Jameson, *The Cultural Turn: Selected Writings on the Postmodern, 1983–1998* (London: Verso, 1998), 15–16.

5. For a gloss on this odd term, see Klinkowitz's preface to *Literary Disruptions: The Making of a Post-Contemporary American Fiction*, 2d ed. (Urbana: University of Illinois Press, 1980), ix–x.

6. Gary Shapiro, ed., *After the Future: Postmodern Times and Places* (Albany: State University of New York Press, 1990).

7. Geoffrey Bennington, "RIP," in *Futures: Of Jacques Derrida*, ed. Richard Rand (Stanford, CA: Stanford University Press, 2001), 1.

8. Ihab Hassan, *Paracriticisms: Seven Speculations on the Times* (Urbana: University of Illinois Press, 1975), 52.

about how to think about futurity.[9] Hassan suggests that "futurology" will emerge as a field to challenge traditional literature departments: "How will the verbal imagination sow its seed?" (166).

At first glance, then, science fiction's interest in cognition and speculative inquiry would seem to be at odds with many of the qualities that we associate most with postmodernism. If postmodernism can be characterized by a loss of confidence in logical inquiry free from political and philosophical bias, then science fiction's speculative structure would seem fundamentally at odds with contemporary culture. Indeed, we might point to certain varieties of contemporary science fiction by writers like Samuel Delany, Brian Aldiss, and J. G. Ballard that go out of their way to explore irrational worlds. And yet, many of the speculative works that have emerged both in popular and in academic consciousness as embodiments of postmodern science fiction are not, in fact, the ontologically ambiguous or contradictory worlds of Delany's or Ballard's fiction, but rather works that seem speculative in more traditional ways. When one thinks of philosophically current science fiction, feminist work by writers like Marge Piercy or Joanna Russ, and the "cyberpunk" writing of authors like William Gibson and Bruce Sterling are likely to come to mind first. This is true not only of academic critics, who write on these works far more often than the more innovative and apparently postmodern narratives of Delany, but also of the image of hip and up-to-date science fiction in popular culture embodied in films like *The Matrix*. Why have these works emerged as embodiments of a postmodern science fiction? And, as a consequence, how do we imagine the cultural, artistic, and intellectual role of the fictionality in a speculative genre?

Reading the Matrix

The Matrix (1999) has come to embody in popular culture a certain type of brainy speculation on the nature of contemporary media culture that tells us a great deal about the apparent relevance of science fiction. Like film adaptations of several Philip K. Dick novels—*Blade Runner* (1982) or *Minority Report* (2002)—*The Matrix* typifies in a popular imagination that otherwise

---

9. Among the many critics who have discussed changing attitudes towards temporality in postmodernism, see Elizabeth Deeds Ermarth, *Sequel to History: Postmodernism and the Crisis of Representational Time* (Princeton, NJ: Princeton University Press, 1992). For a discussion that links utopian futures in the postmodern historical and science fiction novels, see Elisabeth Wesseling, *Writing History as a Prophet: Postmodernist Innovations of the Historical Novel* (Amsterdam: John Benjamins, 1991).

has little contact with science fiction novels what the genre can do. Nowhere is this emblematic use of the film clearer than in its reference to "the desert of the real." The Wachowski brothers, who directed the film, take this line from Jean Baudrillard and insert it into the film as description of the post-apocalyptic world that is the film's setting, and which is hidden beneath the computer-generated "matrix" that most people take for real. In turn, the film's use of the term is picked up on and used by Slavoj Žižek in his collection of essays on the world after 9/11. For him, the film is fascinating because of the belief that there is some "real reality" behind the reality that we experience everyday."[10] Žižek writes,

> Virtual Reality simply generalizes this procedure of offering a product deprived of its substance: it provides reality itself deprived of its substance, of the hard resistant kernel of the Real—just as decaffeinated coffee smells and tastes like real coffee without being real coffee, Virtual Reality is experienced as reality without it being so. What happens at the end of this process of virtualization, however, is that we begin to experience "real reality" itelf as a ritual entity. For the great majority of the public, the WTC explosions were events on the TV screen. . . . (11)

For Žižek, *The Matrix* embodies a broader cultural response to the creeping expansion of virtual reality, an urge to believe that behind our everyday life is something "realer"—even if that realness is itself an imagined condition. *The Matrix* represents a point of circulation between academic and popular thinking about contemporary culture and audiences.

For all that the film announces itself to be a speculation on contemporary culture, however, we need to reflect only briefly on the film to recognize the gap between Baudrillard's theory of postmodern culture and its own speculative donnée. Although in *America* Baudrillard associates hyperreality with the American landscape and utopian aspirations,[11] Baudrillard's theory works best as a characterization of contemporary media culture. Baudrillard's discussion of the increasing prevalence of simulation in this regard is both his best-known theoretical offering and what the Wachowski brothers are invoking by referencing Baudrillard. Indeed, in a blatant tip-off to the viewer about the intellectual context in which the film should be understood, *The Matrix*'s main character, Neo, is shown hiding a diskette containing software in a hollowed-out copy of Baudrillard's *Simulacra and*

    10. Slavoj Žižek, *Welcome to the Desert of the Real: Five Essays on September 11 and Related Dates* (London: Verso, 2002), 15.
    11. Jean Baudrillard, *America*, trans. Chris Turner (London: Verso, 1988).

Simulation. Baudrillard remarks there (although it does not appear in the film), "Today abstraction is no longer that of the map, the double, the mirror, or the concept. Simulation is no longer that of a territory, a referential being, or a substance. It is the generation by models of a real without origin or reality: a hyperreal."[12] Drawing on examples of Disneyland and the Watergate scandal, Baudrillard has in mind an expansion of media representation as part of a capitalism in which use value evaporates under the pressure of omnipresent exchange value. In other words, the domination of simulation is a stage of capitalism in which advertising becomes increasingly powerful and pervasive.

It is clear in that *The Matrix* does not mean anything of the sort in its use of Baudrillard. The film itself tells the story of a post-apocalyptic world in which human beings are hardwired into a computer-generated fantasy world so that their unnoticed bodies can be used by a race of machines to produce energy. This communal world is itself the "matrix" and is recognizable as a construction only when an individual's body is forcibly removed from its connection to the hardware that sustains it and delivers the computer-generated experiences directly to the nervous system. In such a filmic world, "simulation" has no connection to the expansion of capitalism or the prevalence of mass media; the matrix is, instead, a simulation in a much stronger but simpler way. Indeed, in his discussion of the film, Žižek suggests the shift from Baudrillard's description of the simulacrum to this computer-generated "matrix" is a fantasy about the presence of a real world that is waiting for us to claim it. In the film we are told that some people can sense the falseness of the world presented to them; it is this vague dissatisfaction that characterizes Neo at the beginning of the film. The film opens with a restless Neo uninterested in his day job, staying up late into the night searching for scattered information about the matrix. Later, Trinty characterizes Neo's restlessness: "I know why you're here, Neo. I know what you've been doing. I know why you hardly sleep, why you live alone and why, night after night, you sit at your computer; you're looking for him. . . . I know because I was once looking for the same thing, but when he found me, he told me I wasn't really looking for him. I was looking for an answer."[13]

To complain about the Wachowski brothers' literalization of Baudrillard's theory is, I think, pointless as a critique of the film itself; after all, they are under no obligation to make an authentically Baudrillardian film. More

---

12. Jean Baudrillard, *Simulacra and Simulation*, trans. Sheila Faria Glaser (Ann Arbor: University of Michigan Press, 1994), 1.

13. Larry Wachowski and Andy Wachowski, *The Matrix: The Shooting Script* (New York: Newmarket Press, 2001), 13.

interesting, it seems, is to ask what this shift in the meaning of Baudrillard's simulation accomplishes, and how it affects the appeal of the film to its audience. A number of critics writing on the film have noted the irony that so much of the appeal of this film depends on its spectacular action sequences and its innovative use of computer-generated imagining (CGI) technology. In particular, the film uses a sophisticated form of stop-motion photography that seems to rotate the camera around a scene watched in slow motion. Dubbed "Bullet-Time" because of its striking use in filming scenes of gunplay, this technique is important to allowing the audience to sense how Neo and others, aware of the artificial nature of the matrix, are able to manipulate its laws—to walk up walls, dodge bullets, and so on. In her discussion of the "search of wonder" in contemporary film special effects, Michele Pierson describes the impact of *The Matrix* this way: "In contrast to the aesthetically moribund *Phantom Menace*, *The Matrix* featured this technique [of "Bullet-Time"] in a number of key action sequences combining stunts with subtle 2-D and 3-D animation, transforming the cinematographic image into as dynamic and arresting assemblage capable of arousing that old sense of wonder and curiosity about the technology—and art—of cinematic illusion in even some of the most jaded cinemagoers."[14] Although its thematic handling of postmodern themes has been the most frequent occasion for both popular and academic discussion of the film, it is clear that without the striking effects and its overall style, *The Matrix* would not have attracted nearly the attention that it has.

This technique works hand-in-hand with the general theme of the film, that what we take to be reality is in fact a simulation whose rules are only apparently absolute. Indeed, one of the best-known lines from the film is Morpheus's assertion to Neo, "Unfortunately, no one can be told what the Matrix is. You have to see it for yourself" (28). Having made this claim, he "unplugs" Neo from the matrix, recovers his body, and brings it to his ship where Neo has the design and operation of the matrix shown to him. Reconnected to a simulation of the matrix controlled by Morpheus, Neo comes to understand that this is a construct precisely because of the extraordinary things—filmed using bullet time—that he and Morpheus are able to do. Neo, in other words, is impressed in the same way that the audience for the film is by these striking effects. There are a number of ironies here, in that the film is most characteristic and Neo's powers most impressive when he occupies not the real world but the computer-generated world of the matrix. Writing in

---

14. Michele Pierson, *Special Effects: Still in Search of Wonder* (New York: Columbia University Press, 2002), 163.

Cultural Critique, Laura Bartlett and Thomas Byers remark, "recall that, for all the spectacular physical stunts that help make *The Matrix* an eyepopper, the reality of Neo's heroism is both cybernetic and amazingly passive. He is the One not because he is a karate kid, but because he is a supreme hacker. All his amazing defiances of gravity and dodges of death come while he is, in fact, strapped and wired into a chair in a kind of trance."[15] Both the film and its hacker heroes seem to valorize the real world as a site of unlimited possibility not bounded by the rules of computer architecture, but the real appeal of both is based on the matrix and the amazing effects that this sophisticated CGI technology allows. This irony (if not outright contradiction) is not quite the same one that I noted in the way that the film literalizes Baudrillard, but they are clearly related. Both suggest that the film has redirected its critique of simulation in unexpected ways. Indeed, this should be no surprise, since the film itself is, after all, a kind of simulation that mirrors the position of the passive body connected to the matrix. If Neo accomplishes his amazing feats while being strapped to a chair, we participate vicariously while being rooted in our theater seats.

The Matrix depends, then, in a curious and not quite coherent way on its own visual style. Indeed, style is an absolutely central quality of the film. One of the film's best-known images—the one that is used more than any other in promotional material—is the posed and stylized portrait of the sunglass-wearing, leather-clad band of hackers lead by Morpheus. After all, if everything in the matrix is artificial, one can dress whatever way one wants. Style here is of a piece with the amazing physical powers that this band acquires while in the matrix. The film ends with Neo awakened to his unique powers to influence the matrix. The final scene is not, however, one in which the matrix is destroyed and masses of humanity wake from their illusion; it is, instead, of the stylishly dressed Neo alone in the matrix surrounded by everyday life, flying—the very embodiment of matrix-given power and style.

We can see the way that the film links Neo's awareness of the matrix and a certain countercultural style if we consider the film's introduction of Neo and his initial contact with the band lead by Morpheus. We first meet Neo asleep at his desk, with this computer evidently searching for information about Morpheus; newspapers from around the world flash onto the screen, testifying to his notoriety even within the matrix-generated world. Neo is awoken—although why is not clear—when the flashing news reports

---

15. Laura Bartlett and Thomas B. Byers, "Back to the Future: The Humanist Matrix," *Cultural Critique* 53 (2003): 42.

are replaced by a typed message from Morpheus offering to explain what the matrix is and charging him to "follow the white rabbit." As Neo frantically tries to clear Morpheus's message from his screen, he is interrupted by a knock at his door; a group of stylishly dressed twentysomethings have come to buy a diskette of illegal software or data from Neo. Struck by Neo's haunted appearance, the casual leader of this group invites Neo to join them at a dance club: "you need to unplug, man" (13). The line initially carries the double meaning of taking time off and getting away from Neo's apparently obsessive interest in computers—time that we are to sense takes up his leisure as well as work days. At the industrially themed dance club to which Neo is led he meets Trinity, a member of Morpheus's group, while technopunk music blares in the background. The location is clearly one chosen by Trinity and Morpheus, who have somehow manipulated Neo's hacker friends unwittingly into leading him into this meeting.

While this scene does a certain amount of work to establish contact between Neo and Morpheus's group and to make clear Neo's dissatisfaction with his everyday life, more important to the film, I think, is the way that it establishes certain types of emotional links between the futuristic world of the film and the definition of the stylish in late-'90s America. Neo's interest in hacking is metonymically rather than literally related to the themes of the matrix. If, in fact, all of reality is constructed like a computer program, there is no reason to think we would have any access to the structure of this program through the type of information networks that Neo is searching. Although the image of Neo as a hacker suggests his dissatisfaction with his everyday life, the coincidence between the structure of the matrix and his own interest in programming makes no logical sense. Likewise, Trinity's choice of meeting place plays on our contemporary sense of the rebellion of youth culture. As we know when we get further into the film, any sort of rebellion that takes place within the guidelines established by the matrix is no rebellion at all. (Indeed, when Neo goes to visit the "oracle" who promises to reveal his destiny, she appears grandmotherly, baking cookies in what seems to be a low-rent, crowded apartment. More effectively than in the opening scene, the film here reminds us of the gap between how one appears in the matrix and how conventionally one is really behaving in relationship to that system.) Like the leather clothing adopted by Morpheus's outlaw group, such meeting places and interests are metonymically related to the themes of the film, without themselves being causally connected. We might say the same of the role of Baudrillard in the film's subtexts as well: it is not literally embodied in the computer-generated reality of the matrix but rather connected by certain metonymic similarities to the concerns of the film. In all of these cases, superficial similarities (rock music = rebellion = working against the matrix) stand in for causal connections.

To suggest that *The Matrix* is more concerned with style than substance will sound like a criticism, and I am pointing to what are fairly straightforward intellectual incoherencies in the film. This might seem especially important since science fiction is traditionally understood as a genre that depends on logical extrapolation from the present to a hypothetical future. What seems to me important here is that these incoherencies do not touch what has been most compelling about the film; the critique that I have offered here will seem to most fans beside the point. Much more important in understanding the appeal of the film is that precisely the stylishness of the film appears to offer so successful and powerful a way of speaking about contemporary culture. This seems to be true of other science fiction films that have become the subject of both academic and popular discussions about the future. Films like *Blade Runner* and the *Terminator* series certainly raise thematic issues about human identity and our vision of the future, but it seems clear that their place in popular consciousness depends not only on these themes but also on the very stylishness of the films: from the mixture of a noir narrative with the hypercommericalized culture of Ridley Scott's future to the "first computer-generated main character" of *Terminator 2*.[16] As Pierson's quote about the "aesthetically moribund" quality of the recent *Star Wars* films suggests, there is a strange way in which the visual style of these science fiction films comes to determine our sense of their relevance as a portrait of our future. Nothing, of course, could make less sense in the light of our traditional definition of science fiction as a logical extrapolation from the present; according to such a definition, the style of science fiction is much less important than its content—its logical premise and its coherent vision. If *The Matrix* refers to these contemporary issues more in its style than in its substance, we might well ask if this stylishness might not represent a different way of thinking about what science fiction can do in contemporary American culture.

Cyberpunk Style

Larry McCaffery titles his introduction to a 1988 special issue of the *Mississippi Review* "The Desert of the Real: The Cyberpunk Controversy."[17] McCaffery's invocation of Baudrillard makes explicit a structure of allusion in the

---

16. Pierson, *Special Effects*, 77.
17. Larry McCaffery, "The Desert of the Real: The Cyberpunk Controversy," *Mississippi Review* 47/48 (1988): 7–15.

criticism that quickly shot up around cyberpunk fiction that we have already seen in *The Matrix*. I have already noted that the "desert of the real" is both the film's most explicit citation of Baudrillard but also the point at which this film is picked up and used by Žižek as a commentary on our contemporary belief that some "realer" reality is hiding just out of reach.

The similarity is, of course, not accidental. The term *matrix* itself is routinely seen as a reference to William Gibson's *Neuromancer,* where it names what we call cyberspace today: "A graphic representation of data abstracted from the banks of every computer in the human system."[18] Gibson's novel is the ur-text of cyberpunk writing. Indeed, some have claimed that the "movement" called cyberpunk actually consists on only one writer (Gibson) and is really only well exemplified by *Neuromancer* itself.[19] If we think of *The Matrix* as an attempt to use science fiction in a new way constituted by a different style of allusion, it is clear that much of the criticism that has grown up around the concept of cyberpunk (as opposed to Gibson's novel specifically) struggles with exactly the question of the relevance of this fiction. So it is that McCaffery is able to announce in this introduction the importance of science fiction as a vehicle for understanding contemporary life. McCaffery remarks parenthetically, "if my suspicions are right . . . SF and SF-related forms are going to continue to play an increasingly dominant role in the arts: it is a relatively new form of great elasticity whose central motifs and stylistic conventions are evolving *now* in response to what is happening *now.*"[20] He goes on to make a remarkably strong claim about the relevance of this fiction: "And the fact is that cyberpunk seems to be the only art systematically dealing with the most crucial political, philosophical, moral, and cultural issues of our day" (9). The wiggle room created by the word *systematically* in this passage aside, McCaffery claims an extraordinary importance for cyberpunk writing. He does so, at least in part, by following the path that the Wachowski brothers will trod ten years later: by claiming a particular allusive quality that allows this writing to handle broad theoretical problems in the definition of contemporary media, culture, and subjectivity in a narrative form.

We should not, however, single out McCaffery, since the sort of claims that he is making about cyberpunk writing is reflected by most of the contributors to this collection, as well by the general tone of most of the criticism

---

18. William Gibson, *Neuromancer* (New York: Ace, 1984), 51.
19. Samuel Delany cites this criticism without identifying the source in *Shorter Views: Queer Thoughts & the Politics of the Paraliterary* (Middletown, CT: Wesleyan University Press, 1999), 280.
20. McCaffery, "The Desert of the Real," 8–9.

produced at the end of the 1980s and beginning of the 1990s celebrating this writing. So it is that the collection *Fiction 2000: Cyberpunk and the Future of Narrative*, which appeared four years later, assumes that this writing will function as a turning point in storytelling. In this regard, John Huntington's essay, "Newness, *Neuromancer*, and the End of Narrative" is exemplary. Huntington recognizes that Gibson's novel creates a feeling of "newness" whose nature is difficult to pin down: "Those who find the novel significantly new seem to want to read it as a serious meditation on the reality that computers will someday create, but their enthusiasm is not dampened when they find that Gibson does not know very much about technology. One has to suspect that *Neuromancer*'s aura of newness derives from something deeper than its explicit ideas about the future."[21] Huntington goes on to suggest that Gibson's newness consists of the way that cyberspace makes characters aware of their own fictionality. More important for my interest in the reception of the novel and the critical production of the category of cyberpunk fiction is the way that this fiction gets associated with millennial change, even though—as Huntington rightly recognizes—our sense of exactly what is new in this writing is only vaguely formed.

Cyberpunk writing seems to promise, then, a new form of narrative that has a particular relevance to contemporary issues—frequently involving technology, but not exclusively—that critics feel other forms of writing are not addressing directly. Part of the apparent newness of cyberpunk writing no doubt reflects the rapidly increasing importance of computers and computer-mediated communication during the 1980s and '90s. Certainly one of the reasons that Gibson's novel has continued to have influence is because it gets credit for coining the term *cyberspace* and providing the first literary use of what has seemed to readers to be an increasingly ubiquitous part of contemporary life. But as Gibson himself has noted, his own technical knowledge of computing is very limited; critics love to point out that *Neuromancer* was composed not in a word-processing program but on a typewriter. One of the ways that we usually think about science fiction is as projecting likely or possible futures so that we can speculate on them and consider the tensions or issues within the present. This description does not, however, apply particularly well to *Neuromancer*. In interviews Gibson has routinely noted that he did not set out to write this novel as a speculation on emerging technology. In the same issue of the *Mississippi Review* that I have been discussing, McCaffery interviews Gibson and discusses his lack of familiarity with

21. John Huntington, "Newness, *Neuromancer*, and the End of Narrative," in *Fiction 2000: Cyberpunk and the Future of Narrative*, eds. George Slusser and Tom Shippey (Athens: University of Georgia Press, 1992), 133.

technology. In response to McCaffery's question, "So your use of computers and science results more from their metaphoric value or from the way they sound than from any familiarity with how they actually operate," Gibson responds: "I'm looking for images that supply a certain atmosphere. Right now science and technology seem to be very useful sources for these things. But I'm more interested in the *language* of, say, computers than I am in the technicalities of how they really operate. On the most basic level, computers in my books are simply a metaphor for human memory. I'm interested in the how's and why's of memory, the ways it defines who and what we *are*, in how easily it's subject to revision."[22] Gibson claims that his novel is less a matter of speculation than a recycling of certain forms of contemporary language that suggest to him a kind of novelistic atmosphere. Late in this interview Gibson remarks bluntly, "I don't see myself as extrapolating in the way I was taught an SF writer should" (228).

Although we can say, then, that Gibson's importance to critics trying to define science fiction seems initially to be justified by the presence of certain forms of new technology in his books, in fact his treatment of that technology is frequently quite cursory. Likewise, as Samuel Delany has remarked, much of what seems most new in Gibson's technology fits easily within traditions of science fiction, and only seems radical from the outside.[23] To suggest that writers before Gibson had ignored computer technology or had failed to consider the possibilities of the cyborg body is absurd. Delany's favorite point of comparison is between Gibson's character of Molly, who appears in both his story "Johnny Mnemonic" and *Neuromancer*, and Jael from Joanna Russ's *The Female Man*. "The point," writes Delany, "of course, is that these differences and similarities—formal and attitudinal—give these writers' works their meaning. And a sophisticated look at their texts immediately leads on to still other SF writers. The informed SF readership can experience that meaning because they are familiar with the informing range."[24] To suggest, in other words, that Gibson's writing, or that of any of the other cyberpunk authors, is somehow fundamentally different from earlier writing and thus radically

---

22. McCaffery, "An Interview with William Gibson," *Mississippi Review* 47/48 (1988): 224.
23. In "Is Cyberpunk a Good Thing or a Bad Thing?" *Mississippi Review* 47/48 (1988), Delany compares the misinterpretation of cyberpunk to deconstruction: "Within SF discourse 'cyberpunk' is really in the same sort of position that 'deconstruction' is in within the contemporary discourse of literary criticism" (34). He explains: "move it [deconstruction] out of that context [of those for whom 'the problems of literary criticism are of deep and pressing concern'] into *Time* magazine or *The Village Voice* and a brilliant thinker and writer like Derrida becomes a 'nihilisitic philosopher' and a powerful social and literary critic like Fredric Jameson is dismissed as 'a jargon monger'" (34).
24. Delany, "Is Cyberpunk a Good Thing or a Bad Thing?" 33.

more relevant than other science fiction is simply to pick a few works out of a tradition irresponsibly. And yet this simplification has been important to critics when they try to define the particular relevance of science fiction to contemporary literature. It should be no surprise that science fiction emerges as genre of writing with claims to academic attention at precisely the moment when critics are trying to distinguish the particular relevance or difference of cyberpunk. In this regard, McCaffery's decision to use *Neuromancer* as the epigraph to his essay on "The Fictions of the Present" in the 1988 *Columbia Literary History of the United States* is typical: science fiction emerges in this essay for a canon-forming volume as an important element of contemporary writing precisely by using Gibson as a representative of "[t]he growth and maturity of science fiction in the United States."[25]

Most of the traditional ways that we could define the uniqueness of cyberpunk, then, turn out to be false: it does not address some topic unrecognized by other contemporary writers, and it does not extrapolate a future in the traditional science fiction sense. There is, however, one point upon which all the critics discussing cyberpunk agree: the issue of style. Indeed, even Gibson himself remarks in the interview with McCaffery that the concept of cyberspace allows him to establish an atmosphere. Delany is more explicit, writing and speaking frequently about how Gibson's style belongs in a tradition of other writers who have shaken up the conventions of science fiction and created excitement. In comparing the excitement generated by Gibson, Roger Zelazny, and John Varley, Delany remarks on the particular stylistic "quality" of their writing:

> Though an absolutely necessary part of high writerly quality involves a skillfully wrought verbal surface, skill in writing may manifest itself in styles ranging from the simplicity of a Beckett, Hemingway, or Carver to the recommendations of a Joyce, Gass, or Davenport. Nor does the verbal surface exhaust the concept of high quality. Such quality would seem to be, rather, closer to the concept of a skillfully wrought verbal surface generated in a series of narrative situations that clearly and greatly excite a small number of readers comparatively well-educated in the history, in the traditions, and in the conventions of the particular genre.[26]

As in his other comments on cyberpunk and Gibson, Delany is eager to emphasize the science fiction tradition in which this writing should be

---

25. Larry McCaffery, "The Fictions of the Present," in *Columbia Literary History of the United States*, ed. Emory Elliott (New York: Columbia University Press, 1988), 1166.

26. Delany, *Shorter Views*, 283.

considered. This tradition is manifested primarily in the particular narrative "situations" that make up the story, and these situations in turn can be traced back to the particular style of the verbal surface. The same sort of observation about the unique quality of Gibson's style appears in other critics as well, even when they approach cyberpunk without concern for the tradition of science fiction. Writing in the same *Mississippi Review* issue that I have cited frequently, George Slusser describes cyberpunk as "literary MTV": "Images have been condensed, sharpened, creating an optical surface—a matrix of imagines that is more a glitterspace, images no longer capable of connecting to form the figurative space of mythos or story."[27] Even such a breezy comment about Gibson's writing ends up emphasizing style rather than topos, theme, or even narrative.

Critics who want to reject this emphasis on style find themselves swimming against the current of popular interpretation of science fiction. When Andrew Ross discusses Gibson's short story, "The Gernsback Continuum," he notes how this story works to contrast contemporary and past science fiction styles: "Its appeal rests on a contrast between the tough, savvy realism of contemporary SF's fondness for technological dystopias and the wide-eyed idealism of the thirties pulp romance of utopian things to come."[28] Ross goes on to show that the pulp romances so disparaged by these newer writers imagined the future in the context of social progress, and that in severing these links, cyberpunk "disconnect[s] technological development from any notion of a progressive future" (135). In other words, cyberpunk's savvy realism is unwilling to imagine plausible and socially responsible futures. At least part of the reason for this is because the vocation of this "savvy" writing is imagined not as ultimately predictive but as a stylistic exercise. The same move away from the stylistic justification for cyberpunk fictionality is made by Anne Balsamo in her feminist critique of the movement. Citing Fred Pfeil's observation that cyberpunk novels have no political unconscious but are instead acting out neurotic symptoms explicitly, Balsamo turns to Pat Cadigan's novel *Synners* as a feminist alternative to such superficially symptomatic writing: "in constructing this reading of *Synners*, not to emphasize its cyberpunk characteristics but rather to point to its feminist preoccupations, I am implicitly arguing that it expresses some form of allegorical narrative; as a work of the feminist imagination, it narrativizes certain tensions and obsessions that animate feminist thinking across cultural discourses."[29]

27. George Slusser, "Literary MTV" *Mississippi Review* 47/48 (1988): 279.
28. Andrew Ross, *Strange Weather: Culture, Science and Technology in the Age of Limits* (London: Verso, 1991), 102.
29. Anne Balsamo, *Technologies of the Gendered Body: Reading Cyborg Women* (Durham,

Balsamo's appeal to allegory shares with Ross's interest in utopian futures a resolve to read science fiction against the grain of its style and to look for a more traditional justification for its fictionality.

The emphasis on style that we see throughout cyberpunk writing and its reception by critics and fans seems to me especially significant because it prefigures the role of style in that other icon of cyberpunk, *The Matrix*. As I have argued, this film has appealed to critics and viewers as an exemplary cyberpunk artifact, even though thematically and narratively its portrait of reality and simulation is ambiguous or contradictory. As Delany and Slusser suggest, this appeal is based on the style of the verbal surface in cyberpunk fiction; in the film, it is based on the stylish appearance of the characters and the visual innovations of "Bullet-Time." There is perhaps no better example of the importance of style in both artifacts than the relative failure of the first adaptation of Gibson's cyberspace to film: the 1995 film *Johnny Mnemonic*. Based on a script produced by Gibson himself and directly translating the plot and atmosphere of Gibson's short story, this film has attracted considerably less interest from both critics and popular audience precisely because, I think, it lacks that striking visual style of *The Matrix*. This is no doubt related to the reason that the sequels to *The Matrix* have been considered disappointing. Regardless of the films' narrative success or failure, visually their style simply cannot recapture the newness of the original. It is this visual style rather than some theme that makes us feel that particular contemporary science fiction films are relevant to our image of the future.

Postmodern Symptoms

Why this appeal to style in cyberpunk writing? The answer seems fairly straightforward in *The Matrix*. The industrial music at the club where Neo and Trinity meet and which provides much of the soundtrack for the film as a whole, like the stylish black leather worn by most of the characters, reflects a departure of the reality of the "normal" world. The style of the characters' actions is not a political principle so much as an outright rejection of this world. In the world of *The Matrix,* our only political choice is literally to drop out. It is in this sense that the film deserves the problematic term *cyberpunk;* by defining its aesthetic and political action in terms of a style of rebellion rather than a theory of change, *The Matrix* reflects the way that critics have

---

NC: Duke University Press, 1996), 145. Citing Fred Pfeil, *Another Tale to Tell: Politics and Narrative in Postmodern Culture* (London: Verso, 1990), 86.

imagined novels by Gibson and others to be a style rather than a cognitive exercise.

When critics characterize the relevance of cyberpunk fiction, they frequently fall back on a similar language of theory-less praxis, of a stylish rejection of the status quo. McCaffery ends his introduction to the *Mississippi Review* issue by defending this writing against critics who "have constantly pointed towards c-p's appropriation of devices associated with other genres . . . as exhibiting c-p's superficiality and its collective failure of imagination." McCaffery turns this into a positive: "What such criticism ignores, however, is c-p's postmodernist spirit of free play (*jouissance*) and collaboration, its delight in creating cut-ups and collages (à la Burroughs) in which familiar objects and motifs are placed in startling, unfamiliar contexts."[30] Leaving aside the accuracy of McCaffery's characterization, what seems to me most striking about this defense of cyberpunk is the way that it mutes all questions of thematic or narrative innovation for the sake of establishing its "spirit." Appeals to a spirit seem to me precisely what is contained within the characterization of cyber*punk*—what is most important is the style with which things are done. *The Matrix,* Burroughs's fiction and punk music all describe a reality that has been "pulled over our eyes" by those in power; consequently the only possible response is to break down the structures of power and representation, without being concerned about what results. The cut-up in this regard (which I discussed briefly in the previous chapter) is a certain style of writing that explicitly denies the importance of what is said for the sake of how it is said. Whether this is, in fact, what really makes Gibson's writing compelling is another matter. Delany may well be right that the reasons that cyberpunk writing excited fans of science fiction have little to do with such broad claims about resisting power. Nonetheless, it seems to me clear that a significant reason why cyberpunk has attracted the interest of critics working outside of the tradition of science fiction as well as the fascination of the general public through *The Matrix* is precisely because this writing is available to the sort of stylistic characterization that McCaffery offers.

In foregrounding style as a reflection of the broader cultural conditions, cyberpunk is in good company. Indeed, many of the most popular statements about postmodernity treat the characteristics of contemporary texts as symptoms of changing social conditions. Charles Newman's early critique of postmodernist fiction, *The Post-Modern Aura: The Act of Fiction in an Age of Inflation* (1985), exemplifies the tradition of critiquing postmodernist works

---

30. McCaffery, "The Desert of the Real," 14.

as mere symptoms of a larger culture. Newman's account, he announces, is "nothing so juicy as a sensibility, only a dim pathology of the contemporary."[31] It is in this way that Lyotard's description of postmodernism as incredulity toward master narratives likewise is usually understood, as a statement of the way that current forms of writing reflect a loss of confidence in certain philosophical claims.[32] Defining postmodernism as essentially a cultural symptom rather than an aesthetic or political choice has been one of the most controversial elements of Frederic Jameson's revolutionary theory of postmodernism. Perry Anderson notes that the central accomplishment of Jameson's theory is to define postmodernism as a reflection of its economic conditions: "The first, and most fundamental, [decisive move] came with its title—the anchorage of postmodernism in objective alterations of the economic order of capital itself. No longer mere aesthetic break or epistemological shift, postmodernity becomes the cultural signal of a new stage in the history of the regnant mode of production."[33] Defining postmodernism essentially as a symptom of its economic conditions nonetheless brings with it significant problems over which critics have fought ever since. Not only does Jameson's theory have trouble accounting for the timeline of the historical causality that it implies,[34] but it also raises questions about how some elements of culture can reflect on that culture productively. The ambiguities of this sort of symptomatic reading of postmodern artifacts have been critiqued by Brian McHale. Examining the claims made about postmodernism by Linda Hutcheon and Fredric Jameson, McHale notes that both treat some works as merely symptomatic while associating others with commentary or resistance. In particular, McHale asks of Jameson, "If postmodernist texts are, like all cultural products in all periods, from a dialectical perspective both complicit with the dominant culture and critical or resistant to it, then what are the grounds for making the complicit moments stand synecdochically for the text *as a whole* in one case ... while choosing to have the critical moments do so in another case?"[35]

31. Charles Newman, *The Post-Modern Aura: The Act of Fiction in an Age of Inflation* (Evanston, IL: Northwestern University Press, 1985), 5.
32. Jean-François Lyotard, *The Postmodern Condition: A Report on Knowledge,* trans. Geoff Bennington and Brian Massumi (Minneapolis: University of Minnesota Press, 1984).
33. Perry Anderson, *The Origins of Postmodernity* (London: Verso, 1998), 54–55.
34. Anderson notes, for example, "If postmodernism was the cultural logic of late capitalism, should they not coincide fairly closely in time? Yet Mandel's *Late Capitalism,* on which Jameson based his conception of a new stage in capitalist development, dated its general arrival from 1945—while Jameson put the emergence of the postmodern in the early seventies" (78–79).
35. Brian McHale, "Postmodernism, or the Anxiety of Master Narratives," *Diacritics* 22, no. 1 (1992): 28. McHale goes on to note that this is especially a problem in Jameson's dismis-

This problem of exemplarity is implied when we describe postmodernist texts as symptoms of cultural or economic changes. Lyotard, to some extent, avoids these problems by staying at a fairly high level of abstraction—writing about the "postmodern condition" in general without addressing particular contemporary artifacts whose awareness of this condition would need to be defined. This seems likewise to account for the relative success of Linda Hutcheon's considerably less sophisticated explanation of postmodernist works as "using and abusing" their conditions of representation. By according such works a degree of agency, Hutcheon provides critics with a more satisfying account of contemporary cultural production—even if the implications of this "use" are not fully developed. John Duvall describes the contrast between these two critics this way: "Hutcheon's postmodernism, which focuses on the intentions of artists to comment critically on their contemporary moment through their interventions in aesthetics and poetics, is more clearly linked than Jameson's to what he himself means by modernism; in other words, Hutcheon's postmodernism, like Jameson's modernism, represents the arts' response to the material conditions created by modernization."[36] Like so many of the debates about postmodernism, this argument about the relationship between a text and its culture reflects a larger theoretical debate. Giles Gunn notes that this issue of how a text reflects its cultural moment is at the heart of debates about historicism in contemporary literary theory. In *Thinking Across the American Grain,* Gunn contrasts the old and new historicism: "The new historicism can be differentiated from the old by virtue of the way it construes the text as the site of a particular kind of production rather than a specific kind of reflection. The 'old historicism' was—and is—defined most simply, and not inaccurately, in the well-known words from the preface to Edmund Wilson's *Axel's Castle,* as the attempt to provide 'a history of man's ideas and imaginings in the setting of the conditions which shaped them.'"[37] As this passage makes clear, old historicism need not define all texts and individuals as passive dupes of a cultural moment, nor treat every action as a mere symptom of its time. For Gunn, the

---

sive discussion of cyberpunk: "Jameson seems to imply that cyberpunk is somehow the direct expression of late capitalism itself, as though it were unmediated by inherited literary forms or historical genres" (30). While McHale's critique is no doubt right about the incoherence within Jameson's own theory, I would suggest that cyberpunk is a bit of a trap for Jameson precisely because it has been constructed by critics through its symptomatic style.

36. John N. Duvall, "Troping History: Modernist Residue in Jameson's Pastiche and Hutcheon's Parody," in *Productive Postmodernism: Consuming Histories and Cultural Studies,* ed. John N. Duvall (Albany: State University of New York Press, 2002), 2.

37. Giles Gunn, *Thinking Across the American Grain: Ideology, Intellect, and the New Pragmatism* (Chicago: University of Chicago Press, 1992), 163.

old historicism tells a moral story of artists struggling to resist their shaping conditions.

Although we may be tempted to see Jameson's use of "conditions" and "symptoms" as a weakness for his theory, what seems most interesting about the now-tired debate between the virtues of Jameson's and Hutcheon's definitions of postmodernism is the degree to which Jameson's symptomatic reading reflects the way that writers themselves often talk about their work. In this way, Donald Barthelme's comment in a short story, "Fragments are the only forms I trust," was used for years by critics as a way to gloss his disjointed writing style.[38] The manifestoes turned out by writers since World War II frequently reflect this passive language of symptoms. When Raymond Federman describes the future of fiction as a time when "all distinctions between the real an the imaginary, between the conscious and the subconscious, between the past and the present, between truth and untruth will be abolished" it is in part symptomatic of the culture: "real fiction happens, everyday, in the streets of our cities, in the spectacular hijacking of planes, on the Moon, in Vietnam, in China (when Nixon stands on the Great Wall of China), and of course on television (during the news broadcasts)."[39] The sort of symptomatic generalization that is kept at some distance in Federman's theory is embraced much more directly and unproblematically by writers who seek to mediate between popular audiences and literary culture. In his 1975 anthology, John David Bellamy offers an account of American fiction that unreservedly accepts a symptomatic explanation: "But perhaps the most revealing explanation for the recent obsession with forms and visions can be located in the vagaries and intense dislocations of contemporary American experience. As early as 1961 that erstwhile American realist Philip Roth began saying that the toughest problem for the American writer was that the substance of the American experience itself was so abnormally and fantastically strange."[40] In the first chapter I spent some time discussing the reception of John Barth's "Literature of Exhaustion" essay and his insistence that

---

38. Donald Barthelme, "See the Moon?" *Unspeakable Practices, Unnatural Acts* (New York: Farrar, Straus and Giroux, 1968), 169. See Barthelme's witty "retraction" of this aesthetic claim in an interview with Jerome Klinkowitz, which he describes as a misunderstanding of the story by critics eager to find a simple symptomatic justification for his way of writing (Joe David Bellamy, *The New Fiction: Interviews with Innovative American Writers* [Urbana: University of Illinois Press, 1974], 53–54).

39. Raymond Federman, "Surfiction—Four Propositions in Form of an Introduction," *Surfiction: Fiction Now . . . and Tomorrow,* ed. Raymond Federman (Chicago: Swallow, 1975), 8, 6.

40. Joe David Bellamy, "Introduction," in *Superfiction, or The American Story Transformed: An Anthology,* ed. Joe David Bellamy (New York: Vintage, 1975), 4.

it had been misread as a statement of despair. One way to account for this misunderstanding is to suggest that critics came to Barth's essay expecting a symptomatic explanation—postmodernism reflects an exhausted American literary culture—and ignored Barth's insistence that such writing "confronts an intellectual dead end and employs it against itself to accomplish new human work."[41] We can say, then, that the reception of Barth's essay is an example of conflicting definitions of fictionality circulating within American literary culture today.

The language of symptoms reflects not only theoretical issues but also the struggle between various disciplines with a claim to account for writing and culture. The outright embrace of symptomatic explanations of postmodern style often falls to what Andrew Ross calls "Pop intellectuals": "In the mind's eye of the media, the Pop intellectual with new groovy ideas was required to be somewhat hokey, not entirely legitimate, at least not in the mold of the 'eccentric but responsible academic' media type."[42] Good examples of such popular intellectual discourse is Andy Warhol's explanation of contemporary culture discussed in the second chapter, or Robert Venturi et al.'s calls for a postmodern architecture.[43] The language of symptoms seems to appear most frequently when critics, artists, and writers are explaining contemporary texts without recourse to particular disciplinary procedures. Such manifestos reject the traditional discipline of literature or architecture, and so are left without any formal framework for defining their aesthetics. We can say, then,

---

41. John Barth, *The Friday Book: Essays and Other Nonfiction* (Baltimore: Johns Hopkins University Press, 1984), 69–70.

42. Andrew Ross, *No Respect: Intellectuals & Popular Culture* (New York: Routledge, 1989), 114.

43. Venturi et al.'s famous call to embrace popular models like the Las Vegas strip and the motel and move away from sculptural architecture associated with modernism rests on a broad theory of the changing nature of contemporary life: "Learning from the existing landscape is a way of being revolutionary for an architect. Not the obvious way, which is to tear down Paris and begin again, as Le Corbusier suggested in the 1920s, but another, more tolerant way; that is, to question how we look at things" (Robert Venturi, Denise Scott Brown, Steven Izenour, *Learning from Las Vegas*, rev. ed [Cambridge, MA: MIT Press, 1977], 3). In particular, Venturi calls architects to embrace popular modes of construction as an expression of the change in conditions of contemporary life. Noting the distance between a Vegas casino and the road ("near enough to the highway to be seen from the road across the parked cars, yet far enough back to accommodate driveways" [34]), Venturi et al. reach a simple conclusion: "The scales of movement and space of the highway relate to the distances between buildings; because they are far apart, they can comprehended at high speeds" (34–35). The authors' theory is engaged in the history of architecture, but the portions that are most easily digested by a general audience are those that treat contemporary architecture as a symptom of cultural changes. Precisely because this theory has been used as a starting point for discussion not only by architects but also by critics and readers from a variety of fields, it usefully marks the transition to a popular intellectual debate.

that in work by popular spokespersons for and against postmodernism that art and literary works are taken to be symptoms of larger patterns within the society.

When applied to literature, the reading of texts and styles as symptomatic seems especially to mark a dissolution of belief that a particular set of disciplinary techniques is necessary to understand and evaluate a text, and to position this definition of fiction on the tipping point between literary institutions and popular culture. A case in point is Michael Berubé's critique of the popular representation of canon debates during the early 1990s. Berubé is strongest in his condemnation of *The Atlantic*'s decision to publish Dinesh D'Souza's "Illiberal Education." "D'Souza's attack on the academy," Berubé claims, "relies on ignorance—his own, and ours."[44] As an example of this ignorance, Berubé cites D'Souza's breezy characterization that deconstruction is "hostile to all texts" and refuses to deconstruct works by women, minorities, and other deconstructionists. Berubé concludes:

> If someone were to publish an essay which claimed that *Paradise Lost* never really talks about theology, or that psychoanalysis fails to make use of the works of major Greek dramatists, certainly we would recognize such a person as a cultural illiterate. But because no one at *The Atlantic,* including even the journal's fact-checkers, is aware of the past twenty-five years' profusion of deconstruction work on Marx [and others] ... D'Souza is allowed to get away with this series of inanities. ...
>
> That *The Atlantic* would have published D'Souza, and at such length, is an important sign of the extent to which public discussion of American academia is now conducted by the most callow and opportunistic elements of the Right; it's also, sad to say, an important sign of how low are our minimum standards for serious public exchange on the status of American criticism. (141–42)

Regardless of whether his critique of D'Souza is entirely just, Berubé is right, I think, to argue that general culture has lost confidence in the discipline of literature itself and that the canon debates reflect in large part a simplification of theoretical issues by those looking at it from the outside. In this sense, the increasing popularity of book clubs is also a part of this recent trend to deprofessionalize the study of literary works. While any discipline can be restrictive, it seems that an attempt to define an adisciplinary fiction-

---

44. Michael Berubé, "Public Image Limited: Political Correctness and the Media's Big Lie," in *Debating P.C.: The Controversy over Political Correctness on College Campuses,* ed. Paul Berman (New York: Laurel, 1992), 141.

ality likewise leads to problems and restrictions. The equation of texts and symptoms reflects this urge towards a reading of literature that is located within the popular arena and independent of particular disciplinary and institutional rules.

Why Is Science Fiction Symptomatic?

We can say, then, that science fiction emerges onto the scene of American writing at just the moment when the relationship between texts and their culture is at its most theoretically uncertain. When I say that science fiction *emerges* at this moment, I mean simply that in the mid-1970s science fiction begins to achieve some degree of critical respectability that it did not previously have. At the same time, science fiction increasingly appears in popular culture as a vehicle for serious aesthetic interest. As I conclude this chapter, I would like to consider why science fiction of all the varieties of contemporary writing has been chosen to carry the banner of cultural symptoms.

McHale has argued convincingly that cyberpunk writing reflects a dual motion within contemporary fiction: the evolution of contemporary "literature" toward using more of the themes and topoi of science fiction, and the incorporation within this particular strain of science fiction of traditionally postmodern stylistic devices. "Cyberpunk SF," McHale concludes, "can thus be seen . . . as *SF which derives certain of its elements from postmodernist mainstream fiction which itself has, in its turn, already been 'science-fictionalized' to some greater or lesser extent.*"[45] McHale's formulation of science fiction implies a mutual evolution within these two facets of contemporary writing, the primary difference between them gradually fading. Nonetheless, it seems to me that part of the fascination with cyberpunk reflects its particular involvement in science fiction themes. What excites critics about cyberpunk is not only its themes and style but also the fact that it seems to be predictive. This is the logic behind Gibson's prominent place in the predictive collection *Fiction 2000*.

If we consider the uses to which cyberpunk writing, and Gibson's novels in particular, are put, it becomes clear that it is precisely science fiction's traditional role of predicting the future that is essential to its appeal as a critical object. In the cultural studies interest in the cyborg and the posthuman, cyberpunk writers in general, and Gibson in particular, figure largely as occasions to think about technology, society, and subjectivity. Consider,

---

45. Brian McHale, *Constructing Postmodernism* (New York: Routledge, 1992), 229.

for example, the texts cited by Donna Haraway in her well-known "Cyborg Manifesto" (1985): Anne McCaffery's *The Ship Who Sang,* Russ's *The Female Man,* and Delany's *Tales of Nevèrÿon.* Haraway bypasses other texts for the sake of science fiction in part because she is interested in science fiction as an oppositional literature outside of the mainstream: "Students facing Joanna Russ for the first time, students who have learned to take modernist writers like James Joyce or Virginia Woolf without flinching, do not know what to make of *The Adventures of Alyx* or *The Female Man,* where characters refuse the reader's search for innocent wholeness while granting the wish for heroic quests, exuberant eroticism, and serious politics."[46] Whether or not Haraway is right about the difference between modernist and science fiction writing, it is clear that science fiction functions as an example for Haraway because it seems to her more engaged in projecting a political and social future. The same pattern is true in other collections of essays that focus on the future of humanity, like *Posthuman Bodies* (1995) or *The Cyborg Handbook* (1995), where (with a few exceptions) the examples are routinely drawn from science fiction writing.[47] Attending to the issue of the cyborg body, these critics imply, involves an interest in the future of identity and corporeality that science fiction texts are best positioned to address.

Why, we might ask, are science fiction texts the site where these debates are handled? Why not, for example, *Gravity's Rainbow,* which certainly works through a certain kind of cyborg existence? Joseph Tabbi notes precisely this shift in the literary sites where these issues are considered: "If Gibson carried the aesthetic of Pynchon's *Gravity's Rainbow* (and much else from alternative cultures of the seventies and eighties) into the science fiction genre, the motifs in *Neuromancer* now circulate primarily through *The Matrix.*"[48] The answer, it seems to me, is fairly straightforward and speaks to the continuing function of the disciplinary definition of science fiction: novels like *Neuromancer* and Piercy's *He, She and It* are taken to be a form of thought experiment, if not an outright prediction of the future, because they are read first and foremost as science fiction narratives. Because of this, they are understood to raise questions about the literal structure of the future and the ramifications of technology, rather than being parsed for less direct,

---

46. Donna J. Haraway, *Simians, Cyborgs, and Women: The Reinvention of Nature* (New York: Routledge, 1991), 178.

47. Judith Halberstam and Ira Livingston, eds., *Posthuman Bodies* (Bloomington: Indiana University Press, 1995); Chris Hables Gray, ed., *The Cyborg Handbook* (New York: Routledge, 1995).

48. Joseph Tabbi, *Cognitive Fictions* (Minneapolis: University of Minnesota Press, 2002), xv.

thematic engagements with technology like Pynchon's novel. This is of course ironic, since we have seen that at the same time critics justify the importance of contemporary science fiction in terms of its style more than its substance. In this strange formulation, science fiction is important because it promises to predict the future but understanding it as a symptom defines its fictionality without reference to the future. Given the anxieties that I noted at the outset in our notions of the future, this hybrid, compromise definition may be its primary appeal. In this sense, cyberpunk's symptomatic style is a way of negotiating science fiction's predictive function without appealing to the future. Indeed the very nature of the symptom—as an entanglement with the past that predicts the future by causing continuing effects—nicely embodies the contradictions that surround a postmodern future.

Based on my discussion in the previous section, it seems clear that science fiction is the form of contemporary fiction best able to symptomatize contemporary culture precisely because it is thought of as already outside of the norms of literary study. Although many critics praise science fiction for its resistance to institutional norms—as opening up the claustrophobic space of traditional canons and genres[49]—to take science fiction as the model for contemporary fiction in general means to undermine literary institutions and methodologies broadly. This is why, it seems to me, that popular audiences would turn not to general "fiction" less marked by genre categories (like *Gravity's Rainbow*) but instead to a film like *The Matrix* to think about the impact of technology on our lives. *The Matrix* is accessible as a symptom of larger culture in a way that Pynchon's novel is not; as an example of science fiction, it is free from the baggage of institutional expectations that accrue to books labeled "literary." Because it is marked as *popular* rather than *literary*, such fiction is available to ways of reading outside of traditional disciplinary norms. It should also be clear that in the process science fiction is being positioned as an alternative to both the mythical, archival, and lying fictions that I discussed in the first three chapters. While the novels and stories discussed in those chapters were defined through their relation to literary discourse, science fiction is positioned as marginal to this discourse, and thus demanding a form of reading that reflects less disciplinary attention. It is for this reason that this definition of fictionality is a step away from literary institutions and towards alternative contexts and audiences for reception and interpretation.

Science fiction is defined as important for its style, then, and readers

---

49. Joanna Russ defines science fiction as "outsider" art in *To Write Like a Woman: Essays in Feminism and Science Fiction* (Bloomington: Indiana University Press, 1995), 90.

are encouraged to treat it as a symptom requiring no specialized disciplinary training to appreciate. This is how I would interpret the wild popularity of Donna Haraway's essay on the cyborg, an essay and critical concept that clearly struck a cord with readers. In defining the cyborg as an "ironic political myth,"[50] I would argue, Haraway subtly draws on the tradition of associating science fiction and style. Haraway states that these myths are a kind of intellectual tool: "The tools are often stories, retold stories, versions that reverse and displace the hierarchical dualisms of naturalized identities. In retelling origin stories, cyborg authors subvert the central myths of origin of Western culture" (175). Not only do cyborgs provide alternative tool-stories, but they embody storytelling in some more fundamental sense: "Writing is pre-eminently the technology of cyborgs" (176). If the cyborg is a tool for thinking differently, then the myths that Haraway is interested in are less about a set of beliefs—hence the cyborg is ironic—and more about a way of behaving intellectually. In other words, Haraway's cyborg is more a matter of a style of thought than a particular belief or conclusion. That style should form the basis of the cyborg should not be a surprise. We have seen over and over that science fiction—and especially the appeal to style in science fiction—embodies the attempt to think about the relevance of stories to the present after their traditional disciplinary function has been problematized.

Haraway also makes clear—in case it hasn't been clear all along—that the struggle with science fiction's vocation and the attraction to texts as cultural symptoms is ultimately an attempt to define a particular justification for fictionality today. Haraway is quite explicit in associating the cyborg with a shift in our traditional thinking about the line between the real and the imaginative: "A cyborg is a cybernetic organism, a hybrid of machine and organism, a creature of social reality as well as a creature of fiction. Social reality is lived social relations, our most important political construction, a world-changing fiction" (149). As a "condensed image of both imagination and material reality" (150), the cyborg blurs the line between the real and the imagined. Doing so is essential to Haraway's claim that such myths offer intellectual tools. In defining the invented as an expression of a certain style that embodies the cultural moment, Haraway, like other critics and writers concerned with science fiction today, responds to changes in the status of the discipline of literature and offers a new justification for fictionality.

---

50. Haraway, "Cyborg Manifesto," in *Simians, Cyborgs, and Women*, 149.

CHAPTER 5

Role-Playing Games, Possible World Theory, and the Fictionality of Assemblage

Role-playing games developed in the last thirty years primarily in the United States and Britain. In such games, a group of players (at least three but as much as dozen) take on the roles of fictional characters in some alternate universe. They generate basic statistics that represent the acquired skills and physical attributes of these characters. One of these players will serve as the referee and design this universe, creating settings to explore and opponents to confront. Players will usually join these characters into a single group to overcome these conflicts, occasionally using dice to decide the outcome of events—whether a character wins or loses a fight, succeeds or fails at a difficult physical task, and so on. In the end, characters who negotiate these challenges successfully usually receive rewards of some sort—valuable objects, increased abilities, or information that unravels mysteries. Players carry over their characters from one playing session to the next, and the next situation they encounter may continue the action of earlier sessions, or may introduce entirely new events and opponents. Although many players enjoy the game for the challenge of "winning" and developing powerful characters, others see in the game an extended form of acting performance in which they develop characters whose actions are psychologically realistic.

Even from this brief summary, it is clear that role-playing games are fundamentally narrative in nature and that they depend on a very particular understanding of fictionality. Role-playing games are played within a storytelling environment, whose dynamics are primarily narratological: players construct characters, anticipate events and the plot lines they imply, and respond to settings for exploration and adventure. Players as well as referees work to imagine possible actions and to construct storylines. What strikes me as especially interesting is that role-playing games go further than the works of the previous chapter in locating fictionality beyond literary institutions. Indeed, role-playing games are at the extreme of the spectrum opposite of John Barth's myth, since they make virtually no reference to literary institutions for their reception and do not appeal to traditional literary values to justify their fictionality.

In this chapter, I am particularly interested in how role-playing games construct narrative worlds as a way to understand their particular definition of fictionality. We find that these games—and I will focus primarily on the original *Dungeons and Dragons* game itself and its first-generation revisions—define the game world as a collection of objects that allow players to mix characters and situations drawn from a variety of science fiction and fantasy novels. What seems especially important is that these games have a very different relationship to the literary institutions that I have been discussing thus far in this project. Even in the previous chapter, where science fiction writing occupies a somewhat marginal position in relation to mainstream literary study, we still saw an appeal to this writing framed as a form of (culturally significant) literature. Indeed, my whole focus in that chapter was on the way that science fiction emerged as a form of writing interesting to academic critics. In contrast, role-playing games define themselves by appealing to popular genres and by adopting a relationship to these texts that can seem scandalously irreverent. In this chapter, I would like to explain this understanding of fictionality as a response to contemporary market culture. I will go further and apply these conclusions to possible world theory used to describe fictional worlds in literature. Role-playing games and this particular way of understanding fictional worlds have remarkably similar genealogies. Both come to prominence in the early 1970s and reach their full articulation by the end of that decade by transforming models developed in the previous century. Both, I will argue, can be seen as a response to questions about what we can and should do with fictional texts. In this sense, the birth of role-playing games reflects the development of another form of fictionality—one based not on myth, archive, lying or style, but on assembling a world from diverse textual sources.

A World Made of Objects

Role-playing games evolved out of battle simulations that use miniature figures to represent groups of soldiers moved around some kind of playing board battlefield. Role-playing games depart from battle simulations primarily in terms of scale. Where earlier simulations used miniature soldiers or artillery pieces to represent whole army battalions, role-playing games focus on the actions of individual characters.[1] The transitional text in this regard is the 1971 rulebook *Chainmail*, which was the basis for *Dungeons and Dragons* and role-playing games that followed. The majority of the *Chainmail* booklet concerns the large-scale movement and combat of medieval armies, with play built around the strategies for organizing groups of soldiers. Rules are given, for example, to describe the rate of movement of different types of soldiers across different kinds of terrain, the various formations these soldiers can adopt, the number of rows of archers and cannons permitted to fire without danger of hitting soldiers in front of them, and so on. Individual figures moved around a scale battlefield are taken to represent a group of soldiers of the same type. Subsequent editions of the *Chainmail* rules, however, complicate this model. After discussing group combat, *Chainmail* introduces another set of rules for man-to-man combat: "Instead of using one figure to represent numerous men, a single figure represents a single man."[2] A few pages later a third set of rule variations is offered as a "fantasy supplement," applying these combat rules to fantastic creatures (dragons, ogres, elves) and abnormally powerful heroes.

This shift in the *Chainmail* rule booklet from armies to individuals shows that the tactics handled in one way at the level of a large-scale battle must be transformed as the scale is lowered and focus is placed on individual combatants in role-playing games. In the original *Chainmail* rules, military units are generic: every group of archers, for example, is the same. As long as they are still alive on the battlefield and have not lost their morale and fled, they

---

1. This is obviously an abbreviated history. One treatment that is frequently used by critics writing about role-playing games is Lawrence Schick's *Heroic Worlds: A History and Guide to Role-Playing Games* (Buffalo: Prometheus Books, 1991), which provides a good, short overview of this history and evolution of these games.

2. Gary Gygax and Jeff Perren, *Chainmail: Rules for Medieval Miniatures*, 3d ed. (Lake Geneva, WI: TSR Rules, 1975), 25.

behave like any other archery unit. Likewise, combat has only a few possible outcomes: units live or die, kill or miss. Such a blunt combat method is possible when a large number of troops are being used by players; when, however, the scale is reduced and players control a single combatant, having an encounter decided immediately and so finally removes nearly all tactics from the game. As a result, the fundamental innovation of the successor to *Chainmail*, *Dungeons and Dragons*, is the concept of the "hit-point"—a certain number of injuries that a particular player can sustain before dying. Thus, combat tactics are retained at the level of the individual character, since now players can decide when to engage or withdraw from combat based on how many injuries their characters and their opponents have sustained. Thus, the role of chance in the game has been narrowly circumscribed. The concept of the hit-point has become so ubiquitous within contemporary game design for allowing a certain kind of tactical manipulation that it is the basis even of trading-card games like *Pokémon*—games with no direct basis in large troop tactics and little connection to role-playing games.

The development of role-playing games, then, depends on finding a way to endow individual characters with statistical qualities that allow tactical manipulation. For the purposes of my interest in role-playing games, this is the essential quality of these games.[3] As I noted at the outset, the statistics that individual role-playing games use to define characters vary from game to game but usually represent a combination of acquired skills, possessions, and physical and mental attributes. The original *Dungeons and Dragons* rules, for example, take into account the type of weapons and armor worn by a character, his or her level of training, as well as physical strength and dexterity. Subsequent games usually introduce some variations on these terms but rarely depart from them wholesale. These games rarely count as tactically significant many of the qualities that we think of as most significant in the real world: race, class, and gender.[4] Indeed, many games encourage players

---

3. This is, of course, not the only element of role-playing games that might be of interest to narratologists, nor the only way that we might frame the emergence of these games within contemporary culture. Daniel Mackay in *The Fantasy Role-Playing Game: A New Performing Art* (Jefferson, NC: McFarland, 2001) and Kurt Lancaster in *Warlocks and Warpdrive: Contemporary Fantasy Entertainments with Interactive and Virtual Environments* (Jefferson, NC: McFarland, 1999), for example, focus on the nature of performance during the role-playing game session. Mackay in particular develops a phenomenological theory of the difference spheres for player performances (60), and the way these are defined culturally, formally, socially, and aesthetically.

4. Race does have a place within these early games, but this is race conceived in this fantastic landscape by such broad categories as human, dwarf, or elf. Such a definition treats race more as a synonym for species rather than as a matter of the subtle physical and cultural differences that we associate with race. Later versions of *Dungeons and Dragons* do introduce

to make up their own social background as a way of getting into character without necessarily recording this information as one of the central game statistics.⁵ Although some later games like the Anne Rice–based *Vampire: The Masquerade* take class and social structures more seriously, *Dungeons and Dragons* uses as its starting point an essentially middle-class model for subjectivity and ability.⁶ In this latter game, characters succeed or fail based on inherent qualities, learned skills, and personal choices. When the conditions of success are defined in this way, whatever explicit social structure may exist within the world is largely a veneer superimposed on individual bodies endowed with certain abilities and potentials that determine their true power in the game.

This brief description should suggest that these games define the world as a structure not of events but of objects.⁷ Once players have defined the objects in the world and assigned them statistical qualities, what particular players might choose to do with those objects is quite open-ended. The lock

---

subcategories of these groups (different types of humans, dwarves, and so on) that better reflect the way that we use the term *race*. In fact, the recent *Player's Guide to Faerûn* by Richard Baker, Travis Stout, and James Wyatt (Renton, WA: Wizards of the Coast, 2004) lists seven different human ethnic groups and provides detailed charts explaining language and religions (11–16).

5. In the *Dungeon Master's Guide* (Lake Geneva, WI: TSR Games, 1979), Gary Gygax introduces a discussion of social class as follows: "There is no random table for determination of a character's social status to be found here. That is because the inclusion of such a factor will either tell you little or nothing of useful nature, or it will abridge your freedom with respect to development of your campaign milieu" (88).

6. Mark Rein-Hagen, *Vampire: The Masquerade: A Storytelling Game of Personal Horror* (Clarkson, CA: White Wolf, 1992). Gygax describes "adventuring" in essentially economic terms of risk and suggests that such risks are most appropriate for middle-class characters: "adventurers would come from the younger children of aristocrats—those who will inherit little and wish to remain in the favored class. Some would come from the middle group—adventurous persons who aim at becoming members of the aristocracy through successes in such adventures. Few, if any, would come from the lowest class, i.e. the bondsmen and common laborers" (*Dungeon Masters Guide*, 88).

7. Indeed, even when these games describe history, it is as a collection of objects. Originally the "treasure" won upon successful completion of a *Dungeons and Dragons* mission was fairly generic, for example: gold, gems, magical potions of several standard types, magical swords that increased the player's chances in battle, and so on. Over the course of the expansions to the game in 1976, and then in the first mainstream rulebooks in 1977 through 1979, descriptions of treasures in the game increasingly focused on artifacts with very distinctive histories. While most of the description of treasures continues to be concerned with finding more mundane objects of value, the attention given in these rulebooks to particular artifacts increases. One item, the "Jacinth of Inestimable Beauty," for example, comes attached with a legend drawn from the history of one campaign world: "Legend relates that the *Jacinth* was possessed by the fabled Sultan Jehef Peh'reen for a time and then passed into the Land of Ket and southward into Keoland (see *The World of Greyhawk*), where all trace disappeared" (Gygax, *Dungeon Masters Guide*, 158). In no other part of these rulebooks are such histories so important.

on a box might be opened with a key or picked by a skillful thief, but players could also propose prying it open with a tool or carrying it to the top of a wall and dropping it. Some of these activities are covered by standard tables that define chances of success, but even when actions that fall outside of the rules are proposed by players (dropping the box from a height), the result can be interpolated based on other rules. A box, for example, can be assigned hit-points and the damage caused by being dropped from a height might be calculated using combat tables for blunt weapons. It is because players might propose actions that have no precise definition in the rules that all role-playing games have some type of referee who controls no particular character but who constructs the spaces explored, controls the players' opponents, and determines the outcomes of all actions. Precisely the opposite is the case in more traditional board games, where players do not have the option of inventing, for example, a new kind of move in the middle of a game of chess. These games are defined not only by the objects on the board (the pawn, the rook) but also by a very strictly limited range of actions and events.

The contrast between game worlds based on objects and those based on events is nicely exemplified by the game described in Robert Coover's novel *The Universal Baseball Association*. This novel tells the story of Henry Waugh, a man who becomes so obsessed with a kind of baseball simulation game he has invented that he gradually loses contact with all of his social relationships outside of the game. Although Coover's game may at first seem similar to role-playing games because it relies heavily on statistics and complex charts, these statistics describe not objects but events. Coover explains, for example, what happens when dice-rolls call for the Extraordinary Occurrences chart to be consulted: "Two successive throws of triple ones and sixes were exceedingly rare . . . but when it happened, the next throw was referred, finally, to the Chart of Extraordinary Occurrences, where just about anything from fistfights to fixed ball games could happen."[8] The characters of Waugh's game have relatively few individual statistical qualities (they are defined simply as a Rookie, Star, or Regular). Henry, however, comes to identify them as personalities, as he builds elaborate narratives around these random statistical events: "Henry was always careful about names, for they were what gave the league its sense of fulfillment and failure, its emotion. The dice and charts and other paraphernalia were only the mechanics of the drama, not the drama itself. Names had to be chosen, therefore, that could bear the whole weight of perpetuity" (46–47).

8. Robert Coover, *The Universal Baseball Association, Inc.: J. Henry Waugh, Prop.* (New York: Plume, 1971), 20.

What is especially noteworthy about the contrast between role-playing games and the baseball game described by Coover is that they locate agency in very different ways. In both role-playing games and the baseball game Coover describes, we recognize characters acting within an overall narrative. But while the players of role-playing games control these actions and try to manipulate the statistics to produce a desirable narrative end (power, success, discovery), Coover's Waugh is active only in how he records the events. Although Waugh must make certain tactical decisions, throughout the game he quite literally plays both sides of the fence—making decisions for both teams in a particular game that are fair and obey common game management practice. Waugh strives to keep his own desires and agency out of the actual play of the game, allowing the random generation of events to determine the outcome. Indeed, when he invites a friend to play the game with him, he is irritated to find him making illogical or unconventional choices (189); it is clear that Henry's game decisions strive to replicate standard ways of playing. In this novel, narrative worlds are organized around events that proceed by their own logic, but at the expense of creative agency in shaping their direction. For all that he seems to be playing a game, in fact, Waugh's relationship to his baseball league is much closer to that of the reader of a traditional narrative: he observes events and responds to them, participating only to the extent that he gives particular events meaning. In contrast, it is clear that one of the goals of role-playing games is not merely—as is often claimed by proponents—to participate in an ongoing narrative, since this is what Waugh does.[9] Instead, role-playing games give players something to do and make them responsible for the outcome of the adventures that they undertake.

I have focused primarily on the implications of the move from large-scale troop-based to individual combat. The other innovation that we can see occurring in the original *Chainmail* rules—the introduction of fantasy elements—may initially not seem relevant to the issue of player agency. However, without the fantasy elements, these rules would essentially function as a way of recreating an antiquated style of combat, with emphasis probably placed on greater and greater accuracy in the details of moving,

9. Game designers routinely suggest that role-playing games are a way of helping to create shared narratives that we would otherwise consume passively in novels or films. In *Rifts Game Master Guide* (Taylor, MI: Palladium Books, 2001), Kevin Siembieda remarks in his preface to a recent role-playing game manual: "We role-playing gamers use our power of imagination to create and tell stories. Stories each and every player in the group helps to mold through his or her character's actions and interaction with others in the gaming group. Together, we create a *shared experience* visualized in our heads. Together we shape an epic story of adventure and heroism" (9).

using, and maintaining various military units. Such historical simulations do have a small but loyal following as part of the gaming community but are not usually considered role-playing games.[10] What strikes me as important is not merely that extraordinary things happen in role-playing games, but that the nature of these extraordinary things seems to line up directly with precedents laid down by a variety of popular and literary subgenres. Daniel Mackay notes that after the appearance of *Dungeons and Dragons*, "Many new role-playing games reflected the literary influences of the designers": "The trend was to create role-playing games based on works of literature. The worlds of Jules Verne, J. R. R. Tolkien, or Michael Moorcock ceased to function as a generic fantasy model and became the very thing that the role-playing game intended to simulate. This trend also applies to the comic-book influence in role-playing."[11] The emphasis is not on the fantastic in general but on fantastic elements whose origin is clearly in a certain kind of speculative or fantasy literature.

If one considers the various types of role-playing games, one is immediately struck that they are directly connected to various subgenres of contemporary popular writing. Lawrence Schick's catalogue of role-playing games compiled in 1991 reads like a list of subgenres within popular literature; he groups them into categories like superhero, espionage, fantasy, horror, humor, mystery, science fiction, westerns, swashbucklers, and pulp adventure stories. Mackay goes further and suggests that role-playing games have a reciprocal relationship with fantasy literature, and that the industry as a whole has evolved towards cross-marketing: the "strategy of using novels to stimulate interest in role-playing successfully brought new role-playing gamers into the fold. Readers were drawn to the game to discover what they were missing. In turn, the publication of novels based on role-playing games influenced the literary genre itself as new authors used the game as inspiration for their own tales" (20). Good examples of this reciprocal relationship are the very popular "Forgotten Realms" novels produced by TSR, the publisher of *Dungeons and Dragons*. Such novels not only obey the general milieu of the game but also describe a particular world whose maps and histories players can purchase to use in their own *Dungeons and Dragons* game. Characters

---

10. Greg Costikyan notes the different audiences for role-playing games and historical war games in his history of the game company SPI. Noting the narrow but loyal audience for war games, he points out that "[i]n 1982, the 30,000 subscribers of Strategy & Tactics, SPI's flagship magazine, were the most avid wargame enthusiasts on the globe. More than 50% of them, per SPI's own feedback, owned 100 or more wargames; most of them bought a dozen or more games very year, not counting the games they received as subscribers to the magazine" ("A Farewell to Hexes," http://www.costik.com/spisins.html).

11. Mackay, *The Fantasy Role-Playing Game*, 16, 17.

and situations described in these novels then appear, in full statistical detail, in game information about the "Forgotten Realms" setting.[12]

Role-playing games, then, are fundamentally a way for players to engage in favorite books and popular subgenres, to make beloved texts into a place where one can play. Although many recent role-playing games are fairly strict about defining their world through close attention to the texts that inspire them—*The Lord of the Rings, Star Wars,* Lovecraft's horror fiction—what is remarkable about the original *Dungeons and Dragons* is how catholic its sources are.[13] To read through the original 1974 rules for this game is to be struck by how much these rules are a system for intertextual connections. Probably the simplest example of this intertextual quality is the list of creatures that the game offers up as antagonists for play. The original 1974 rulebook draws its creatures from a variety of myths and legends. While some of these creatures are generic enough that they betray no particular textual or mythological origins (giants, ogres, trolls, goblins), others clearly come from particular sources.[14] Mummies and vampires, for example, can be traced back to modern horror films, while creatures like medusae and chimeras are obviously lifted from Greek mythology. When this list of creatures is expanded to create the *Monster Manual* (1978) as part of the launch of the game into mainstream toy- and bookstores, the creatures become even more heterogeneous: from vaguely naturalist creatures like dinosaurs and sharks to others imported from various mythological categories like djinni and leprechauns.[15] The intertextual logic of these borrowings becomes more apparent in the explicit treatment of mythology in the game. The last of the first-generation "supplements" to the game, *Gods, Demi-Gods & Heroes* (1976), describes deities using standard game statistics (the Egyptian god

---

12. Such is the case in particular of the novels describing the adventures of Drizzt Do'Urden written by R. A. Salvatore (see, for example, *The Crystal Shard* [Renton, WA: TSR, 1988]). Salvatore created this character based on the *Dungeons and Dragons* milieu, and TSR has included game statistics about him in subsequent publications like Ed Greenwood et al.'s *Forgotten Realms Campaign Setting* (Renton, WA: Wizards of the Coast, 2001).

13. See Steven S. Long, John Rateliff, Christian Moore, and Matt Forbeck, *The Lord of the Rings: Roleplaying Game: Core Book* (Norfolk, WV: Decipher, 2002); Bill Slavicsek, Andy Collins, and J. D. Wiker, *Star Wars Roleplaying Game: Revised Core Rulebook* (Renton, WV: Wizards of the Coast, 2002); and Sandy Peterson and Lynn Willis, *Call of Cthulhu: Horror Roleplaying in the Worlds of H. P. Lovecraft,* 5th ed. (Oakland: Chaosium, 1995).

14. Gary Gygax and Dave Arneson, *Dungeons and Dragons: Rules for Fantastic Medieval Wargames Campaigns Playable with Paper and Pencil and Miniature Figures,* 3 vols. (Lake Geneva, WI: Tactical Studies Rules, 1974).

15. Gary Gygax, *Advanced Dungeons & Dragons Monster Manual,* 3d ed. (Lake Geneva, WI: TSR Games, 1978).

Set, for example, has 275 hit-points).[16] What is perhaps most remarkable in this strange book is that alongside traditional pantheons of deities (Egyptian, Greek, Norse, Indian, and so on) are descriptions of deities from fantasy worlds like the Robert E. Howard's Conan novels. This book shows how fundamentally the game is rooted in allowing players to bring elements from many different fantasy books together. And what allows these games to make such intertextual connections is the way that the objects that make up these game worlds have been defined statistically. A regularized statistical definition allows objects from a variety of textual worlds to be combined and compared. Having read *Gods, Demi-Gods & Heroes*, for example, players know that while the Egyptian god Ra can move a third faster than the Greek god Apollo, the latter is a slightly better fighter (17th vs. 16th level).

Because it is built on such a messy intertextuality, *Dungeons and Dragons* is the best available model for how these games draw on literary sources. Although games based on a single literary world (such as Anne Rice's vampire novels or H. P. Lovecraft's horror stories) frequently have the reputation within gaming communities of being better games for more serious players, it seems to me that role-playing games inherently involve borrowing from various sources.[17] The very idea of *playing* in such a world means bringing one's experiences to bear and connecting these worlds to other sources of inspiration.[18] Again Mackay is helpful in summarizing the way that such games are performed by players. Mackay describes gameplay sessions as "hypertextual": "The shifting ... from frame to frame in the role-playing game performance is analogous to navigating from link to link in a hypertextual space. Just as the navigation between links in cyberspace presents the possibility of continuing on to new links and never returning, so too in sessions

---

16. Robert Kuntz and James Ward, *Dungeons & Dragons Supplement IV: Gods, Demi-Gods & Heroes* (Lake Geneva, WI: TSR Games, 1976).

17. Complaints about the heterogeneous nature of *Dungeons and Dragons* go back almost to its beginnings. Bruce Galloway complains in his guidebook *Fantasy Wargaming* (New York: Stein and Day, 1981) about the odd mixture of creatures and objects that populate the game world and concludes, "Motive is the key word. D&D scenarios exist in a vacuum, and that is why we call them unsatisfactory. To be satisfying, a fantasy scenario must contain its own intrinsic and consistent logic. There are a variety of ways of achieving this. One ... is to choose a fantasy world which already 'exists,' complete with its own geography, history, opposing deities and races. These can be found within the course of dozens of paperback fantasy novels" (x).

18. So it is that Gygax remarks in 1979 about the problems of setting role-playing games in nonhuman worlds: "Those works which do not feature mankind in a central role are uncommon. Those which do not deal with men at all are scarce indeed. To attempt to utilize any such bases as the central, let alone sole, theme for a campaign milieu is destined to be shallow, incomplete, and totally unsatisfying for all parties concerned unless the creator is a Renaissance Man and all-around universal genius with a decade or two to prepare the game and milieu" (*Dungeon Masters Guide*, 21).

where the setting, story, and characters are not sufficiently engrossing, there is the danger of digressing into out-of-character anecdotes and free association of popular-culture references from which the players never return" (75). Mackay suggests that performance in role-playing games frequently involves borrowing from a variety of cultural sources and texts, even when the game world itself strives to be less hybrid than the original *Dungeons and Dragons*. The statistical construction of objects in role-playing games allows them to carry their worlds with them in order to make intertextual combinations possible.

Although I have focused entirely on role-playing games in this discussion, what I have noted about the way that statistics are used in these games has implications for a wide variety of contemporary narrative practices. Certainly the most obvious relevance is to computer and video games, which are becoming an increasingly important and mainstream form of entertainment. Not only are some of the most important titles in these games directly descended from the statistical systems defined by *Dungeons and Dragons* or indirectly by from the war games that inspired it, but the ways in which activities and narrative are imagined in these games are usually statistical in nature. It is an unremarkable part of any of the ubiquitous first-person shooting games that fill publishers' lists that players will be able to sustain a number of injuries before dying, that different weapons will do different amounts and kinds of damage, and so on.[19] This is quite a contrast to first-generation arcade video games like *Pac-Man* or *Space Invaders*, in which the player was defeated the moment his or her icon was struck by an opponent. A more interesting example of the way in which the worlds and creative practices imagined in role-playing games can influence narrative play in general is in fantasy sports, which has no direct genealogical link to role-playing games. Like role-playing games, fantasy sports are built around collections of objects—in this case, players from various professional teams. In a particular fantasy sport—the most popular in America are baseball and football—players assemble a team made of up of real-life professional athletes. Players determine the success of their assembled teams and win games against other players based on the success that the real-life athletes had with their own teams in real-life games. In his introduction to the rulebook *Rotis-*

---

19. While a relentlessly mundane computer game like *The Sims* seems to be the very antithesis of the fantasy world that I have been describing, precisely the same sorts of statistical definition of characters takes place in that game, since players receive job promotions by increasing a variety of core skills and bodily attributes (mechanical, logic, charisma, etc.), which will remind us a great deal of the *Dungeons and Dragons* core attributes of strength, intelligence, and so on.

serie League Baseball (1984)—the first rule system for fantasy sports—Daniel Okrent emphasizes the way that such fantasy games build on and transform the nature of being a fan by allowing players within this game to act, to become agents rather than passive spectators. He writes, "One could say we merely wanted to raise the ineluctable movements of generations enthralled by baseball to another, higher plateau. Assembling a collection of baseball cards, playing two-man stoopball while doing an eight-year-old's version of play-by-play, proposing trades to hypercritical radio talk-show hosts—what were all these preadolescent endeavors but preparation for the Rotisserie League?"[20] While role-playing games may be the best example of this contemporary shift towards narrative built around statistically constructed objects, the use of the same basic type of narrative object in fantasy sports makes clear that such narratives are a broad contemporary phenomenon.

Invention, Accounting, and Agency

I have argued that role-playing games provide a framework in which players may adopt a more active relation to fictional texts and genres. In the process, I would like to suggest, these games imply a very different way of understanding fictionality. This shift in thinking about agency and fictionality is evident not only in role-playing games and fantasy sports but also in the ways that critics think about narrative texts in fictional world theory.

We can see what is at stake in this discussion of fictionality in statistics-based games by turning to a study of the relationship between statistics and creativity in narrative—Mark Seltzer's study of American naturalist writing, *Bodies and Machines*. Seltzer sees naturalist writing arising out of a cultural crisis about the nature of identity in industrialized society precipitated by the division of labor. Once production divides those who make the machine from those who use it, we can no longer be sure "what exactly it means to produce some thing."[21] According to Seltzer, this "uncertain agency of production" leads to a fascination with imitation and reproduction. If industrial production treats individuals as mere elements in a larger process over which they have no control and which they may not even understand, they can easily wonder whether they are not themselves just as much the product of the economy as the tables and chairs that they are making. Furthermore,

---

20. Daniel Okrent, "The Year George Foster Wasn't Worth $36: An Introduction to Rotisserie League Baseball," in *Rotisserie League Baseball*, ed. Glen Waggoner (Toronto: Bantam, 1984), 4.

21. Mark Seltzer, *Bodies and Machines* (New York: Routledge, 1992), 51.

increasingly expansive advertising works to shape and direct the desires of these workers as consumers, just as production fills stores with more and more items to desire. Seltzer's comments on Henry James's *The American* are helpful to understand the link between the making of workers and the fostering of workers' desires: "this logic of equivalence between bodies and objects, between persons and things, and between the passions and the interests defines the logic of the market and of market culture. The logic of the market and of market culture projects a fantasy of perfect reciprocity—the equation of interior states and economic conditions, of desires and goods" (57).

In this cultural environment, Seltzer argues, naturalist novels become fascinated with the mechanical qualities of writing—for example, the "birth of the newspaper," which for Mark Twain is the birth of writing of "a mechanical sort . . . not written by hand, but printed."[22] Seltzer explains:

> The naturalist mechanics of writing is . . . not simply a reduction of action to "the scene of writing" (that is, to the scene of the writer's self-absorption or self-reference); nor is the naturalist mechanics of writing simply a transparency through which appears the materiality of writing in general. . . . The foregrounding of the scene of writing and the materiality of writing in these cases indicates how writing and mechanics in naturalist discourse refer back to each other in circular fashion; it registers the fascinated, and at times excruciated, coupling of the work of writing and the workings of the body-machine complex. (19–20)

Interest in the physical act of printing can manifest itself explicitly as Twain's fascination with the typewriter and Paige typesetting machine ("designed to work on the model of the person, imitating the movements of the compositor" [9]) or subtly as the description of a dead soldier's shoe as paper-thin in Stephen Crane's *The Red Badge of Courage* (111–12). According to Seltzer, naturalist writers search for sites where they can observe a discrepancy between the subject's will and the social or economic structure that he or she inhabits; there is "no end to the work of disclosing and accounting for the discrepancies between what things and persons look like and what they 'are'; no end to the work of 'adjusting' subjects and structures, coordinating the everyday practices, disciplines, and dispositions of the body and the formal and juridical principles in relation to and against which these practices

---

22. Ibid., 8. Citing Mark Twain, *A Connecticut Yankee in King Arthur's Court*, ed. Allison R. Ensor (New York: Norton, 1982), 151; Seltzer's ellipsis.

function" (90). The result is an image of agency that dwells on the points of crisis. For Seltzer, "if agency in modern culture appears always in the form of a crisis of agency, such a panic about agency makes for the ritualized reaffirmations of individuality and self-possession that motivate and mobilize these contradictions" (145).

The paradoxes of the mechanical body and the problems of agency that Seltzer describes have obvious similarities to the statistical objects of role-playing games. Indeed, in the culture that Seltzer describes, individuals seek out statistical standards precisely as a way to define their individuality: "The shifting measures of persons and things redefine typicality and the meaning of the standard, such that the statistical average and norm serve to correlate measure and humanity, that is, measure and individuality. The correlation of persons and measures makes possible the cases and classes and sizes that, in turn, individualize individuals" (82). Much the same paradox is evident in the statistical qualities of role-playing games, where stories of the extraordinary and dramatic are translated into numbers that make the genuinely unexpected more and more difficult to make part of the game. Indeed, I have already noted that role-playing games are built around controlling chance: depending on random events but narrowly limiting the effects of chance to overrule player tactics. When players know, for example, precisely their number of hit-points and the possible damage caused by an opponent's weapon, they can calculate all possible outcomes of a particular encounter. This predictability can help to explain why many handbooks warn players against knowing too much about the rules of the game. The 1978 revisions to *Dungeons and Dragons* split the reference books into a player's book and a book for the referee.[23] In the preface to the latter, Gygax warns, "As this book is the exclusive precinct of the DM [Dungeon Master or referee], you must view any non-DM player possessing it as something less than worthy of honorable death."[24] The desire not to allow players to calculate the odds of every action can be seen as a recognition that doing so robs the game of the feeling that something extraordinary might happen. Obviously, outside of the scope of actions covered by numerically based rules, the game can still stage surprising events and introduce unlikely characters. But since these rules are often used to determine the outcome of particularly important events (a climactic battle, for instance), allowing them to be entirely predictable seems to some designers to set an inappropriate tone for the game as a whole.

23. Gary Gygax, *Advanced Dungeons & Dragons Player's Handbook* (Lake Geneva, WI: TSR Games, 1978).
24. Gygax, *Dungeon Masters Guide*, 8.

The image of creativity in naturalism and role-playing games will certainly seem to be a peculiar one, since play is built around forms of imagination that will seem decidedly secondary. Creativity here means the creative use of predetermined statistical rules. George Steiner's discussion of how our ways of thinking about creativity have changed in the twentieth century in *Grammars of Creation* can illuminate the issues of agency that I have been describing here. Steiner's most relevant distinction is between creation and invention. Where the former implies that something has been created out of nothing, by a pure act of will—"'creation,' properly understood and experienced, is another word for 'freedom,' for that *fiat* or 'let there be' which has meaning only in its virtually tautological relation to 'let there not be'"— the latter is connected to its circumstances and immediate needs.[25] Steiner explains:

> The crux is this: "invention," in our social history, in industry and technology, taken in their comprehensive sense, is, more often than not, applied mathematics. Invention is answerable, as Edison emphasized, to specific needs, to pragmatic possibilities as these are offered by the availability or manufacture of new materials (re-inforced concrete for the modern metropolis, titanium for the Museum at Bilbao). Invention fills a niche in evolving totality as do rare metals in the table of elements. It is, again in the best, most energized sense, "interested" and "useful." (183)

Invention, Steiner goes on, is ultimately combinatorial and subject to the "sovereignty of the pre-fabricated" (153); it is quite unlike genuine creativity, which is "organic and transcendental in that no anatomy of their constituent elements, no technical dismemberment of their gestation and possible sources can account for the vitality of the whole" (167). Clearly these two ways of thinking about imaginative "making" imply different notions of agency. In creation agency is supreme and independent of all circumstances; in invention agency is subservient to conditions, which provide the "needs" that the invention satisfies. Steiner sees a shift—which he attributes to Dada in general and Duchamp in particular—by which creativity loses its validity and contemporary artistic practice is seen more and more as a form of invention. Much as Seltzer suggested, the prominence of invention is for Steiner a product of modern industrialized economics.

The similarity between the creativity expressed by players in role-playing games and invention's reliance on pre-formed elements should be

---

25. George Steiner, *Grammars of Creation* (New Haven, CT: Yale University Press, 2001), 130.

obvious. Indeed, one of Steiner's examples of the shift in contemporary thinking about creativity is Duchamp's pursuit of chess: "*Invention is identified as the primary mode of creation in the modern world.* It follows that art is becoming amateurish indulgence, that a Marcel Duchamp is better employed at chess. Here also, if the pun is allowed, the move is perfectly calculated and significant. Like art, poetry, or music, chess is transcendentally trivial.... The Surrealist indignation that so important an artist as Duchamp should have relinquished art for a board game wholly missed the point" (331). I have, of course, suggested that role-playing games are more complex in their imagining of creativity and their use of statistics than board games, but the point is generally the same: industrial production seems to turn all making into a form of invention. If this is the case, some of the features of role-playing games become more significant. Not only do these games clearly work with predetermined elements—the story components drawn from the narrative tradition that makes up the game system—but they also embrace statistical ways of representing action and character. To play such games creatively is to use statistics and manipulate prefabricated objects in unexpected and resourceful ways.

I have suggested that role-playing games allow fans to become involved in and work with literary subgenres; they can, in other words, claim for themselves a certain agency in fandom. Indeed, I would go so far as to suggest that the game exists to make these sorts of comparisons of books within a subgenre (fantasy, science fiction) possible. Naturally, critics who talk about these games assume that their appeal is either psychological (allowing players to create powerful alter egos) or narrative (pulling players into a story whose resolution they hope to discover).[26] It may be, however, that a part of the pleasure of these games is organizing and combining the various stories and subgenres that players enjoy. Since players usually come to these stories as fans of the subgenre of writing that they emulate (medieval fantasy, futuristic science fiction, westerns), play is less a matter of escape and more a matter of sifting through the relations between genres and what it means to be a

---

26. In note 9 I observed the appeal to the shared construction of narratives. Other designers and proponents of the game have emphasized the psychological and personal value of role playing. In the rulebook for *Vampire,* Mark Rein-Hagen describes the formation of identity through role playing in childhood and remarks, "This is why it is impossible to fully leave yourself behind when you roleplay. Part of your character will certainly be different from yourself—in fact, quite frequently you will play someone with traits entirely different from your own—but always, in some essential way, that character will reflect some aspect of yourself" (23). A better-known articulation of this psychological value of role play is Sherry Turkle's influential discussion of role playing in online environments, *Life on the Screen: Identity in the Age of the Internet* (New York: Simon & Schuster, 1995).

fan. In this regard, role-playing games are exemplary artifacts of fan culture and reflect the cultural work done by objects that achieve cult status. In trying to define what makes a film suitable for cult status, Umberto Eco settles on its ability to be broken into components: "I think that in order to transform a work into a cult object one must be able to break, dislocate, unhinge it so that one can remember only parts of it, irrespective of their original relationship with the whole."[27] It seems to me that something similar is going on in role-playing games, where objects from fictional texts or subgenres are being removed and transplanted into the game world. Cultural studies like Janice Radway's *Reading the Romance* have gone a long way toward changing how we think about popular fiction by emphasizing the personal and social work that is done by reading this fiction.[28] Likewise, a number of critics have claimed that the phenomenon of fan fiction—the continuation of storylines by fans of a television show or movie—is a way for everyday people to take some control of a media culture that seems beyond their control.[29] Role-playing games in this regard are a form of cultural practice that allows players to intervene productively into popular genres of fiction.[30]

Objects and Agency in Possible World Theory

I have described a kind of fictionality that positions itself intentionally outside of the categories of literary institutions that have otherwise defined my other strands of contemporary fictionality. It may seem inevitable that this understanding of fictionality will be limited to popular literature, and that it will have no relevance to academically respected methods of literary analysis. In fact, I would like to argue, the concept of fictional worlds developed out of a possible-worlds model of literary semantics similarly allows critics to emphasize their agency in relation to literary works. Although at first glance

27. Umberto Eco, *Travels in Hyperreality: Essays*, trans. William Weaver (San Diego: Harcourt Brace & Co., 1986), 198.
28. Janice A. Radway, *Reading the Romance: Women, Patriarchy, and Popular Literature* (Chapel Hill: University of North Carolina Press, 1984).
29. See Henry Jenkins, *Textual Poachers: Television Fans & Participatory Culture* (New York: Routledge, 1992).
30. Likewise, although a full discussion of the issue is beyond the scope of this chapter, the evident desire of fans to be involved with the professional sports in ways other than simply attending games and following news of their favorite teams may well reflect alienation from the changing economics of professional sports. It may be that there was a time when agency was not a significant part of being a fan of a particular sport; the desire to claim agency may result from the sort of anxieties that Seltzer describes earlier in the century manifesting themselves now in professional sports.

this recent way of thinking about fictional worlds seems miles away from the consumption of popular fiction that characterizes role-playing games, both emphasize the objects that make up their narrative worlds in order to answer the question, what do we (readers, critics, fans) *do* with the stories we love? More generally, this interest in fictional worlds reflects a similarly irreverent stance towards the literary.

The idea that fictional works imply some "world" that readers intuitively grasp is a very traditional way of thinking about our experience of literary texts. This concept has undergone significant change over the last three decades through the influence of literary semantics, which describes how fictional statements can refer to nonexistent objects. When critics define a literary work as a "possible world," they argue that within such a hypothetical context such references can indeed be meaningful. It is clear, of course, that fictional worlds cannot be considered possible worlds strictly, since fictional worlds are created by an author and possible worlds are simply identified by logic.[31] Nonetheless, the possible-world framework allows the traditional idea that a novel contains a world to be made more meaningful; as Marie-Laure Ryan remarks, "in being borrowed and returned by philosophers, the dead metaphor [of the world of a book or author] receives a new influx of life. The concept comes back to textual semiotics sharpened by a repertory of analytical tools which reveal new territories to be explored."[32]

Interest in fictional worlds understood in the context of possible-world theory tries to describe the logic that animates a particular world and gives it coherence. The search for a way of speaking about fictional worlds is the attempt to describe the particular kinds of coherences that exist even in narratives that violate our traditional sense of the realistic. As Richard Routley notes, "In general, *each work will have its own internal logic.*"[33] I find Lubomír Doležel's distinction between extensional and intensional narrative worlds especially useful, both because it is more concrete than most possible-world theory, and because it marks a limit to the kinds of textual features that possible-world theories can attend to. Like the statistical structure of role-playing games, the basic building blocks of Doležel's theory are entities: "A possible world is not a random assemblage of entities; it is constructed in accordance with certain postulated global principles.... By

---

31. See Robert Howell, "Fictional Objects: How They Are and How They Aren't," *Poetics* 8 (1979): 139.

32. Marie-Laure Ryan, *Possible Worlds, Artificial Intelligence, and Narrative Theory* (Bloomington: Indiana University Press, 1991), 3.

33. Richard Routley, "The Semantical Structure of Fictional Discourse," *Poetics* 8 (1979): 11.

imposing global restrictions, we construct a narrative world whose entities are semantically homogeneous in some respect(s). Under this interpretation, narrative world appears as an organized macro-system of constituents (entities)."[34] Such worlds are characterized by Doležel as "extensional"—that is, concerned primarily with the simple existence and enumeration of narrative entities. He contrasts this to intensional narrative worlds, which we become aware of through the "texture" of the story ("[t]exture is our term for the 'wording' of the text" [201]). Narrative worlds achieve texture when regularities of description can be noted. Doležel's macrosemantic method "is interested in *global principles of sense organization*. Since we assume that text sense is determined by the forms of the texture, principles of sense organization will be determined by global regularities of texture" (201). Doležel's example is the use of proper names and descriptions in *Robinson Crusoe*. Although all of the characters in the book are equally part of its extensional world, the particular way that Defoe describes these characters distinguishes between those given proper names like Crusoe and Xury from those defined simply by their profession, family relation, or nationality, like "my father" or the "English captain's widow." Doležel argues that this pattern of description forms the texture of the novel, which sorts characters into two types and creates a "two-value function" (201–2) that contributes to the sense or meaning of the novel.

It should be clear that role-playing games substitute the statistical description of its entities for the "texture" of traditional fictional worlds described by Doležel. As Doležel suggests, what transforms a set of objects into elements of a value system is the differential way of describing them. In role-playing games, in contrast, value and differentiation reside within the statistical construction of the objects. Both ways of appealing to worlds, however, share an interest in breaking the text down into the building-block elements that Steiner associates with invention. In doing so, both also define and emphasize the agency of players and critics who interact with these texts and create their own mixtures while comparing works. Doležel's example of naming in *Robinson Crusoe* is especially significant, since it suggests the underlying differences between these two ways of thinking about textual worlds and marks what I will argue is a boundary beyond which the appeal to fictional worlds no longer emphasizes agency in the way that role-playing games do. So long as texture is a way to grasp more fundamental fictional objects, it is the equivalent of statistics in role-playing games; when texture begins to take

---

34. Lubomír Doležel, "Extensional and Intensional Narrative Worlds," *Poetics* 8 (1979): 196.

on a life of its own and transcend the objects it describes, I will show, the agency of the critic becomes more problematic.

For Doležel, the objects of the textual world are primarily recognizable from the actual world; they are given meaning by the texture of the narrative, the particular ways they are described. The laws organizing these entities are subtle and to be inferred from the texture of the narrative. Although not working from a possible-worlds basis, Félix Martínez-Bonati notes that much of our understanding of narrative worlds is a matter of inference: "The novelistic narrator's universal judgment is a commentary on, not a constitutive determination of, the world he is speaking about. Such commentaries can be, and often are, inadequate to the corresponding fictional world. The nature of the fictive world is determined by the universal *implications* of non-universal judgments."[35] Indeed, recent theories of fictional world influenced by possible world theory have taught us to recognize that one of the games that fictional narratives play is pretending to refer to real-world objects, while subtly smuggling in judgments that we grasp through the implications of the texture of those references.[36] The concept of texture describes how readers are able to grasp the aesthetic principles that transcend simple references to real objects. Objects in written narrative, then, have a dual identity: as we read we shuttle between all that we know about these objects in the real world (fathers, captains, widows) and their more limited use in the texture of the narrative (their difference, for example, from Xury and Crusoe). The tension between these two definitions of the same object helps us to grasp the contours of the fictional world, what Doležel describes as the general patterns of contrasts that make up the intensional world. In the case of *Robinson Crusoe*, we recognize the two-value opposition between types of characters. Quite a different thing happens in role-playing games, where

---

35. Félix Martínez-Bonati, "Towards a Formal Ontology of Fictional Worlds," *Philosophy and Literature* 7 (1973): 186.

36. It is at least in part for this reason that speech-act theory has continued to be an important, if usually background, part in developing a notion of fictional worlds through literary semantics. Peter J. McCormick characterizes speech-act theory as providing the "standard" view of fictionality (*Fictions, Philosophies, and the Problems of Poetics* [Ithaca, NY: Cornell University Press, 1988]), even though the claim that fictional reference is "pretended" or "nonserious" has little intuitive sense for how fictional language works outside of the philosophical traditions out of which this theory has been developed. Thomas Pavel concludes his discussion of speech-act theory in *Fictional Worlds* (Cambridge, MA: Harvard University Press, 1986) by suggesting that fiction contains "a mixture of pretended and genuine statements" and arguing "in fiction one does not always need to keep track of pretended and genuine statements, since global relevance is apparent in spite of such distinctions" (25). Such pretended references do seem to get at fiction's ability to appeal both to real-world objects and to the way that they have been limited by the narrative.

the evaluation of the entity—in this case, characters and their opponents—is itself an explicitly defined constituent of those objects. In role-playing games the statistical construction of the object functions as the equivalent of texture in a written narrative, as objects from popular genres are transformed into objects that can become part of the game.

In focusing on entities as his starting point, Doležel is typical of the way that possible-world thinking and the broader field of literary semantics have defined fictional worlds. Uri Margolin notes that many critics have seen such individual objects as the basic building blocks of fictional worlds,[37] and quotes Martinéz-Bonati: "the fundamental compass of narrative is a world of individuals."[38] Why this focus on entities? One explanation is that the field as a whole has its roots in philosophical debates about the validity of reference to nonexistent objects;[39] in other words, how can we have a meaningful debate about a fictional character, since such a character obviously does not exist in the real world? Nonetheless, this does not seem adequately to explain the prevalence of objects as the bedrock of fictional worlds. There is no reason, after all, that we might not speak about narrative world as a structure of events. But when these recent theories of fictional worlds do discuss events, they usually treat them through a theory of modalities and thus define them as a state of affairs modifying the objects of the world. Modalities describe logical constraints that frame a state of affairs: alethic constraints define the possibility, impossibility, or necessity of a state of affairs; deontic constraints, the proscriptive or prescriptive norms for a state of affairs; axiological constraints, the valorization of a state of affairs; epistemic modalities, the knowability of a state of affairs. A good example of this treatment of events through modalities is Doležel's recent possible-world theory of fiction, *Heterocosmica*.[40] Because it describes the conditions under which events come about, a modal theory of narrative events emphasizes the objects and spaces that frame these events. Indeed, each of the types of modal restrictions that Doležel describes is observable primarily through its effects

---

37. Uri Margolin, "Individuals in Narrative Worlds: An Ontological Perspective," *Poetics Today* 11 (1990): 846.

38. Félix Martínez-Bonati, *Fictive Discourse and the Structures of Literature: A Phenomenological Approach,* trans. Philip W. Silver (Ithaca, NY: Cornell University Press, 1981), 24.

39. See Charles Crittenden, *Unreality: The Metaphysics of Fictional Objects* (Ithaca, NY: Cornell University Press, 1991).

40. Doležel's discussion of modalities in *Heterocosmica* draws heavily on a much earlier essay; see Lubomír Doležel, "Narrative Modalities," *Journal of Literary Semantics* 5 (1976): 5–14. Modalities continue to be an important way to explain the structure of events in fictional worlds. See, for example, Marie-Laure Ryan's use of Doležel's modality theory in *Possible Worlds* (111).

on characters. For example, Doležel describes alethic constraints as able to "determine the character of all the world's entities, particularly of its persons. Fictional persons of the natural world are possible counterparts of humans, their properties and action capacities are fictional projections of actual persons' attributes."[41] Treating events in terms of modalities allows Doležel to link multiple narrative worlds. At the end of his chapter on modalities in *Heterocosmica,* Doležel describes cross-world journeys, where characters who obey different modal structures (who may, for example, reflect different definitions of the possible) interact. In such situations, it is narrative objects (characters) that allow the mixture of modal structures. Doležel offers an example: "The devil of Le Sage's *Le Diable boiteux* . . . travels . . . to observe, and to comment on, the natural world. But in several episodes he succumbs to the temptation to intervene in the human world by physical acts. He thus follows a time-honored tradition that gives supernatural beings the capacity to act in the natural world" (131). The structure of what is possible in the supernatural and the natural worlds are combined and compared here precisely by allowing an entity from the one to travel to the other. Recent work, then, has defined fictional worlds as primarily comprised of objects because doing so provides a way to compare and mix texts—just as we have seen role-playing games use statistically defined objects as meeting points for many fictional sources.

This turn to mixed worlds is not unique to Doležel's study. Indeed, one of the most influential applications of possible-world theory to fiction in recent years, Thomas Pavel's *Fictional Worlds* (1986), ends with a very similar image of mixed narrative worlds. Pavel argues, "the world view of a given community may divide into several *ontological landscapes.* European society at the end of the eighteenth century was still keeping the Christian element as an essential component of its ontological territory. This territory was, however, much wider than the Christian world: even among those not primarily interested in the progress of science, the rumor would circulate that new and disturbing cosmological theories were being proposed."[42] Pavel's conclusion that "[o]ntological landscapes foster the plurality of worlds" seems to be the most important and far-reaching claim of his book, since it paints a rich image of the give-and-take between fiction and science, tradition, and invention. Such pluralities are created when societies are willing to tolerate entities drawn from a variety of sometimes-overlapping, sometimes-conflicting worlds: "At the margins of ontological landscapes, one finds leisure worlds, or worlds for

---

41. Lubomír Doležel, *Heterocosmica: Fiction and Possible Worlds* (Baltimore: Johns Hopkins University Press, 1998), 115.

42. Pavel, *Fictional Worlds,* 139.

pleasure, which often derive from older discarded models. Each culture has its ontological ruins, its historical parks, where the members of the community relax and contemplate their ontological relics" (141). Pavel's claim about the mixture of worlds is remarkably similar to the way that Doležel ends his section on narrative worlds in *Heterocosmica,* and I would suggest that the similarity is not accidental. This recent interest in fictional worlds is at its most powerful when it describes the interaction between many different, seemingly contradictory macrosemantic regions. And a crucial component of this theory's ability to describe the interaction between these regions is its focus on narrative entities. Because theories of fiction influenced by possible-world theory define narrative as a mixture of objects, critics pursuing this theory are especially able to account for heterogeneous texts—combining realistic humans and devils, to use Doležel's example—and our movement as readers and critics between many different texts.

The mixture of worlds through attention to narrative entities ultimately, I would suggest, helps to explain what it is that critics *do* with fictional texts. Answering this question has seemed especially important because earlier structuralist theories have defined the agency of critics and writers very problematically. In *Fictional Worlds,* Pavel's point of departure is the reductiveness of the structuralist intervention into the literary text. Taking his example of Lévi-Strauss's analysis of the Oedipus myth and its subsequent reworking by other structuralists, Pavel writes, "it is difficult to believe that all myths, stories, or texts can be reduced to single elementary semantic structures consisting of four terms in a proportional relationship. Semiotic objects are complex constructions, overloaded with meaning; to postulate so rudimentary a sense involves a considerable loss of information" (7–8). In contrast, Pavel suggests that a semantic approach to fiction better respects the complexity of the text and its relation to the culture in which it is written and read: "Freed from the constraints of the textualist approach, theory of fiction can respond again to the world-creating powers of imagination and account for the properties of fictional existence and worlds, their complexity, incompleteness, remoteness, and integration within the general economy of culture" (10). In *Heterocosmica,* Doležel makes a similar point about how interest in fictional worlds allows for a different type of involvement in the text: "The art of the folk storyteller or popular crime-fiction writer produces variations on stock tales and characters and can thus be described by a 'narrative grammar.' But the creative energy of literature is beyond the grasp of such a restrictive model. Literary narratology needs a theory of *poiesis,* of the invention of new stories in and through new texts" (ix). Doležel's description here is an attempt to understand the creation of and how to intervene into fictional texts—just as the popular writer finds ways to intervene productively into earlier works and time-tested formulae.

If we think of theories of fiction influenced by possible-world theory as essentially methodologies for intervening into texts, then focus on transtextual objects becomes understandable. But we can already see the limits of this approach even with Doležel's essay. Taken to an extreme that he wisely avoids, Doležel's description of texture as a subtle network of values implied by the way that entities within a text are described could make the critic subservient to every subtlety of the text, implying that lifting objects out of a narrative would constitute a kind of heresy of paraphrase since the organizing texture would be absent. In fact, this type of close analysis of the specific texture of a world is not at all typical of theories of fiction influenced by possible-world theory, which usually range over a wide variety of texts and take most of their theoretical energy from the connections and comparisons they can make between disparate narratives.[43] By paying less attention to texture and more to the entities that make up their worlds, theorists interested in fictional worlds are able to make cross-textual comparisons much more easily. Doležel's theory of how texture contributes to a narrative world actually has more in common with discussions of fictionality that focus on style. Erich Auerbach's discussion of Homer at the outset of *Mimesis*, for example, attends to fictional worlds as a direct product of texture: Homer's poem "ensnares us, weaving its web around us, and that suffices him. And this 'real' world into which we are lured, exists for itself, contains nothing but itself; the Homeric poems conceal nothing, they contain no teaching and no secret second meaning."[44] When Auerbach compares *The Odyssey* to the description of the sacrifice of Isaac in *Genesis*, he does so not by focusing primarily on characters and settings but by attending closely to the texture of both works—what is described and in how much detail. Something of a middle point between Auerbach's attention to texture and possible-world theory's focus on objects is instanced by Roland Barthes's *S/Z*, which analyzes texture (the particular lexia that make up *Sarrasine*, some as short as a single word)

---

43. Pavel's discussion of fictional worlds opens, for example, with the example of references to Samuel Pickwick and geographical features of London (11), but then goes on to talk about philosophical issues raised by these references rather than to describe the texture of Dickens's novel. A few pages later Pavel is in the midst of the sorts of transtextual comparisons typical of fictional world theory: "During the reading of *The Pickwick Papers* does Mr. Pickwick appear less real than the sun over Goswell Street? In *War and Peace* is Natasha less actual than Napoleon?" (16). For an example of close analysis focused on a particular author and text, see Lubomír Doležel, "Intensional Function, Invisible Worlds, and Franz Kafka," *Style* 17 (1983): 120–41.

44. Erich Auerbach, *Mimesis: The Representation of Reality in Western Literature*, trans. Willard Trask (New York: Anchor, 1957), 11.

while at the same time breaking the text up into various codes (such as the semantic code "femininity") that appear in many other texts. Barthes's assertion in this study that such an analysis is endless—"it is a nomination in the course of becoming, a tireless approximation, a metonymic labor"—reminds us that focus on texture emphasizes not our actions in bringing texts together, but the endless reservoir of codes contained in the text, which can never be turned into the manipulable building blocks that narrative objects seem to be.[45]

Theories of fictional world based on possible world thinking do not, then, follow Barthes in attention to texture but instead assign to the objects themselves the job of bringing texts together. More typical of possible-world theory is Doležel's description of "secondary narrative worlds" in his essay on extensional and intensional narrative worlds: "Narrative worlds defined as sets of compossible actants shall be called *secondary* narrative worlds. The comparison with cross-world identification is, then, based on the construction of a secondary world embracing a set of primary narrative worlds" (199). More so than the concepts of texture and intensional worlds, Doležel's theory of secondary narrative worlds is typical of the eagerness we can observe in many critics working with the concept of narrative worlds to pull examples from a wide variety of texts, frequently jumping between characters drawn from different works. Doležel's description of secondary narrative worlds as critical constructions prefigures the way he describes the popular fiction writer two decades later. Just as a novelist creates a world by intervening into a genre, so too the critic creates a world by intervening into narratives written by novelists.[46] In other words, interest in possible world accounts of fiction arise in part from an anxiety about the proper way to engage with fictional texts in the wake of structuralism, much as role-playing games reflect a struggle to engage with literary subgenres in an age of mass-produced media. For both, worlds offer translation as the creative—or, following Steiner, we should say inventive—principle for engaging with such texts.

In role-playing games and fictional world theory, then, we can see a fifth distinct strand of contemporary fictionality. Not only does this strand mark a

---

45. Roland Barthes, *S/Z*, trans. Richard Miller (New York: Noonday, 1974), 11.
46. Although not strictly a matter of fictional worlds, I would put Menachem Brinker's definition of theme in the same category as Doležel's secondary narrative worlds: "our quest for a theme or themes *of* a story is always a quest for something that is not unique to this specific work. The theme is understood as potentially uniting different texts" ("Theme and Interpretation," in *The Return of Thematic Criticism*, ed. Werner Sollors [Cambridge, MA: Harvard University Press, 1993], 21). Brinker's essay appears in a book about the "return of thematic criticism" after structuralism and seems to reflect the same attitude about how critics intervene into texts.

different way of thinking about the value and use of fictional narrative that I have described in other chapters, but it also completes a trajectory that began with the highly literary debates about postmodernism in the first chapter. Over the course of these five strands I have shown a variety of fictionalities that reflect in large part different relations to literary institutions. Where Barth's myth was a direct restatement of traditional mid-century literary values, Alice Walker's archive adopted a position just outside of that tradition in the hopes of transforming the nature of the literary canon and the disciplines for studying it. Subsequent definitions of fictionality in metafiction and science fiction have adopted increasingly outside positions, frequently citing literary institutions as a mere framework for individual performance (chapter 3) or celebrating the value of extra-literary narratives for symptomizing the culture (chapter 4). In the role-playing game we have finally arrived at a form of fictionality positioned distinctly outside of literary institutions, in which the practice of picking and choosing literary and genre material does things with text that traditional literary study would deem inappropriate. The range of definitions of fictionality, then, reflect the range of positions that can be adopted toward literary institutions.

CHAPTER 6

Institutional Sutures in Electronic Writing

I have demonstrated what I call distinct "strands" of fictionality in contemporary American literary culture. These strands are not independent, of course, and part of the story that I have told in this book is about how these different definitions have jostled up against each other as they compete for institutional predominance. The tendency within America today for fictionality to diverge into these distinct strands in part reflects the different subgroups operating within and across literary culture. In the fourth chapter, for example, I described the appeal to cultural symptoms in science fiction, a definition of fictionality that reflects trends within more mainstream writing and the marginal location from which science fiction is produced and consumed. In addition, I have shown that the divergence of fictionality also reflects competition between different forces and groups within literary institutions. This is especially the case in the appeal to "myth" and "folklore" that I discussed in chapters 1 and 2. These appeals, which seem similar if not outright congruent, actually reflect a conflict between two contrasting canons of contemporary writing and two different ways to legitimate critical practice.

In attempting to tease apart these different strands and to examine their distinct appeals to literary authority and legitimacy, I have not paid particular attention to the interaction between these competing definitions within particular literary works or movements. I would like to correct that gap in this final chapter by turning to an area of contemporary writing that displays these competing definitions of fictionality especially well—electronic writing. By electronic writing I mean works designed to be experienced through a computer screen.[1] The institutionally simplest instances of electronic writing are literary hypertexts and poetry, works often written by practicing novelists and poets designed to be read and interpreted within fairly traditional literary terms. At its boundaries, electronic texts include computer games, which not only are the most successful instances of the dissemination and consumption of electronic texts, but which provide many of the aesthetic models that more explicitly literary electronic artists draw on and define themselves against.

Electronic writing is an especially valuable concluding example for this book because it is so obviously positioned on the boundary between several competing institutions that promise to legitimate it. In this chapter I particularly focus on works that make some appeal to literary seriousness, since those works reveal the point at which literary institutions are most energetically at work. My examples will include not only literary hypertexts and poetry designed by writers who have also produced more traditional print writing but also games like *American McGee's Alice,* which rewrites the *Alice in Wonderland* story as a first-person combat game. Such works reveal designers and authors struggling to appeal to literary models and inherited texts while at the same time accommodating themselves to the particular demands of electronic textuality. As these writers and designers struggle to bridge these two worlds, they turn—as we might expect—to a variety of ways of defining fictionality. These various definitions nicely summarize the chapters of this book. Questions about how to define fictionality will be asked with particular force and energy when a new form of writing emerges.

---

1. This is by design an amorphous definition. I am not interested in deciding which sorts of works should be categorized as game or text but rather in looking at how these works position themselves. While early hypertexts were quite obviously a distinct form of textuality, recent dissemination of even more traditional writing by electronic means further complicates this distinction. One important qualification for my examples should be noted, however: I have chosen electronic works that locate themselves primarily in the context of writing, rather than those that seem more dependent on other media. For example, many games frame themselves cinematically, such as the many game versions of the *Star Wars* films. While my discussion here might have some relevance to such games, my focus is on those electronic works that appeal in whole or in part to writing and reading as a framework for understanding them.

I have also argued that fictionality is most noticeable when we are aware of how the text is being used and by what institutions and disciplines. The issue of use and agency is especially powerful in electronic writing since this work frequently defines its newness by claiming to produce agency where other literary forms deny it. Indeed, in raising the issue of reader/player agency in the context of contemporary fictionalizing, we could say that electronic writing embodies current debates and anxieties about what invented stories are good for.

Literary Activity in *Arteroids* and *Alice*

A good place to start this discussion of agency and literary institutions in electronic writing is with a work that is both extremely game-like and self-consciously literary. Jim Andrews's *Arteroids* straddles the line between poem and game. It echoes and rewrites the early arcade game *Asteroids* in which the player maneuvers a spaceship in two-dimensional space to avoid and destroy asteroids, which fly across the screen in different directions. Andrews rewrites this game by replacing the spaceship with a word (usually *desire*) and having the player shoot not at asteroids but at words and phrases that move across the screen.[2] When the player successfully shoots a word or phrase it explodes into a shower of random letters that remain scattered across the screen for several minutes.

Andrews explains his aesthetic justification for this odd mixture of poem and game in a companion essay, "Games, Po, Art, Play, & Arteroids 2.03." Andrews frames this work in familiar avant-garde terms: "Arteroids is about cracking language open. William S. Burroughs said about audio tape that when you cut it, the future spills out. When writers and artists use cut-up techniques of all kinds on all types of media ... then language is indeed cracked open in the sense that the fundamental symbols of writing are no longer simply the letters in the alphabet and other typographical marks. Writing is now a larger thing." Andrews describes his work as "the battle of poetry against itself and the forces of dullness," clearly framing his work as an attempt to rejuvenate writing in the standard sense of the avant-garde. Indeed, it is no accident that Andrews should appeal to Burroughs in his justification for this work. Not only is Burroughs himself usually recognized

---

2. *Arteroids* is available at http://www.vispo.com/arteroids/index.htm. In version 2.5 players are able to edit the word representing the player as well as the target texts. Andrews discusses the reasons why player-editing game conditions is important in his essay, "Games, Po, Art, Play & Arteroids 2.03," http://www.vispo.com/arteroids/onarteroids.htm.

as a (sometimes misunderstood) avant-garde writer, but his work is particularly defined by the meeting point of several media. As someone influenced by collage in visual art and interested in audio recording, Burroughs is clearly a model for Andrews, whose work both claims to have literary significance and at the same time worries that it will be dismissed because of its cross-media position. In this, Andrews reflects the kinds of institutional conflicts that will affect any definition of fictionality that electronic texts adopt.

Arteriods exemplifies the tension between literary and game justifications for electronic texts by foregrounding two different sets of qualities. These justifications in turn imply different contexts, institutions, and protocols for dealing with its particular instances.[3] Exemplary, too, is the way that Andrews works to balance these two sets of contexts, institutions, and protocols. Indeed, Andrews signals his attempt to appeal to both literary and game contexts at the outset of his essay. He describes *Arteroids* as "[k]ind of an 'end of language' piece. Yet only the small death, for the most part: the id entity and the executed texts are resurrected as per usual in computer games after the player succumbs to the mortal distress of texts with legs and eyes. And as much is created as destroyed in the language wars between sense and strong, dynamic language." Andrews is not simply creating a compromise between the aesthetic demands of play and the traditional contemplative understanding of poetry. Instead we see an attempt to reinterpret the traditional limitations of one form of textuality in terms of the other. Thus, the necessity of allowing players to return and replay a game in which they have "died" is not simply explained away but is used as the basis for the literary significance of the game text. In Andrews's interpretation, the resurrection of the text is not a quirk of the game, a necessary compromise in the nature of play, but rather a reflection of the permanence of language. What Andrews is accomplishing here in relation to the literary and game contexts for his work seems to be a model for all electronic works: he finds some way to bind together these two ways of framing the work by constructing particular elements of his text in ways that appeal to both.

The best language for discussing this combination of game and literary context is *suture*, a term that will be familiar to many from Lacan as inter-

---

3. Although the contentious debates among proponents of different ways of defining electronic writing have usually meant that critics must decide on a single framework for defining the text, some critics have noted that games can make multiple appeals to different kinds of reading and play. See, for example, Nick Montfort and Stuart Moulthrop's "Face It, Tiger, You Just Hit the Jackpot: Reading and Playing Cadre's *Varicella*" (*Fineart Forum* 17, no. 8 [August 2003], http://nickm.com/if/varicella.pdf), which discusses the appeal to reading and play in an adventure game.

preted by Jacques-Alain Miller. In particular I am interested in the way that the term has been picked up by Ernesto Laclau and Chantal Mouffe in *Hegemony and Socialist Strategy* as a way to talk about the constitution of a field of ideology. Slavoj Žižek summarizes Laclau and Mouffe: "the multitude of 'floating signifiers,' of proto-ideological elements, is structured into a unified field through the intervention of a certain 'nodal point' (the Lacanian *point de capiton*) which 'quilts' them, stops their sliding and fixes their meaning."[4] Sutures (Lacan's *point de capiton,* Žižek's quilting point) create bindings at certain points within an ideological field that give the whole a solidity. Especially important is Laclau and Mouffe's observation that such suture points function only to the degree that there is some openness within the field. In the context of electronic writing, sutures are especially important because the meaning of key terms like reading, text, and creativity are so obviously open.[5] Laclau and Mouffe explain in more detail in a note: "Hegemonic practices are suturing insofar as their field of operation is determined by the openness of the social, by the ultimately unfixed character of every signifier. This original lack is precisely what the hegemonic practices try to fill in. A *totally* sutured society would be one where this filling-in would have reached its ultimate consequences and would have, therefore, managed to identify itself with the transparency of a closed symbolic order. Such a closure of the social is, as we will see, impossible."[6] As John Cayley remarks about a particular form of electronic textuality, codework poetry, "Reading codework as code-in-language and language-in-code also risks stunning the resultant literary object, leaving it reduced to simple text-to-be-read, whereas there are real questions of how such work is to be grasped as an object: is it text, process, performance, instrument?"[7] As artistic justifications for this writing intervene into these ideological fields, they create such binding points by suturing together multiple institutions, contexts, and protocols for use.

Using the concept of the suturing of literary and game protocols makes it possible to interpret many of the choices that Andrews has made as he

---

4. Slavoj Žižek, *The Sublime Object of Ideology* (London: Verso, 1989), 87.

5. A good example of the openness of this field is the debate between critics who see electronic works as best exemplified by hypertexts (and thus a form of textuality) and those who take as the primary example games. See, for example, the rancorous exchange in the *Electronic Book Review* over Espen Aarseth's *Cybertext*: Markku Eskelinen, "Cybertext Theory: What an English Professor Should Know Before Trying"; Katherine Hayles, "What Cybertext Theory Can't Do"; Nick Montfort, "Cybertext Killed the Hypertext Star"; all in the *Electronic Book Review* (http://www.electronicbookreview.com).

6. Ernesto Laclau and Chantal Mouffe, *Hegemony and Socialist Strategy: Towards a Radical Democratic Politics* (London: Verso, 1985), 88n1.

7. John Cayley, "The Code Is Not the Text (Unless It Is the Text)," *Electronic Book Review* (2002), http://www.electronicbookreview.com/thread/electropoetics/literal.

constructed *Arteroids*. This is especially evident in the way that Andrews describes the functioning of sound in this game: "The sounds of exploding arteroidal texts are male, female, young and old, human and semi-human, semi-human and animal. Every sound in *Arteroids* is my voice and nothing but—with a little help from Sound Forge." These sounds are played at random, with a randomized pitch change, every time a player "executes" a text. Andrews goes on to explain the logic of sound: "As you can hear in the MP3's linked to the Arteroids home page, sound recordings I made of games I played, the audio, when the game is played well, is listenable in its own right as a kind of sound poetry punctuated into different 'verses' between the explosion of poetry.... Part of the idea of the audio is to create a high energy sound track for a game, and make it ultra human, or hyperhuman, as the case may be. Really alive, in any case, and lively." Sound in *Arteroids* sutures together the game and the literary protocols. The sounds not only reflect typical game design features—things must make a sound when destroyed—and depend on imminently computerized features like randomization of pitch change. These sounds also reference the traditional features of literary discourse—the belief that a poem is "alive" in some organic way. In describing these sounds as "hyperhuman," Andrews echoes traditional beliefs that artworks take our everyday experience and amplify it; such a description of the text's sound clearly works to bind together game and literary features. This is not simply a matter of compromise—of striking a middle ground between two divergent media, or of keeping the lowest-common-denominator features—but rather of linking together particular features in game and literary objects.

We should notice that in his literary sutures Andrews emphasizes the activity of the reader/player. This issue emerges with particular importance when Andrews writes about the use of the gun as an organizing principle. Noting that the gun is the central, "kinaesthetic" component of the game, Andrews writes,

> There are enough guns in enough real hands, and enough computer game guns that the making of guns in computer games must attain the next level of message passing as the real structural nexus of the activity of programming "first or second person shooter games," i.e., it isn't really the gun that is the most strongly dynamic and appealing element (though guns are primal and it becomes an imaginary life-and-death situation), it is the real-time/game-time control over the activity of interaction with objects that you pass messages to kinaesthetically via the keyboard, plus primal drama.

Andrews concludes that "[g]uns are primally dramatic" and proposes a figurative reading of their presence in future electronic texts: "The games that will emerge that are the Web's own games (not tired retreads) will take advantage of message passing figuratively and literally, to fuller playful communications between people, and between people and media objects." Andrews is clearly trying to interpret the central gun of his game in a way that sutures together game and literature, play and artistic statement. What seems especially important here is that the means of this suturing is the reinterpretation of the activity of the player/reader. Guns are the central issue of Andrews's work (and his essay justifying that work) because they are the point at which the activity condoned by both the game and the literary institution is justified. Games depend on the activity of the player, promise to challenge that player, and position the accomplishments of that activity in a community context (a score, finishing a level) that makes that performance meaningful. Literary activity, conversely, emphasizes composition and reading as a process of communicating experience. Andrews interprets the gun of his game as the point at which both are accomplished: experience is crafted kinesthetically, but that experience in turn becomes a metaphor for the process of exchanging information.

What is most important in Andrews's sutures, then, is that they bind together the features we expect of games and literary works by addressing the activity demanded by each. That such sutures work on reader activity should not be a surprise. Indeed, critics have routinely understood that institutions are most powerful when they shape practices, the sort of work that Andy Warhol described in chapter 2 or that Pierre Bourdieu defines through the *habitus*. *Arteriods* is remarkable for foregrounding this appeal to activity, and for making clear that these sorts of sutures will work by moving back to what is "really" happening in the work. Note that I have emphasized the categorization of the work, rather than its essential properties. Much of the debate about electronic writing has focused on the question of its narrativity conceived in quite general terms. For example, Jesper Juul argues that electronic games cannot be fundamentally narrative because they are necessarily set in the present: "it is impossible to influence something that has already happened. This means that *you cannot have interactivity and narration at the same time.* And this means in practice that games almost never perform basic narrative operations like flashback and flash forward. Games are almost always chronological."[8] In this chapter, instead, I have emphasized

---

8. Jesper Juul, "Games Telling Stories? A Brief Note on Games and Narratives," *Game Studies* 1, no. 1 (July 2001), http://www.gamestudies.org/0101/juul-gts/.

how we have sorted the work into an institutionally defined category. In this context, we should ask not "is it narrative?" but instead "is it a story?"[9] These questions are determined by the categories that are available to writers and readers, developers and players, and are the product both of explicit institutional definitions like ideas of literary value inherited from the academy or the types of games defined by the game industry, but also of the more subtle sorting that goes on when audiences for games and texts define themselves as certain types of players or readers. This sort of categorization is especially important in the case of computer and video games, where players are often quite explicit about what kinds of games they like and dislike, and consequently define themselves as part of one fan base rather than another. In such an environment, asking about the essential narrativity of a game seems to me to make much less sense than asking whether players think that they are experiencing a story or whether they think that they are doing something else—testing their stills, trying on other identities, meeting friends, and so on.

I would like to offer one other introductory example of this sort of suturing before I turn to the issue of fictionality and a more systematic list of varieties of suturing below. American McGee's reworking of *Alice in Wonderland* as the 3D combat game *Alice* (2000) seems to me to be doing much the same suturing that we see in *Arteriods* but in a way directed at a popular audience.[10] *Alice* opens with its titular character as a young woman in the 1870s, confined to a mental hospital and virtually comatose after a fire in her home killed her family. We are shown a cutscene (a non-interactive mini-movie) about the death of Alice's parents and her time in the mental hospital, and then see her falling downward into Wonderland, where the player takes control of her. Alice's progress through the game follows many of the most conventional models for first-person combat games. She acquires a variety of weapons that she uses to kill opponents (from unique characters like the Red Queen to the ubiquitous red and black card guards) while sustaining as little personal injury as possible, performs complex leaps and movements to avoid dangers, and must solve occasional puzzles to move forward in the game. Although the 3-D environment in which she moves is designed to feel

---

9. This is the same kind of question asked by recent cultural histories of the novel. At the outset of *Cultural Institutions of the Novel,* Deidre Lynch and William Warner note that their interest in the institutional definition of the novel was initiated by the question, "is this a novel?" asked in historical courses like "The Eighteenth-Century English Novel." See Deidre Lynch and William B. Warner, "Introduction: The Transport of the Novel," in *Cultural Institutions of the Novel,* eds. Deidre Lynch and William B. Warner (Durham, NC: Duke University Press, 1996), 1–10.

10. *American McGee's Alice,* CD-ROM (Redwood City, CA: EA Games, 2000).

open-ended, there is a single route through each of the levels that Alice faces, and a particular goal whose accomplishment ends the level and moves the game forward.

Even this brief summary of the game reveals it to be a rather odd hybrid, a mixture of almost all of the most conventional features of current game design and a literary background that will be familiar to most players. As we see in *Arteriods,* McGee works to suture these two protocols together. Borrowing a background story like *Alice in Wonderland* is, of course, relatively common in computer game design. Indeed, the pervasive use of franchise tie-ins among games—there have been dozens of *Star Wars*–themed games produced over the last twenty-five years, for example—makes clear how useful such borrowed stories are to creating interest in character and a sense of emotional involvement in the game.[11] What seems especially important in this game is less its decision to borrow a story than its appeal to a literary classic. The technique that *Alice* uses to accomplish this is familiar from *Arteriods:* it finds particular features of the game and sutures those to a literary context. In this case, that context is provided not by Andrews's language of hyperhumanism but by the discourse of psychological struggle. At the end of the game we discover that Alice's battles in the game world reflect her psychological struggle to emerge from her comatose state. The suture between game world and literary world is based on the metaphor of wrestling with one's personal demons.

Alice also draws our attention to its heroine's agency and the institutions that promise to define, circumscribe, and explain it. Indeed, the game itself ships with a facsimile "casebook" that records the psychiatric observations of Alice's doctor over the course of the ten years she spends in the mental hospital. This casebook specifically invokes the institutions of psychology through which Alice's illness is understood. Setting Alice's commitment in the 1870s particularly allows the game designers to distance us from this institution, since the explanations given to her behavior and the treatments proscribed (laudanum and camphor) are discredited by modern psychiatry. The movement into the game itself and away from this introductory material serves to shift our methods of inquiry—our agency in trying to cure Alice—from such obviously failed psychological institutions to the combat defined by the game itself. The game substitutes an imagined journey inside Alice's psyche for these institutional methods, all the while retaining an appeal to an overall psychological explanation for her actions. In the substitution of combat

---

11. I discuss how borrowed stories create narrative involvement in "Involvement, Interruption, and Inevitability: Melancholy as an Aesthetic Principle in Game Narratives," *Sub-Stance* 33, no. 3 (2004): 80–107.

for analysis, *Alice* works to reshape player agency. Indeed, the central story told by the casebook is that of the failure of the psychiatric institution to help Alice, despite the efforts of a doctor who takes particular interest in her case. The doctor's casebook suggested an exhausted agency; near the end he writes, "Everything I can think of, I have done. Treatments, remedies, disciplines and pleasures—nothing makes a difference. Alice speaks when and about what she wants, recites poetry on a seeming whim, draws pictures at her own pleasure. She does nothing at my command, instruction, entreaty or request. She's become very willful and nothing I do or say makes a difference." The casebook ends with the doctor ceding agency to Alice (and by implication to the player who controls Alice during the game): "I truly do, however, become immersed in her fantastic tales of Wonderland. I wait for the day when she claims victory over the Red Queen and her minions, when Wonderland will be restored. Perhaps by this Alice will cure herself, regain her balance, and leave this place of her own volition."

Alice is not, however, simply a response to psychiatric institutions; it is the product of a very complicated relationship to literary institutions as well. Not only is the game itself a rewriting of the Alice story, but the very shift from psychiatric to game treatment of Alice is accomplished by appealing to the value of made-up stories—to fictionality. As the doctor's response to Alice's story suggests, fiction has the power to affect psychological change by playing out the events of her life in a different way. The principle of translation is at work not only in Alice's translation of her personal struggles into the combat game but also in the translation of the book into the game. The opening cutscene for the game specifically invokes the book, showing it amid the fire.

McGee may have in mind simply providing a psychological motivation for Alice's association of trauma and the world of Wonderland, but it also seems important that the game employs the principal translation not only on a psychological but also on a textual level. The agency that Alice claims in producing her own cure is echoed by the game's agency in (re)claiming the book for new purposes. The game's transformation of the literary institutions surrounding the classic Alice story parallels Alice's own transformation of the demands placed on her by psychiatric institutions.

I would note, finally, that *Alice* embodies literary institutions in the artifact of the book itself. Although the decision to do this may seem a quirk of the game's opening cutscene, Andrews does something similar when he has the player destroy "dull words" that embody traditional poetry. The artifact of the literary text haunts this game as a reference point against which transformations of the institutional uses of the story can be measured. Such artifacts seem to be a common component of electronic works like *Alice* that explicitly position themselves against disciplinary expectations. Jay David Bolter and Richard Grusin's influential theory of electronic texts, *Remediation* (1999), has made the presence of other and especially older media a defining characteristic of electronic media: "we call the representation of one medium in another *remediation,* and we will argue that remediation is a defining characteristic of the new digital media."[12] As long as we see echoes of previous media primarily as a quality of the medium itself rather than a facet of how an individual work adopts an institutional position, I would argue, we are bound to misinterpret the work being done by these echoes.[13] The differences between these two ways of thinking about electronic texts can be seen in strongly historical combat games like *Metal of Honor: Allied Assault* (2002), for example, where artifactuality points to disciplines rather than media.[14] As a squad-based first-person combat game, *Allied Assault* sends the player with a small group of fellow soldiers into missions based on actual World War II battles. History exerts its force on the game not only in the particular tasks assigned to the player, but also in the materials made available for combat. Indeed, one is struck that the game works so hard to create a sense of artifactuality—menus replicate the texture of old metal, game information appears to be printed on period-style letterhead, and so on.

Our sense of agency involves working with what appear to be actual artifacts from the period, since players use specific weapons and tools that are meant to reflect the setting. Much the same is being accomplished by the game: just as players get to create new events within the boundaries defined by historical artifacts and situations, so too the game is trying to find a new

12. Jay David Bolter and Richard Grusin, *Remediation: Understanding New Media* (Cambridge, MA: MIT Press, 1999), 45.
13. In addition to Bolter and Grusin, see also Lev Manovich's *The Language of New Media* (Cambridge, MA: MIT Press, 2001), which likewise sees the "transcodable" quality of digital elements (47) as making remediation more natural to electronic texts. For a critique of *Remediation* as neglecting the particular historical and institutional position of individual electronic works, see Jan Baeten's review of the follow-up book by Bolter and Grusin, *Windows and Mirrors,* in the *Electronic Book Review,* "A Remediation's Remediation?" (http://www.electronicbookreview.com/thread/imagenarrative/designflaw). More in keeping with the kind of transmedia relations that I am describing here is the appeal to analog "mourning" in subsequent media. In "Digital Incompossibility: Cruising the Aesthetic Haze of the New Media" for *Ctheory* (2000), http://ctheory.net/text_file.asp?pick=121, Timothy Murray remarks that new media works "open themselves to the virtuality of the future only in relation to their dedicated refashioning of past codes of similitude and resemblance." Murray concludes that new media "look[s] back to the past to reach into the future."
14. *Metal of Honor: Allied Assault,* CD-ROM (Redwood City: EA Games, 2002).

CHAPTER 6

use for history and its artifacts. Player agency again echoes the agency of the game design itself in its relationship to the institutions of history. This artifactuality carries over even into games without real-world historical reference. In fantasy games based on *Dungeons and Dragons* like *Baldur's Gate*, for example, player maps are represented as stained and torn at the edges to create the illusion that the player is interacting with physical artifacts and thus is connected to a history independent of the game.[15] Artifactuality in these games is less a reflection of its digital qualities and more a sign of its awareness of the institutions and disciplines that have a prior claim on its topic.

Fictionality and the Varieties of Suturing

Electronic texts must negotiate, then, the expectations placed on them as both games and literary works. They do this, as I have suggested, by defining reader/player agency in strategic ways. Because games and narratives imply different types of agency, this emerging form of textuality must carefully suture together these two different sorts of expectations. As we might expect, these works draw on many of the same definitions of fictionality that are at work in other forms of contemporary literary production. Indeed, I would like to suggest here that we can see all five of my "strands" of contemporary fictionality woven in these various texts. It should be no surprise that these electronic works tend particularly to move between a variety of ways of defining and legitimating their own fictionality, since such works are positioned at the very margins of contemporary literary production.

In this second section I would like to examine briefly five electronic works that draw on my five strands of fictionality before turning to works that strive to balance these against each other in the final section.

MYTH

Lionhead Studios's computer game *Black & White* (2001) is an excellent example of how electronic works appearing within a field that is not yet independent of earlier analogues like games and stories define themselves in the context of a variety of institutional frameworks.[16] Indeed, this game is significant both because of its pedigree and because of its critical reception.

---

15. *Baldur's Gate,* CD-ROM (Edmonton: Bioware, 1998).
16. *Black & White,* CD-ROM (Redwood City, CA: Electronic Arts, 2001).

The game was produced by Peter Molyneux, whose earlier games included several influential civilization simulations like *Populous* (1989); *Black & White* is also one of the most talked-about recent simulation games.

Black & White draws on and reworks many influential trends within the short history of computer games and thus functions in part as a commentary on the genres of current gaming. *Black & White* is a tactical resource-gathering game in the tradition of *Civilization*, *SimCity*, or *Age of Empires*. In games like these, players control a civilization and are responsible for directing its economics, military, and diplomacy. Traditionally such games demand that players gather some type of resource—such as raw materials like wood and stone or tax money drawn from the population—that will be used to further develop the society. Such games are often described as "god games" both because players have no particular identity within the game and because they control every aspect of the civilization directly and view the game world at a neutral distance looking down on the city or terrain. *Black & White* literalizes this concept of the god game, making the player an actual deity who must inspire reverence in his or her followers—either through benevolent acts or fear-inspiring malevolence. As civilizations grow and more citizens spend their time on worship, the player's power grows.

Several innovations in game design allow *Black & White* to function as a critique of the god game. First, there is no simple position from which the viewer watches the events of the game. The player can indeed pull back the perspective on the game until the island world appears to be a featureless green mass. But to interact with this world, the player must zoom in until the particular features of the landscape—buildings and peasants—are large enough to manipulate. Because the player has control not only of the scale of the image but also of the perspective—allowing us to rotate around the features of the ground, approaching the island from any angle—in some ways players seem to be much more powerful than in a traditional god game, where viewing position is traditionally constrained to a single isometric point of view. But because the player must spend so much time controlling this point of view, the effort of moving around the island is much more obvious. Second, the player's intervention into the world of his or her worshipers is not as effortless as it is in most games. To change the task that a particular peasant is doing at one time, the player must grab that person, carry her across the sky and deposit her at the site of the new task. Letting her go from too high in the air will make her plummet to her death—inspiring fear from one's villagers, but wasting one particular resource.

Black & White is, consequently, a difficult game to play for reasons that are quite different from what we would traditionally expect in a god game.

Much of the learning curve in the game depends on the quite physical job of moving around the island, changing perspective, and manipulating objects on the ground—tasks that most games try to make as effortless as possible. It seems clear that part of the point of this game is to make the interface between player and units to be manipulated less transparent. On a thematic level, this game raises questions about power in general. Given a player so obviously out of proportion to his or her charges, what is the difference between benevolence and malevolence? Most players are likely to try initially to play the game as a "good" deity, but when one is grabbing peasants away from tasks and flying them through the air to other locations, when one is treating workers like any other resource, how significant is the difference between good and evil, black and white? If any game—indeed, any form of bureaucratic control—involves treating subordinates as means to larger ends, is what we usually think of as goodness even applicable? Molyneux makes this point when discussing the origins of *Black & White* in an interview. Explaining that his inspiration for the game was the disproportion of god and peasant in a film ("this image of a colossus standing over a horde of tiny creatures"), he remarks, "The really interesting thing about this is that if you're worshipped with that level of devotion, you're basically a god, and you can, in the eyes of your followers, do no wrong. So you can rule your people, be they alien bugs or humans, in the manner you choose. From this came the idea of *Black & White*. A world that takes the form you wish on it; a world where you aren't judged, and a world where good and evil are simply different ways of doing things."[17]

How does *Black & White* imagine its fictionality? In other words, what does this made-up game accomplish, and how does its imagined reality function as a means to that end? It should be clear that the relationship between means and ends is one that is dramatized throughout the game. Indeed, this is a question frequently raised about simulation games in general. Marie-Laure Ryan distinguishes between the goal-directed play of most computer games and the open-ended freeplay of undirected exploration.[18] Even in simulation games there is a teleology that players can use to evaluate their performance; game designer Hal Barwood remarks that "people don't want to be in charge unless there's something to be in charge of—unless we can meet a challenge. The equation seems pretty simple to me: interactivity minus goals equals

---

17. James Leach and Christian Bravery, *The Making of Black & White* (Roseville, CA: Prima Games, 2001), 4.

18. Marie-Laure Ryan, *Narrative as Virtual Reality: Immersion and Interactivity in Literature and Electronic Media* (Baltimore: Johns Hopkins University Press, 2001), 175–99.

boredom."[19] *Black & White* pushes this question somewhat further by taking quite literally the premise of simulation games: that the tedium of regulating these virtual lives is redeemed by the pleasure taken in the challenge and by the experience of control that the player enjoys. Precisely that balance between work and control is dramatized in the game, which constantly points out the slippery line between the apparently benevolent goal of building up a civilization and the ultimately selfish pleasure of controlling others. Within the mimetic world of *Black & White,* what this game accomplishes is obviously the former, while reminding us of the latter at the more basic level of the work of the game. In other words, this game dramatizes the clash between two different ways of thinking about what this game *does,* what its imagined world is good for.

In doing both kinds of work *Black & White* sutures together two very different ways of understanding the invented stories. Indeed, we could read the tendency of gameplay to slide towards evil as a way of pointing out the moral pretensions of narrative and fictional worlds. For all that stories seem to promise a narrative of redemption or insight or reconciliation, the motivations behind writers and readers need not be so noble. John Bender, for example, has linked the rise of the novel with the disciplining of the individual by the penitentiary,[20] and other critics writing about the eighteenth-century novel have recognized our often ambiguous moral relation to literary characters.[21] We might also recall John Fowles's image of the controlling author in *The French Lieutenant's Woman* (1969), who asks, "Now could I use you? Now what could I do with you?"[22] Insight into the lives of others here is not sympathetic so much as objectifying. Likewise in *Black & White* the work of manipulating this game world constantly directs us back to the other uses of writing and stories. In this, *Black and White* appeals to the game context for play, the traditions of god games in which players will naturally place the experience of play. The game, then, sutures together the literary

---

19. Randy Sluganski, "LucasArts Speaks Out—Part 1: A Discussion with Hal Barwood," http://www.justadventure.com/Interviews/Hal_Barwood/Hal-Barwood2.shtm.

20. John Bender, *Imagining the Penitentiary: Fiction and the Architecture of Mind in Eighteenth-Century England* (Chicago: University of Chicago Press, 1987).

21. Deidre Lynch remarks in *The Economy of Character: Novels, Market Culture, and the Business of Inner Meaning* (Chicago: University of Chicago Press, 1998) about the mechanical quality of character in Fanny Burney's fiction: "Because it blurs the lines between a person and a thing, between intentional and coerced action, automatized motion sets in relief what is equivocal about literary character, made particularly equivocal after real or 'round' characters are thought of as animated, as escaping the discursive conditions of their meaning and acquiring lives of their own. Automatized motion highlights the difficulty of saying where literary character ends and the contriving author begins" (197–98).

22. John Fowles, *The French Lieutenant's Woman* (Boston: Little, Brown, 1969), 405.

claims to moral lessons and the game claims to power and accomplishment, using each to reflect on the other and to place the game in the context of two completing institutions.

Black & White accomplishes this nifty bit of institutional suturing by appealing to a definition of myth that I described in the first chapter. There I noted that early postmodernist manifestoes defined fiction as myth because both depended upon and transcended its particular moment of writing. This definition of fiction worked to place particular forms of contemporary writing in the literary forefront and to exclude others from the nascent canon of postmodernism. It seems to me that myth does something similar in *Black & White,* since appeals to belief and control embodied in the player's manipulation of peasants are treated as an attempt to transcend immediate tasks. Indeed, it seems that *Black & White* is in large part about just the irony that we noted in John Barth's *Friday Book*. Like Barth's desire to transcend the occasion of writing, the benevolent goals of caring for a civilization in *Black & White* reach their limit in the mundane work of manipulating that civilization. At issue in both cases is the relationship between ends and means: how much can we escape our occasion, how much can we move beyond to some larger end? This is true not only about gameplay but also about the game itself. While most simulation games try to locate themselves historically, *Black & White* aspires to a mythical generality—a battle between good and evil that promises (but never quite manages) to escape its occasion.

ARCHIVE

M. D. Coverley's multimedia hypertext *Califia* (2000) occupies a very different position within the range of electronic writing.[23] Where *Black and White* was developed out of computer game traditions and marketed directly to a gaming audience, *Califia* is more obviously a literary work. Unlike most early hypertext narratives, which frequently are constructed of linked words and passages (lexia), Coverley's work is much more visual, frequently placing only a few words on each screen and supplementing the reading with images and a soundtrack keyed to different parts of the text. The text itself opens by introducing California as "an island where . . . dreams come true." The reader is invited to "come ashore" by clicking on a footprint icon, which is designed to look as if it were part of the seashore landscape that provides the backdrop for the words. Following the footprints leads to a series of screens

23. M. D. Coverly, *Califia,* CD-ROM (Watertown, MA: Eastgate Systems, 2000).

that introduce a mystery of buried gold coins: "Ah, fellow searchers... so begins Augusta's journey to find the treasure of Califia. You are invited to join us" (ellipsis in original). We are given a more explicit description of the project on the next screen: "We are seeking assistance in discovering a cache of gold. The gold was originally mined in the Sierras, then brought to Los Angeles in the 1850's. It was re-buried in the Southern California hills, but, through foul play or a California mixup, knowledge of the actual location was lost.... Here we bring together the legends, photos, maps, and documents that lead us to believe that there was good reason for generations of Californians to keep searching for the secret treasure." *Califia* is, then, a kind of treasure hunt. Subsequent screens introduce us to a variety of archival resources assembled by different characters seeking the gold: "Calvin has designed the Archives pages to hold the contents of Father's study we now think are important. He and Kaye have had some fun—embroidering it all in Docudramas. But I have requested that he not add unnecessary junk to my pages. He tends to get carried away."

It is clear, then, that *Califia* is a collection of documents that the reader is expected to sort through. Woven through these documents is a series of conflicts over the nature of the investigation ("Because it is three-dimensional, and because it is evolving, Augusta, Kaye, and I see the outline [of the project] differently..."). Movement through the hypertext is motivated by the mystery of the gold's disappearance and the task of finding it. It is not difficult to see in this emphasis on solving a mystery a suturing together of game and literary protocols. Lev Manovich has argued that the opposition between database and narrative is a fundamental one for electronic texts: "As a cultural form, the database represents the world as a list of items, and it refuses to order this list. In contrast, a narrative creates a cause-and-effect trajectory of seemingly unordered items (events). Therefore, database and narrative are natural enemies."[24] Coverley's hypertext is both a story and a combination of many stories, both a work of literary art and a means of accessing other stories contained within it. In this, *Califia* reflects some of the contradictions in the idea of an electronic text and thus works to redefine the context in which this story should be understood. We have seen something of the same sort of response to contradictions accomplished by *Black and White,* which likewise responds to some of the contradictions in the god game to produce a work positioned very differently between literary and game institutions. In doing so, *Califia* works to define its own fictionality. This invented text is valuable not so much because it teaches a lesson or because it creates sympa-

24. Manovich, *The Language of New Media,* 225.

thy—two of the more conventional definitions of fictionality—but because of the insight that moving through the book can produce. This goal for writing and reading is articulated in the section defining the overall design of the project: "Our hope is that, as you choose your way among the paths, you will discover more than we know. In the end, your created stories will determine the real location of the Treasure of Califia." Coverley suggests here that the movement of the reader through the text itself is creative and produces an experience that becomes a story in its own right.

This idea that reading a hypertext is comparable to producing a story is a common theme in early manifestos about the value of electronic writing,[25] but I would suggest that *Califia*'s claim that readers produce something not anticipated by the author is important as a component of its definition of fictionality as an archive. In chapter 2 I noted that writers cite (neglected) texts as the source of new writing, and that this appeal to the archive promises a form of future writing that harks back to and amplifies this archival resource. Particularly important in appeals to the archive is that this future work will transcend the disciplinary protocols that surround it. Much the same thing occurs in this hypertext, since Coverley appeals to the hypertext archive as a way to describe potential fiction, a story that emerges in the course of the reader's choices. Indeed, in some ways *Califia* is an even better example of the odd temporality of the archive, which we have noticed always points to the future. Futurity here is embodied in the nature of the hypertext which, rather than being a simple object to be studied, is a mechanism for reading.

Califia is unique neither in functioning as a database nor in appealing to the experience of reading to justify its fictionality. But what does make it especially valuable for our inquiry into the institutional positioning of electronic writing is that it draws attention to curious status of the text itself—is it the whole work, or is it the component documents?—which is implicit in all hypertext. The fluctuation between tool and text, between means of reading and fully formed story, is what makes this hypertext able to occupy the paradoxical futurity of the archive.[26] Although overblown claims about

---

25. This perspective is exemplified by Silvio Gaggi when he claims in *From Text to Hypertext: Decentering the Subject in Fiction, Film, the Visual Arts, and Electronic Media* (Philadelphia: University of Pennsylvania Press, 1997) that in hypertext "the distinction between reader and writer is attenuated, perhaps even dissolved entirely" (103). The most influential critique of this understanding of hypertext is Espen J. Aarseth's *Cybertext: Perspectives on Ergodic Literature* (Baltimore: Johns Hopkins University Press, 1997), which rightly notes that electronic works can constrain readers more than traditional codex texts (see particularly 76–86).

26. The definition of electronic works as tools is a frequently entertained although rarely fully explored possibility. Marie-Laure Ryan considers the definition of the electronic medium as a tool in *Narrative as Virtual Reality* (38). More recently, I have written a brief

how readers participate in authorship when reading a hypertext might make us miss it, there is a surprising link between this understanding of hypertext and Alice Walker's decidedly untechnological search for Hurston's grave. Both see fiction as the experience of an archive.

LYING

Talan Memmott's *Lolli's Apartment* is organized around the layout of the Knossos Labyrinth.[27] Readers move through this space, which has a loosely three-dimensional quality, encountering text and images. Particularly striking in contrast to more conventional hypertexts like *Califia* is that readers access these texts and images not just by clicking on clearly marked pathways but also by simply moving the cursor over parts of the screen. The images and text, too, obey a more complex screen logic than in most hypertexts, since in places it is possible to have several texts overlaid so that none is readable.

Thematically, *Lolli's Apartment* opposes the professor, who is the specialist concerned with reconstructing the past, to the Sophomore, who looks towards the future unrealistically. Describing "the professor's aliment," Memmott notes, "Specialists suffer from fear—always, already a ruin in contrast with the exuberant nature of the Sophomore. In effect, the capitulating professor, performing as the Dean's, [sic] mule, serves to buttress the crumbing walls of history, the shrinking time between now, nostalgia, and forgetting." This opposition between nostalgic interest in ruins and optimistic embrace of possibility parallels the tension in the work between reconstructing a story and moving through a visual space. When Memmott tells a story—as he does in his preface to the hypertext—he invokes the language of ruin and loss: "Lolli's Apartment is an experiment in the ruination of contexts and the reconstruction of this ruin; or, the gathering of its fragments.... As I developed the space, the actual UI for Lolli's Apartment, I abandoned my notes—all the narrative fodder I had collected was off limits. This is the first loss, forgetting culture... " (first ellipsis mine; second Memmott's). In contrast to this loss is the exuberant playfulness of visual text—the movement between objects that disregard the three-dimensional space of the labyrinth, and the overall sense that Memmott has created an object to be experienced more than a story to be reconstructed: "You will get lost. Maybe find yourself

---

essay on the topic for the *Electronic Book Review* (1997) called "Texts and Tools" (http://www.electronicbookreview.com/thread/electropoetics/spunoff).

27. *Lolli's Apartment* is available at http://www.heelstone.com/meridian/memmott.html.

going in circles. . . . Most everything is active and will take you somewhere else" (Memmott's ellipsis).

Although the playful nature of the text seems to be merely part of a common hypertext celebration of reader involvement that we see in *Califia,* in fact Memmott's work offers a much more specific explanation for the experience of reading that focuses on secrecy. Indeed, the labyrinth that provides the structure for the hypertext works to mislead the reader. Part of the nature of our investigation is to reveal secrets that others would prefer to be hidden. One path of particular significance launches by announcing, "the quickest way to gain a secret is through the initiation of scandal." Following this path leads to an investigation of "Frederick," apparently a reference to Nietzsche, the embodiment of the professor. We are shown a brief image of a woman, and then told, "Where Fredrick thought he'd seen a woman we find only words . . . " (Memmott's ellipsis). We are given a series of notebook entries that are described as "the fulcrum scurry toward the desired most." The screen is divided into two parts, one describing Frederick's struggle with the Sophomore, the other blank until rolled over, questioning, "What secrets do I keep?" It seems clear that the structure of Memmott's hypertext reflects this interest in revelation. Indeed, the emphasis on roll-overs rather than different hypertextual paths seems essentially a way of using screen space not as a way of moving from fragment to fragment and demanding reader choice but rather as a means of revealing information gradually. Several times in this hypertext Memmott has parts of a text that are gradually added to the screen as the user rolls-over or clicks on different words. Moving through *Lolli's Apartment,* in other words, is a matter of revealing secrets hidden among the fragments of this narrative.

The appeal to fragments and secrets reflects in a general way the understanding of fiction as a kind of a lie that I discussed in the third chapter. There I noted that when writers describe storytelling as a form of lying, it is in part a way to think about the nature of agency in composition, especially about the relationship between writing and the artifact of the page space. In Memmott's hypertext, likewise, writing is defined as misleading. Certainly it is true that Memmott is more interested in the revelation of secrets—and thus the nature of truth—than many of the contemporary writers that I discussed earlier. As I noted in chapter 3, lying is a way of defining creativity in the context of other restrictions; the best example of creating within the framework of institutional boundaries is the "fake book." Memmott's emphasis on play rather than reconstruction makes clear the difference between defining fiction as a lie and an archive. The superficial similarity between *Califia* and *Lolli's Apartment* gives way to different definitions of fictionality beneath. This definition of fictionality is obviously crucial to the institutional suture that Memmott accomplishes in *Lolli's Apartment*. The agency of investigation and play is invoked in some ways as it is in *Califia*, but the nature of scandal seems to me to give this text a very different framework for this agency. Memmott's text itself is a scandal—a borrowing and a ruining of received texts and objects. Our playful movement through the text is likewise a means of revelation. We are not investigating an archive in the way that we are in Coverley's story but rather allowing a lie to be revealed. This is why actual screen space is so much more important for Memmott. More generally, our interaction with the text plays not on the same features of searching and reading but on the movement of the text, the physical act of manipulating the mouse and moving across the screen.

STYLE

Wes Chapman's *Turning In* (1997) is an earlier and somewhat more conventional hypertext narrative.[28] Indeed, like Michael Joyce's influential *Afternoon* (1987), Chapman's story is constructed entirely of text and organized simply as a series of click-to-follow hyperlinks.[29] Readers pursue the plot, are given occasions to go in various narrative directions, and are sometimes forced to double-back to pick up other story lines. The story focuses on the many personal and career failures of Adri Sumner, a directionless Cornell graduate managing a pizza parlor. The principle structuring element of the story is a surreal trial—in which the author himself is called to the witness stand—that attempts to assign blame for Adri's failures. The novella reaches its climax when the author admits that the trial is a "farce" and abruptly ends the story (the section titled "Cavalry 10").

More than other hypertexts that I have discussed in this chapter, Chapman's story reflects the metafictional goal of drawing our attention to the composition of the story. Indeed, Chapman opens by characterizing himself as the author struggling with the keyboard on which he is composing this work:

> So here I am, typewriter in frnt of me again, with a box of blank pages and a head full of crusted-over nuggets of filled time. I don't know what it is that I need to write, nor why I am writing. I feel—not compelled, exactly, but

---

28. Wes Chapman, *Turning In*, diskette (Watertown, MA: Eastgate Systems, 1997).
29. Michael Joyce, *Afternoon: A Story*, diskette (Watertown, MA: Eastgate Systems, 1987).

CHAPTER 6

rather congested, the past running from me like snot from a runny nose. A delightful image, Adri, glad to see you're setting a proper tone. . . .

Once I would have claimed that I was writing a novel or a story, but time has cured me of that delusion.

The r key sticks.

The irony of composing a hypertext on a typewriter draws attention to the larger issue of the medium in which Chapman is working. As the sticking *r* key obviously reminds us, this is a work of words first and foremost. On the next screen, Chapman connects the composition of this work to the problems of imagining a beginning to his story: "But how should I begin? If this is really a journal, then there shouldn't even be any beginnings, only middles. Writing out a journal entry one should think only of capturing the moment, exprssing prcisely that one small moment of self-honesty or self-delusion; to think of a whole journal, as one might think of a novel, is to disrupt that process of getting the moment down honestly. The moment then has a place, a meaning foretold and a futur to forshadow. Life is falsified even as it is given a definite shape." As this introductory section goes on, it becomes clear that this concern for the future will be reflected in the story of Adri: "For I have spent my life waiting to begin, waiting for the moment. And then of course to write it out, to captur once and forall, where people could see, the completed Adri, the Adri who has begun. And that book would only be a beginning, the first in a long series of books that would transmit to their readers the rabid contentment of the already begun; and thus to become famous and loved, merly as supplement of course to the rbid contentment of the already begun."

Clearly Chapman's hypertext draws in part on the definition of fiction as a lie, and yet in other places his story seems to be trying to reconstruct experience. After all, at the end of this section the author announces, "I suppose that I could do worse than to begin by telling myself the trth, whether or not I am capable of believing it: that, like it or not—like my past or not—I have always already begun." Although lying is a theme here, the real struggle is neither to see through those lies to a real past (as in *Califia*) nor to thematize lying and scandal (as in *Lolli's Apartment*). Instead, *Turning In* describes a life stuck waiting to begin and woven of lies themselves. Chapman sees the intertwined and nonlinear nature of his hypertext as a way to understand the complex temporality of any human life. The trial that Adri endures attempts to assign blame and to define the present as a simple product of past wrongs. As the trial unravels, hope for such a simple revelation is shown to be misplaced. Instead, we have the experience of moving back and forth through time. Indeed, Chapman manages to make clever aesthetic use of one of the central qualities of hypertext writing—that individual textual elements will mean something very different depending on the order in which they are read. Although Chapman clearly wants to control our reading of the story to some extent—he specifically warns us against reading pages out of turn in the index—in fact a large part of the experience of the story depends on rereading, on encountering Adri's life as a mixture of events that reflect on both past and present. His life, in other words, is oddly timeless. The style of the hypertext here reflects the condition of human life as Chapman sees it. It is, in other words, a symptom of our own messy existence in and between times.

This belief in the impossibility of beginnings translates to the central parody of literary authority in the hypertext and thus its main suture. The court case that provides the most important conclusion to the story claims that "Mrs. Leah Summer, was an alcoholic, and was, while she was drunk, guilty of repeated abusive and neglectful behavior, and that her co-defendant, Mr. Adrian Sumner, Sr. abetted this behavior by not only failing to intervene but effectively abandoning them to their suffering." This investigation into Adri's background not only invokes the issue of parental authority (in his opening remarks, Adri's lawyer remarks that his parents are "invoking the forms of parental authority to make compulsory the child's attendance at a spectacle of drunken accusation and remorse"), but also that of literary authority. The defense attorney discovers a poem written by a much younger Adri, which he believes helps to explain his upbringing. To interpret this poem, the attorney calls to the witness stand Professor Gravely B. Little, an expert on poetry at a "Major University." This expert goes on to offer an elaborate interpretation of the poem only to have that interpretation in turn discounted by a second expert who offers a very different interpretation. In the end, even the second critic ends up unable to offer an explanation of guilt, limiting herself to an interpretation of the poem itself. Attempting to use such literary works for a practical purpose turns out to be fruitless. Through the lens provided by the institutional suturing that I have been describing in this chapter, it is easy to see Chapman's parody of literary authority in *Turning In* as a way of positioning his hypertext. The failure of this authority is its inability to understand the temporality of real human life, the fact that our lives have no simple beginnings and no direct causality. The playfulness of our interaction with this hypertext, our movement through various lexia at will, sutures the computer interface to the literary themes of this work. Chapman's invocation of the typewriter at the beginning of this story seems crucial in framing this story not as the product of a new media but as an aesthetic response to thematic problems that could have been produced even in older technologies. In other words, the game quality of this story is defined as an extension of a more prior concern for time whose roots are firmly in a literary tradition. More than any of the electronic texts that I have discussed in this chapter, *Turning In* uses its suturing to game protocols first and foremost as a critique of literary authority. This should be no surprise, since the other uses of the fiction-as-symptom definition that I described in chapter 4 likewise adopted a marginal position relative to literary authority.

ASSEMBLAGE

The final definition of fictionality circulating today in America is as a form of bricolage, as an act of creatively combining elements borrowed from other texts. This assemblage, I argued, reflects a response to market culture in which invention rather than creativity is the norm. Further, I noted that thinking about fiction as assemblage implies a position distinctly outside of literary institutions, since taking apart works is disrespectful. As Umberto Eco suggested in chapter 5, breaking texts down into component parts is something that you do with cult classics of a particular fan base rather than with the classics included in an institutionalized canon. This definition of fiction has an especially important role in how electronic media suture game and literary institutions. Indeed, few films that appeal to any part of the youth market fail to come to market accompanied by some sort of computer or video-game crossover. Likewise, the role-playing games that I discussed in that chapter have been directly translated to computer games. In this instance, little explanation seems necessary of how a particular definition of fictionality serves to bridge game and literary institutions.

I would like to close this overview of the varieties of fictionality circulating in electronic writing by considering a more explicitly literary example of the kind of bricolage that chapter 5 discusses. The need to create sutures between game and literary protocols means that these electronic works cannot adopt the position as outside of literary practices that *Dungeons and Dragons* adopts. Shelley Jackson's *Patchwork Girl* (1995) is a frequently discussed hypertext that rewrites Mary Shelley's *Frankenstein*—a work that itself is usually interpreted today as a commentary on the ways literary establishments marginalize female creativity.[30] As a hypertext that also stitches together materials from other sources into some new entity, *Patchwork Girl*

---

30. Shelley Jackson, *Patchwork Girl*, CD-ROM (Watertown, MA: Eastgate Systems, 1995).

is obviously an attempt to use the sort of borrowing that I have discussed in the previous chapter to do more explicitly literary work. Jackson herself announces at the outset of the hypertext, "I am buried here. You can resurrect me, but only piecemeal. If you want to see the whole, you will have to sew me together yourself." This introductory section ends with the reader "burdened with body parts" leaving the graveyard and announcing "[a] kind of resurrection has taken place." In several places the reader's choices through the text are represented as parts of a body.

It is clear that the central metaphor of the hypertext is that of joining. The monster remarks to the speaker of this story specifically about the nature of scarring. They are not merely cuts but also points of juncture, we are told. "More than that," says the monster, "Scar tissue does more than flaunt its strength by chronicling the assaults it has withstood. Scar tissue is new growth. And it is tougher than skin innocent of the blade." These junctures clearly parallel the hypertextual links that Jackson herself has created. Jackson is quite explicit on this point:

> Assembling these patched words in an electronic space, I feel half-blind, as if the entire text is within reach, but because of some myopic condition I am only familiar with from dreams, I can see only that part most immediately before me, and I have no sense of how that part relates to the rest. When I open a book I know where I am, which is restful. My reading is spatial and even volumetric. I tell myself, I am a third of the way down through a rectangular solid, I am a quarter of the way down the page, I am here on the page, here on this line, here, here, here. But where am I now? I am in a here and a present moment that has no history and no expectations for the future.

Such a form of writing, Jackson continues, means that her work has no history, no story, or "as many stories as I care to put together." The implication for *Patchwork Girl* is clear: reading a hypertext on the screen (rather than in the more tangible and spatially stable form of the codex book) means experiencing the complex temporality of life.

Jackson uses this definition of hypertext to position herself relative to literary institutions differently from the other hypertexts I have discussed. Unlike Chapman's hypertext, where temporality becomes the central issue through which the innovations of the electronic medium are understood, for Jackson what is important is the way that the impossibility of history means that any story is a composite of many. Likewise, in emphasizing mixture rather than source documents, *Patchwork Girl* departs in fundamental ways from *Califia*'s appeal to the archive. Indeed, *Patchwork Girl* is ultimately addressed to the nature of creativity and what it means to be an author. It is for this reason that Jackson's story reworks the themes defined by Mary Shelley's novel; justifying fictionality in *Patchwork Girl* means explaining how a certain kind of writing is produced and institutionalized. Consequently, Jackson understands the playfulness of her hypertext—its participation in game protocols—in a very different way. Play for her is not a matter of style as it is for Chapman but rather a whole new way of thinking about the creation of stories. Moving through *Patchwork Girl* is ultimately a matter of retracing the steps that Jackson has walked as she created her story. Thus, because of its need to create institutional sutures, *Patchwork Girl* tries to use the fictionality of assemblage not to adopt a position outside of literature like the games I discussed in chapter 5 but rather as a way to claim more traditional literary legitimacy.

In thinking about the game-like quality of *Patchwork Girl* as a matter of redefining how we make new stories, Jackson shares a great deal with the role-playing games that I discussed in chapter 5. There we saw that such games work by borrowing older stories and creating new forms of creativity out of their component parts. Jackson's hypertext is especially useful in contrast to Chapman's because they seem initially so similar: both were produced by the same publisher using the same interface (Eastgate's Storyspace program for writing and publishing hypertext) within two years of each other, both appeal to older literary technologies (the journal, the typewriter), and for both reading is a matter of moving from one discrete lexia or writing to another. Despite all of these superficial similarities, these two texts understand their aesthetic significance in very different ways; they define their own fictionality differently.

Putting It All Together in *Myst*

I have argued that electronic works are positioned between literary and game cultures, and that one of their central challenges is defining a notion of reader/player agency that sutures together these two institutions. In creating these sutures, writers must also define fictionality, since the purpose of creative writing will obviously shape the nature of reader agency. Since electronic works come out of many of the same populations within contemporary American culture—writers with literary aspirations, science fiction fans, and so on—that produced the works discussed in other chapters, it should be no surprise that when these works define fictionality they draw on the same sorts of definitions that I have been describing throughout this book.

In describing five "strands" of fictionality in this book as well as in this chapter, I no doubt have suggested that these definitions of fictionality are distinct. It should also be clear, however, that many texts either mix several definitions or invoke several before deciding on one. Although I have distinguished the definition of fictionality as a lie from fictionality as a myth, for example, it is clear that many works invoke both. Robert Coover's *Universal Baseball Association,* which I discussed briefly in chapter 5, clearly has some relationship to role-playing games.[31] At the same time, however, Coover's work draws heavily on myth; along with Barth, his oeuvre is the best example of the mythic justification for writing in postmodern fiction.[32] In chapter 5 I noted that Coover's novel does not appeal to the objects that make up role-playing games but instead places more emphasis on narrative events. This point of divergence is crucial to Coover's appeal to myth, since it is in such events that others find mythical meanings. We will recall the way that Barth appeals to the events that transcend their occasion when he defines his mythical writing. Coover's flirtation with role-playing games, we could say, is a point at which one definition of fiction comes up against and considers a competing definition. The result is less a kind of a hybrid form than a definition that remains aware of its alternatives. The same is true of the electronic works that I have been discussing. When Jackson describes reader choice, it is hard not to think of the alternative ways of thinking about reader agency explored by Chapman, Memmott, and Coverley. It is for this reason that I have defined fictionalizing in contemporary America as a series of "strands"—independent elements that twist together, frequently strengthening themselves by the differences between alternatives.

I will close by discussing *Myst* (1993), an influential computer game whose impact on subsequent literary/game suturing in electronic texts is hard to overestimate, and which seems to me to embody a kind of productive ambivalence about which definition of fictionality it wants to adopt.[33] *Myst* is famous not only for its early use of photorealistic three-dimensional environments, which at the time were a stunning departure from computer graphics, but also for its refusal to build in any of the sort of action and confrontation that we associate with video games. In *Myst,* players move around

---

31. Robert Coover, *The Universal Baseball Association, Inc.: J. Henry Waugh, Prop.* (New York: Plume, 1971).

32. See Kathryn Hume, "Robert Coover's Fiction: The Naked and the Mythic," *Novel* 12 (1979): 127–48.

33. Rand and Robyn Miller, *Myst,* CD-ROM (Novato, CA: Brøderbund, 1993).

a variety of deserted worlds solving puzzles but never facing danger (it is impossible to "die" in the game) or being forced to perform actions or motions that depend on hand-eye coordination. This is clearly a thinking person's game; indeed, the image of the intellectual creator is woven into the game itself. Atrus has created the various worlds that the player visits in *Myst* by writing longhand in old-fashioned books using a power that is never explained.

These books remain links to the worlds that are created, and on several occasions the reader must figuratively place a hand (actually the cursor) upon the book to be transported to this world. As the game progresses, it becomes clear that Atrus's two sons have become trapped in a book, and the game concludes by asking the player to choose which brother to trust and free. A number of critics have noted that this game is positioned quite explicitly as a literary product. This is true not only of the way that the game is packaged—the two brothers who created the game are listed as "authors" rather than directors or producers—but also in the justification that is given for the game as a whole.[34] The liner notes to the game explain its appeal: "You are about to be drawn into an amazing alternative reality. The entire game was designed from the ground up to draw you in with little or no extraneous distractions on the screen to interfere with the feeling of being there. Myst is not linear, it's not flat, it's not shallow. This is the most depth, detail and reality you've ever experienced in a game. Myst is real. And like real life, you don't die every five minutes." This game is justified on the basis of its realism conceived as literary mimesis: it is true to life not because it borrows specific historical facts like *Metal of Honor* but because our style of interaction in the game reflects the real world.

Several strands of fictionality circulate through this game. Clearly the game is imagined first and foremost as a style of experience: playing is like real life. Likewise, the game is also being offered up as an artifact, an artificial construction. Indeed, one of the most remarkable things about the game is that our ingress into the world is defined by a book that we (as the reader/narratee) are supposed to have found and used to enter into the world. Books are also the means of travel in *Myst,* so that the game as a whole constantly stages the act of being "caught up" in a book. In thinking about such artificial constructions, we are obviously confronting a work that draws our attention to its invention, its lie. *Myst* takes this even further by repeating the concern with page space that I noted in chapter 3; here the movement from place to

---

34. Steven Jones discusses literary appeals in *Myst* as well as its use of the book artifact in "The Book of *Myst* in the Late Age of Print," *Postmodern Culture* 7, no. 2 (1997), http://muse.jhu.edu/journals/pmc/v007/7.2jones.html.

place is imagined as selecting page space. Indeed, our pointer in the game echoes the pointing-finger dingbat that Steve Katz's *Exagggerations of Peter Prince* used to draw our attention to page space. The game also appeals to myths, both in its title and in the stories that inhabitants generate about the origins of their worlds. Atrus creates worlds by writing with a kind of quasi-divine power. Likewise, the game regularly invites us to explore books and archives as a way to understand the history of these worlds and to decide what our course of action should be. Indeed, to navigate these challenges players need to spend time in a partially destroyed library simply reading books and journals that provide the backstory for these worlds. Of the five strands of fictionality that I have discussed in this book, the only one that *Myst* does not invoke is the appeal to the bricolage that I associated with the role-playing game. This may at first seem surprising, since I noted above that such role playing is probably the most common thread in computer games. But it is clear that *Myst* wants to define itself as a literary alternative to what it sees as popular combat games; thus, its rejection of a fictionality based on role-playing games is natural. Indeed, role-playing games usually adopt a position outside of traditional literary reading protocols, while *Myst* clearly wants to emulate a literary experience.

How do these four remaining strands interact in *Myst*? Each offers its own way of suturing game and literature; indeed, we might see the game as betraying a kind of schizophrenia in its self-definitions. If *Myst* is important primarily because of the experience that it generates independent of the medium through which we view it, why then foreground the role of the book, through which we gain access to these worlds? If writing has a kind of mythical power to create worlds, such sweeping powers seem at odds with the detective work necessary to understand the archival origins and construction of these worlds. *Myst* is a game in which worlds are contained in archives, and their inhabitants live a strangely shadowy existence: they are both brought into existence by the power of the writing, and at the same time mere characters whose origins can be traced back to authorial notes. Indeed, precisely this conflict is the theme of the second of the *Myst* sequels, *Exile*. In this game the player is called back to Myst to help recover a book stolen by one of Atrus's creations—a person bitter because he feels abandoned by his creator, who is unable to return to his world because the book that would take him there has been destroyed.[35] Here clearly the mythical dimensions of writing come up against their archival limits, and the inhabitants are both products of writing and miraculously alive.

35. *Myst III: Exile*, CD-ROM (San Francisco: Ubisoft, 2001).

Appeals to such divergent definitions of fictionality will seem to mark *Myst* as an aesthetic failure, but the popularity of the game and the way in which it has become a model for a generation of games that has followed belie this problem. It may be the *Myst* was so influential in part because it created a space where all of these definitions of fictionality meet. This game is both style and myth, both lie and archive—just as the electronic medium seems to promise all these things to the nascent genre of computer games. Such a special location is the unique position from which *Myst* launches its claim that computer games can have literary aspirations. As such, it is a site of uniquely powerful suturing. More than anything, *Myst* reminds us that these strands of fictionality are means of defining the institutional identity of texts. *Myst*'s appeal to several mutually exclusive justifications for its fictionality embodies the debates about fictionality across contemporary literary culture in America.

CONCLUSION

Fictionality in the Public Sphere

Struggles over the nature and value of fiction are clearly one of the points where the concerns of literary critics become meaningful for a broader American public. The general trajectory of this book has been from the very literary arguments over postmodernism that provided the subject matter of the first chapter, to the intentional misuse of popular genre fiction in the role playing game in the fifth chapter. Throughout this book I have suggested that the struggle to define fiction means (among other things) defining the nature and the scope of literature. Competing definitions like the archive or the symptom suggest different ways that individuals can make fiction meaningful and provide different ways of negotiating the disciplinary expectations that usually come with literary study. Defining fictionality, in other words, is as much a matter of the larger public sphere as it is a matter of jockeying for power within publishing and academic institutions.

Although the way that I have approached the topic of contemporary fictionalizing depends heavily on social categories and emphasizes the competing claims to power by various groups within and just outside literary

CONCLUSION

institutions, often individual works of fiction are most politically important when their fictionality is ignored. In fact, if we think about the American fiction of the last half-century that had generated the greatest political discussion—if not actual political effects of the scope of *Uncle Tom's Cabin*—few of the works that I have discussed in this book will come to mind. The most rancorous debates about fiction frequently focus on issues of obscenity—first the famous court cases over *Ulysses* (1921) and *Tropic of Cancer* (1961), and then later over *Naked Lunch* (1966). Such novels generate public discussion and actual legal changes because of issues that have little to do directly with their own fictionality. This is true of other novels that have been described as scandalous despite not being directly involved in obscenity legislation, novels like Erica Jong's sexually explicit *Fear of Flying* (1973) or Bret Easton Ellis's story of recreational torture, *American Psycho* (1991).

One of the things that characterizes all these controversies is that they pay relatively little attention to the act of fictionalizing in the works. Indeed, many of these controversies focus not on whether or not a writer may (or should) *invent* stories about torture or sexual experimentation, but rather whether any representation of such topics should be allowed into the public sphere. Shifting the topic back towards aesthetic concerns can in fact shut down discussion of such political issues. One defense of *American Psycho*, for example, is to insist that it be judged as art rather than as an engagement in contemporary sexual politics. Norman Mailer's *Vanity Fair* essay on the book asks directly, "What is art? What can be so important about art that we may have to put up with a book like this?"[1] In her analysis of the controversy, Rosa Eberly argues that in forcing these debates back from broad public topics towards specialized concerns of artistic value, their ability to spark public discussion is muted: "In the twentieth century, literary public spheres have been most robust when institutional, expert literary critics have had the least cultural authority. The rise of English studies and the professionalization of something call first 'literary critic' and then 'literary theorists' relegated the opinions of nonexpert or citizen critics to a position of relatively little cultural authority."[2] In this context, Mailer's question about the aesthetic value of Ellis's novel—while an appropriate and perhaps even essential question for members of literary and academic institutions—works to render irrelevant the public debates that surrounded the novel. As Eberly remarks, "Despite the way Mailer's argument changes the contours of the nation-wide literary

1. Norman Mailer, "Children of the Pied Piper: Mail on 'American Psycho,'" *Vanity Fair* (March 1991), 159. Cited in Rosa A. Eberly, *Citizen Critics: Literary Public Spheres* (Urbana: University of Illinois Press, 2000), 124.

2. Eberly, *Citizen Critics*, 9.

public sphere that formed in response to the publication of *American Psycho*, these discourses demonstrate that literature can serve a social function, even today, by engendering rational-critical debate in a discursively formed public sphere among real individuals who share substantial common interests" (130).

It seems, then, that fiction enters most powerfully into public debate when it pretends not to be fiction at all—or, to the extent that it suspends questions of its truthfulness or inventedness—for the sake of the issues raised by the work. Such works neither insist on their veracity nor do they make a strong claim for themselves as the product of invention. This is the direction that Ronald Sukenick's later work went. In his collection of essays, *Narralogues: Truth in Fiction* (2000), Sukenick suggests treating narrative as a form of argument: "My point is that all fiction can be profitably regarded as argument. When you define fiction by representation you end up confining it to realism at some level and arguing that fiction, as a form of make-believe, is a way of lying to get at the truth, which if not palpably stupid is certainly round-about and restrictive. My approach frees fiction from the obligations of mimesis."[3] Sukenick sees defining narrative as argument as a way to reclaim a public importance for narrative: "While not conceding the realm of pleasure, narrative as rhetoric, in its consideration of relation to an audience, is interactive, the Wordsworthian 'man talking to men,' as it were, and more frankly democratic in its literary aspect than narrative as entertainment, which encourages a hidden intellectual passivity" (5). Whether or not Sukenick's definition of narrative as argument is valid, it is easy to see it as a response to the issue of this book, the need to define the nature and usefulness of fiction. In choosing to forego a theory of fictionality for the sake of rhetoric, Sukenick claims a direct role in the public sphere.

There are ways that fiction can be used for public debate without rejecting the category entirely and foregoing the issue of invention. Martha Nussbaum argues for the importance of fiction as a component of public debate in *Poetic Justice* (1995). In making a claim for "the characteristics of the literary imagination as a public imagination, an imagination that will steer judges in their judging, legislators in their legislating, policy makers in measuring the quality of life of people near and far,"[4] Nussbaum depends on a very traditional definition of fiction as the imagining of possible people: "Why novels and not histories or biographies? My central subject is the ability to imagine

---

3. Ronald Sukenick, *Narralogues: Truth in Fiction* (Albany: State University of New York Press, 2000), 2.
4. Martha C. Nussbaum, *Poetic Justice: The Literary Imagination and Public Life* (Boston: Beacon Press, 1995), 3.

what it is like to live the life of another person who might, given changes in circumstances, be oneself or one of one's loved ones. So my answer to the history question comes straight out of Aristotle. Literary art, he said, is 'more philosophical' than history, because history simply shows us 'what happened,' whereas works of literary art show us 'things such as might happen' in a human life" (5). Nussbaum's explicitly classical theory of fiction may reflect an antiquated understanding of literary creation, but it makes possible very straightforward claims about the value of literary study.[5] Even among the five definitions of fictionality that I have discussed in this book, some make possible fairly straightforward public debate. Treating fiction as an archive of lost material has enabled canon debates that made their way into broad public awareness. Likewise, the willingness to borrow characters and settings from fiction evidenced in the role-playing game can become the stuff of broad public discourse. Benjamin Hoff's popular *The Tao of Pooh* (1982), for example, borrows a popular fictional character for the sake of articulating Eastern philosophy for a nonspecialist audience. Like Nussbaum's appeal to Victorian fictionality, both of these strands of contemporary fictionality seem to make possible forms of public debate.

Other definitions of fictionality will seem to have little role in the public sphere, even though they are quite clearly political in some sense. To take an example from the first chapter, if John Barth's definition of postmodernism as myth denies this writing a direct engagement with contemporary political reality—and we might recall that Barth claims in *The Friday Book* that his novel *Chimera* "has nothing to do with politics"—it is also clear that this definition does a certain kind of work in including some writers and excluding others. That work is political to the extent that it is about the disposition of power and authority in a public space—in this case, in the literature classroom and the postmodernism anthology. These appeals to invention reflect and in some cases justify larger patterns of making in the culture as a whole—as I suggested in the fifth chapter. More than this, these debates over canonicity and the proper use of fictionality reflect struggles over the nature of literary study. It seems quite obvious, however, that this understanding of literary politics is quite different from the politics described by Eberly. Such debates are less accessible to a general public than those prompted by the fictionality of the archive or assemblage.

    5. Although I cannot digress into a discussion of nineteenth-century fictionality, it seems to me that even in Dickens's *Hard Times*, which Nussbaum uses as her main example, fictionality is not so simple. See, for example, Nina Auerbach's discussion of fictionality and the ghostly immortality accorded to fictional characters by Dickens's contemporaries in *Woman and the Demon: The Life of a Victorian Myth* (Cambridge, MA: Harvard University Press, 1982), 192.

It may seem natural, then, to suggest two fairly distinct facets of literary politics: the narrow political struggle over literary institutions and the larger public policy debates into which literary writing may intrude in specific circumstances. We might refer to these two strains as the Pierre Bourdieu and Jürgen Habermas interpretations of literature in the public sphere. As I have noted throughout this study, Bourdieu describes literary production as a matter of position taking within a "force-field" of social power: "A number of the practices and representations of artists and writers . . . can only be explained by reference to the field of power, inside of which the literary (etc.) field is itself in a dominated position. The field of power is the space of relations of force between agents or between institutions having in common the possession of the capital necessary to occupy the dominant positions in different fields (notably economic or cultural). It is the site of struggles between holders of different powers (or kinds of capital)."[6] Habermas, in contrast, sees the advent of literary writing as one of the foundations for the modern public sphere:

> The criteria of generality and abstractness characterizing legal norms had to have a peculiar obviousness for privatized individuals who, by communicating with each other in the public sphere of the world of letters, confirmed each other's subjectivity as it emerged from their spheres of intimacy. For as a public they were already under the implicit law of the parity of all cultivated persons, whose abstract universality afforded the sole guarantee that the individuals subsumed under it in an equally abstract fashion, as "common human beings," were set free in their subjectivity precisely by this parity.[7]

These are, of course, quite different descriptions of the nature of literary discourse as a component of larger social struggles. For Bourdieu, literature is a site of struggle; for Habermas, literature (or letters) is a protected sphere where the abstract claims of all individuals can be weighed. As Elizabeth Harries remarks, "Unlike Habermas's idealized model of Enlightenment discourse, a unified linguistic universe where all ideas can be lucidly and forcefully presented because all the participants are rational equals, Bourdieu's model reflects his understanding of the charged and stratified space in which

---

6. Pierre Bourdieu, *The Rules of Art: Genesis and Structure of the Literary Field*, trans. Susan Emanuel (Stanford, CA: Stanford University Press, 1995), 215.

7. Jürgen Habermas, *The Structural Transformation of the Public Sphere: An Inquiry into a Category of Bourgeois Society*, trans. Thomas Burger (Cambridge, MA: MIT Press, 1989), 54.

ideas are exchanged and placed in competition with each other."[8] The strength of Habermas's theory is the suggestion that fictional discourse moves beyond the particular conflicts that define jockeying for canonicity to take on a role within debates that transcend literary reputation and cultural capital. It is in this latter context that fictional discourse can address most directly political issues.

Such a blunt duality between Bourdieu and Habermas seems to me, however, to simplify the dynamics of fictionalizing that I have described in this study. In particular, I would return to the example of the American imaginary as described in the second chapter. There I noted that Warhol offers work as an antidote to the aura, and more generally describes the way that attention to the material conditions of production and social performance seems to transcend the simpler matter of cultural capital and institutional position taking. This emphasis on work dovetails with recent American studies research on the social imaginary as a collection of objects through which we negotiate in our everyday lives. We become aware of the work of social or artistic performance on the cusp between institutional positions—just where our accidents become fictional or where our archival starting point promises to produce a discipline. Such a process of "becoming fictional" describes a social condition where the categories of literature can be glimpsed in their operation. Such glimpses seem to be somewhere between Bourdieu's image of a hermetic literary world where writers and critics struggle among themselves for cultural and economic capital and Habermas's description of an abstract sphere for public debate.

The recognition of work and the process of becoming-fictional seems to me to describe the general cultural milieu of contemporary American literary culture. In the previous chapter I noted the work of institutional sutures, and this kind of suturing together of overlapping, possibly contradictory definitions of fiction is another place where work can be recognized. In that chapter I emphasized what we might describe as Bourdieu's side of this equation—the way that these sutures define positions within a literary institution. But we can also describe these sutures through Habermas's conception of the public sphere as well, since these sorts of game-like texts become the means by which we can discuss the nature of play and reading. A better example is *The Matrix*, a work which my fifth chapter shows largely fails to cohere as an articulation of Baudrillardian postmodernism, but which clearly provides a tool for viewers to think about media and reality. The best argument

---

8. Elizabeth W. Harries, "'Out in the Left Field': Charlotte Smith's Prefaces, Bourdieu's Categories, and the Public Sphere," *Modern Language Quarterly* 58 (1997): 471.

for *The Matrix*'s power to provoke thought about philosophy outside of the discipline itself is an academic book like *The Matrix and Philosophy* aimed at popular audiences. As one of a series of books discussing philosophical issues raised by popular culture texts—others include *The Simpsons and Philosophy* and *Seinfeld and Philosophy*—this book clearly sees a fictional text as providing the occasion to articulate issues debated by academic philosophers for a nonspecialist audience.[9] Indeed, these books are quite explicitly offered up as discipline-crossing exercises. *The Matrix and Philosophy* specifically defines itself as an alternative to philosophy courses taught by professors: "Not everyone attends college and, sadly, not everyone who attends college takes a philosophy course. While Philosophy 101 is an ideal setting in which to study closely and discuss passionately the life of Socrates, there's no need to wait for an opportunity that may never come."[10]

This kind of intermediary use of fictional texts in a public forum reflects the stranded nature of contemporary American fictionality. Indeed, part of the appeal of a book like *The Simpsons and Philosophy* is its playful way of negotiating the border between definitions of fiction. The same is true of the popular series of academic overviews of philosophy like *Derrida for Beginners* written using comic-book formatting.[11] These sorts of books are not, I think, so much a dumbing down of philosophical or literary discourse as a playful reflection on the different ways in which literary texts can be used. We might contrast them to *CliffsNotes,* which do much the same thing but have a clearly defined institutional purpose: to prepare students for difficult or neglected subjects. To place these two series of popular quasi-academic books side by side is to recognize how important the tension between popular-fictional and academic-literary discourse is to the success of a book like *Introducing Derrida*. No matter how clear and direct a nongraphic version of this book might be, removing the transgressive page design would destroy the institutional positioning that is essential to its appeal. In a book like *Derrida for Beginners* or *The Matrix and Philosophy* a question is implicitly being asked: what do you do with a fictional text? What do you pay academic-style attention to, and why can't subjects be handled by (popular) styles usually

---

9. William Irwin, Mark T. Conard, and Aeon J. Skoble, eds., *The Simpsons and Philosophy: The D'oh! of Homer* (Chicago: Open Court, 2001); William Irwin, ed., *Seinfeld and Philosophy: A Book about Everything and Nothing* (Chicago: Open Court, 1999).

10. William Irwin, "Computers, Caves, and Oracles: Neo and Socrates," in *The Matrix and Philosophy: Welcome to the Desert of the Real,* ed. William Irwin (Chicago: Open Court, 2002), 5.

11. Jim Powell, *Derrida for Beginners,* illustrated by Jan Howell (Danbury, CT: ForBeginners, 1997), 47.

reserved for fiction like cartoons?[12] In this sense, a book like *Derrida for Beginners* is not really an attempt to use a marginalized narrative form for serious purposes—like the use of the graphic novel format in Art Spiegelman's *Maus*. It is, rather, a way of creating a space for inquiry into topics marked by institutionally overdetermined forces.

Such questions are not exactly the position taking that we would associate with Bourdieu—indeed, the cultural capital acquired by reading *The Matrix and Philosophy* strikes me as rather limited—but nor are they a matter of the broad public topics that Eberly describes using Habermas. These works raise nonliterary topics while at the same time gesturing to the problems in our definition of the fictional, the literary, and the popular. These works use these problems as a way to clear some space for themselves amid conflicting disciplinary claims and to get to issues (Derrida's philosophy) otherwise crushed beneath academic expectations. These works are not in this regard parodies of academic studies but rather earnest books that nonetheless evoke conflicting definitions of fictionality (what, really, are we supposed to get out of watching a film like *The Matrix*?) in order to raise real issues that may be difficult to approach from outside the academy. A book like *The Tao of Pooh* is possible, I would suggest, only because the nature of fictionality in a classic children's book like this is in question. What is the point of a book like this? Is it merely to entertain children? To teach moral lessons? Pooh emerges here as a figure available for reuse—somewhat like the literary creatures that make up a *Dungeons and Dragons* game that I discussed in the fifth chapter—but also as a personal, remembered reference point from childhood that also invokes the archive of the second chapter. This is part of the joke that makes these sorts of books possible—the uncertainty about just what appropriate uses fiction can be put to. As the author Benjamin Hoff remarks to Pooh in his introduction, "When informed of my intentions, the scholars exclaimed, 'Pre*pos*terous!' and things like that."[13] This ambiguity may seem to be a problem, and attempts to reclaim a classical justification for fiction by philosophers like Nussbaum suggests a nostalgia for a broadly accepted definition that gives legitimacy to fiction. Looking at the messy fictionality of *Dungeons and Dragons*, *The Tao of Pooh*, or *Myst*, however, it is difficult not to feel that these ambiguities and conflicts are also energizing and empowering. If a book like *The Matrix and Philosophy* strikes some academic critics and philosophers as trivial, it also suggests the real possibility of bringing

12. Another good example of this sort of playing with disciplinary boundaries is the series of literary theory trading cards produced by Theory.org.uk (http://www.theorycards.org.uk/).

13. Benjamin Hoff, *The Tao of Pooh*, illus. Ernest H. Shepard (New York: Dutton, 1982), x.

into debates about traditionally academic issues readers who normally would be excluded by disciplinary rules.

I hope that this book has also made clear that speaking of *the* literary institution is a mistake. My discussion has shown that many different institutional investments make up the contemporary writing scene, and that even writers who want to position themselves against the literary establishment often mean different things in doing so. Alice Walker critiques literary institutions in the form of the canon of American literature when she investigates Hurston's life and burial. Steve Katz critiques literary institutions when he confronts the corporate board that would push his novel into certain well-known directions beyond his control. There is some overlap between the academic institution that Walker challenges and the publishing institution that Katz criticizes; at the same time, these are clearly distinct entities and opposing them necessarily takes different forms. In this regard, William Paulson is surely right when he argues that literary culture is "a nonstandard term, one that brings together the several related ways in which literature is part of culture and in which there is a culture associated with literature."[14] It is because of this multiplicity of literary culture that Bourdieu's description of the way that institutions police their boundaries seems to me not merely mistaken but fundamentally misleading. While there is no doubt that such boundaries are an element of contemporary literary practice, it is equally clear that there are many groups with equal claim to hegemony and consequently many different, frequently conflicting boundaries at work within contemporary writing. Individual literary works frequently draw their energy by adopting a position that references several different institutions and consequently appeal to several different definitions of fictionality. It is for this reason that Robert Coover's *The Universal Baseball Association* can invoke fictionality as myth and fictionality as assemblage as I noted in the sixth chapter. The game described in this novel in some ways appears to be an early version of fantasy baseball, since the events described are randomly generated using dice, and yet at the same time those events come to take on mythic significance in the life of its creator, as the quirky death of a promising young player becomes the basis a religion among later generations.[15] In mixing together these definitions of fictionality, novels like this have the power to help readers think through many elements of our experience of stories, and many ways of justifying their value.

14. William Paulson, *Literary Culture in a World Transformed: A Future for the Humanities* (Ithaca, NY: Cornell University Press, 2001), 26.
15. Robert Coover, *The Universal Baseball Association, Inc.: J. Henry Waugh, Prop.* (New York: Plume, 1971).

CONCLUSION

Even more important than the multiplicity of institutions at work in contemporary American culture is the fact that there is no simple *outside* to these institutions. In the fourth chapter I argued that "cyberpunk" science fiction got much of its energy from its position both outside and inside of our literary expectations. More importantly, the debates that surrounded this movement reflect a broader shift away from many of the authorities that defined literature and its meaning in the past. Such oppositional forms of literary practice remain grounded in their critique of these same institutions. Even the role-playing games that I discussed in the fifth chapter participate in theoretical patterns that are evident in academic criticism as well, linking popular and university uses of fictional stories in unexpected ways. This mixture of the literary and nonliterary contexts for using contemporary fictionality is especially evident in the electronic textuality that I discussed in the final chapter. Many of these works have explicitly literary aspirations, while others claim to be nothing more than games. My discussion showed that there is no particular difference between how these works define their fictionality: a game like *Metal of Honor* can appeal to physical artifacts in storytelling just as much as Katz's metafictional novel *The Exagggerations of Peter Prince*. And these are not merely incidental similarities unrelated to the literary appeals of the two works; instead, both works define the power of their fictionality by referencing the object that provides the disciplinary grounding for their fiction making. Both works understand their fictionality against and through our expectations about literature.

Finally, as the example of electronic textuality suggests, the literary framework for thinking about fictionality is not immediately or fundamentally changed by the introduction of new technologies. In recent years a small industry has grown up among critics who link the passing of literary experience with the changing technological means by which we encounter the story. Sven Birkerts, for example, has celebrated a traditional "shadow life of reading" intimately connected to the printed book as a physical artifact. He opens *The Gutenberg Elegies* (1994) by describing a world changed by technology: "Suddenly it feels like everything is posed for change; the slower world that many of us grew up with dwindles in the rearview mirror. The stable hierarchies of the printed page—one of the defining norms of that world—are being superseded by the rush of impulses through freshly minted circuits."[16] Even critics more sympathetic to technological changes have, at times, been guilty of assuming that the introduction of new media will auto-

---

16. Sven Birkerts, *The Gutenberg Elegies: The Fate of Reading in an Electronic Age* (New York: Fawcett Columbine, 1994), 3.

matically produce a change in the nature of textual experience.[17] My discussion has shown, however, that what Birkerts calls the "displacement of the page by the screen" (3) does not immediately produce a different definition of fictionality or a rejection of literary institutions. Indeed, what is particularly striking in the sixth chapter is that the same definitions of fictionality that we could observe in decidedly printed texts can also be observed in electronic stories and games. The narratives that I discussed in that chapter are not, of course, independent of their medium; all of the works were concerned with exploring the organizational possibilities opened up by their electronic form. But new technologies do not immediately produce new forms of fictionality. As Paulson notes, it is "crucial to remember, when thinking about the role of literature, print culture, or any cultural product or formation from the past, that many institutions, practices, and assumptions associated with the print era are likely to persist for a long time, just as books are still being printed and read today."[18] I have shown that the definitions of fictionality created in print culture do more than just persist into electronic textuality; they provide the basis for thinking about what it means to tell a made-up story in these new forms. In this sense I agree with those critics working on "media ecologies" that see continuities between print and electronic media, since they both reflect more basic questions about knowledge, information, and imagination.[19] If technology does lead to changes in the nature of reading and interacting with fiction, new forms that emerge will do so by initially referencing the existing definitions of fictionality that are available.

In the end, what is most important about the study of fictionality is that it reminds us how much our experience of made-up stories is entangled in the way that we define literature, media, publishing, and popular culture. Each of the strands of fictionality depends on a complex mixture of definitions, and each involves adopting a complex position inside and outside different contemporary institutions. The five strands of fictionality that I have defined in this book are not simply five different possibilities but also components of a single contemporary American milieu in which our understanding of what fiction is and what it's good for is both ambiguous and, for that reason, fertile.

17. A good example of this is Mark Hansen's suggestion in *Embodying Technesis: Technology beyond Writing* (Ann Arbor: University of Michigan Press, 2000) that changing technology fundamentally alters the nature of human experience (1). Hansen goes on to argue that critics have denied what he sees as a fundamental extradiscursive change that can be directly attributed to the technology itself.

18. Paulson, *Literary Culture*, 138.

19. See, for example, Matthew Fuller, who in *Media Ecologies: Materialist Energies in Art and Technoculture* (Cambridge, MA: MIT Press, 2005) describes literature as "a part of a subset of media, and thus of discursive storage, calculation, and transmission systems" (4).

WORKS CITED

Aarseth, Espen J. *Cybertext: Perspectives on Ergotic Literature*. Baltimore: Johns Hopkins University Press, 1997.
Abish, Walter. *How German Is It?* New York: New Directions, 1980.
Acker, Kathy. "Devoured by Myths: An Interview with Sylvère Lotringer." In *Hannibal Lecter, My Father*, edited by Sylvère Lotringer, 1–24. New York: Semiotext(e), 1991.
———. *Empire of the Senseless*. New York: Grove, 1988.
American McGee's Alice. CD-ROM. Redwood City, CA: EA Games, 2000.
Anderson, Benedict. *Imagined Communities: Reflections on the Origin and Spread of Nationalism*. Rev. ed. London: Verson, 1991.
Anderson, Perry. *The Origins of Postmodernity*. London: Verso, 1998.
Anderson, Walter Truett. *Reality Isn't What It Used to Be: Theatrical Politics, Ready-to-Wear Religion, Global Myths, Primitive Chic, and Other Wonders of the Postmodern World*. San Francisco: Harper & Row, 1990.
Andrews, Jim. *Arteroids*. http://www.vispo.com/arteroids/index.htm.
———. "Games, Po, Art, Play & Arteroids 2.03." http://www.vispo.com/arteroids/onarteroids.htm.
Aristotle. *The Complete Works of Aristotle*. Edited by Jonathan Barnes. Princeton, NJ: Princeton University Press, 1984.

Auerbach, Erich. *Mimesis: The Representation of Reality in Western Literature.* Translated by Willard Trask. New York: Anchor, 1957.

Auerbach, Nina. *Woman and the Demon: The Life of a Victorian Myth.* Cambridge, MA: Harvard University Press, 1982.

Baeten, Jan. "A Remediation's Remediation?" *Electronic Book Review* (2004). http://www.electronicbookreview.com/thread/imagenarrative/designflaw.

Baker, Richard, Travis Stout, and James Wyatt. *Player's Guide to Faerûn.* Renton, WA: Wizards of the Coast, 2004.

Baldur's Gate. CD-ROM. Edmonton: Bioware, 1998.

Balsamo, Anne. *Technologies of the Gendered Body: Reading Cyborg Women.* Durham, NC: Duke University Press, 1996.

Barth, John. *Chimera.* New York: Random House, 1972.

———. *The End of the Road.* 1958. Rev. ed. Garden City, NY: Doubleday, 1967.

———. *The Friday Book: Essays and Other Nonfiction.* Baltimore: Johns Hopkins University Press, 1984.

———. *Further Fridays: Essays, Lectures, and Other Nonfiction, 1984–94.* Boston: Little, Brown, 1995.

———. *Giles Goat-Boy: Or, The Revised New Syllabus.* 1966. Garden City: Anchor, 1987.

———. *LETTERS: A Novel.* 1979. Normal, IL: Dalkey Archive, 1994.

———. *Lost in the Funhouse: Fiction for Print, Tape, Live Voice.* 1968. New York: Anchor, 1988.

———. *Sabbatical: A Romance.* New York: G. P. Putnam's Sons, 1982.

———. *The Sot-Weed Factor.* Rev. ed. Garden City, NY: Doubleday, 1967.

Barthelme, Donald. *Come Back, Dr. Caligari.* Boston: Little, Brown, 1964.

———. "The Joker's Greatest Triumph." In *Come Back, Dr. Caligari,* 147–58. Boston: Little, Brown, 1964.

———. *The King.* New York: Penguin, 1990.

———. *Unspeakable Practices, Unnatural Acts.* New York: Farrar, Straus and Giroux, 1968.

Barthes, Roland. *S/Z.* Translated by Richard Miller. New York: Noonday, 1974.

Bartlett, Laura, and Thomas B. Byers. "Back to the Future: The Humanist *Matrix.*" *Cultural Critique* 53 (2003): 28–46.

Baudrillard, Jean. *America.* Translated by Chris Turner. London: Verso, 1988.

———. *Simulacra and Simulation.* Translated by Sheila Faria Glaser. Ann Arbor: University of Michigan Press, 1994.

Baumbach, Jonathan. "Who Do They Think They Are? A Personal History of the Fiction Collective." *TriQuarterly* 43 (Fall 1978): 625–34.

Bellamy, Joe David. "Introduction." In *Superfiction, or The American Story Transformed: An Anthology,* edited by Joe David Bellamy, 3–20. New York: Vintage, 1975.

———. *The New Fiction: Interviews with Innovative American Writers.* Urbana: University of Illinois Press, 1974.

Bender, John. *Imagining the Penitentiary: Fiction and the Architecture of Mind in Eighteenth-Century England.* Chicago: University of Chicago Press, 1987.

Bennett, David. "Wrapping Up Postmodernism." *Textual Practice* 1, no. 3 (1987): 243–61.

Bennington, Geoffrey. "RIP." In *Futures: Of Jacques Derrida,* edited by Richard Rand, 1–17. Stanford, CA: Stanford University Press, 2001.

Bercovitch, Sacvan, ed. *Reconstructing American Literary History.* Cambridge, MA: Harvard University Press, 1986.

Berlant, Lauren. *The Anatomy of Nation Fantasy: Hawthorne, Utopia, and Everyday Life.* Chicago: University of Chicago Press, 1991.

Bertens, Hans. *The Idea of the Postmodern: A History.* London: Routledge, 1995.
Berubé, Michael. "Public Image Limited: Political Correctness and the Media's Big Lie." In *Debating P.C.: The Controversy over Political Correctness on College Campuses,* edited by Paul Berman, 124–49. New York: Laurel, 1992.
Bhabha, Homi K. "DissemiNation: Time, Narrative, and the Margins of the Modern Nation." In *Nation and Narration,* edited by Homi K. Bhabha, 291–322. London: Routledge, 1990.
Birkerts, Sven. *The Gutenberg Elegies: The Fate of Reading in an Electronic Age.* New York: Fawcett Columbine, 1994.
Black & White. CD-ROM. Redwood City, CA: Electronic Arts, 2001.
Bloom, Allan. *The Closing of the American Mind.* New York: Simon and Schuster, 1987.
Bloom, Harold. *How to Read and Why.* New York: Scribner, 2000.
Bolter, Jay David, and Richard Grusin. *Remediation: Understanding New Media.* Cambridge, MA: MIT Press, 1999.
Boorstin, Daniel J. *The Image: A Guide to Pseudo-Events in America.* 1961. New York: Atheneum, 1975.
Bourdieu, Pierre. *The Logic of Practice.* Translated by Richard Nice. Stanford, CA: Stanford University Press, 1990.
———. *The Rules of Art: Genesis and Structure of the Literary Field.* Translated by Susan Emanuel. Stanford, CA: Stanford University Press, 1995.
Brinker, Menachem. "Theme and Interpretation." In *The Return of Thematic Criticism,* edited by Werner Sollors, 21–37. Cambridge, MA: Harvard University Press, 1993.
Brown, Homer Obed. *Institutions of the English Novel: From Defoe to Scott.* Philadelphia: University of Pennsylvania Press, 1997.
Brown, Norman O. *Life Against Death: The Psychoanalytical Meaning of History.* Middletown, CT: Wesleyan University Press, 1959.
Butler, Judith. *Bodies That Matter: On the Discursive Limits of "Sex."* New York: Routledge, 1993.
Capote, Truman. *In Cold Blood: A True Account of a Multiple Murder and Its Consequences.* New York: Random House, 1965.
Carby, Hazel V. "The Politics of Fiction, Anthropology, and the Folk: Zora Neale Hurston." In *New Essays on* Their Eyes Were Watching God, edited by Michael Awkward, 71–93. Cambridge: Cambridge University Press, 1990.
Casper, Scott E., Joanne D. Chaison, and Jeffrey D. Groves, eds. *Perspectives on American Book History: Artifacts and Commentary.* Amherst: University of Massachusetts Press, 2002.
Castoriadis, Cornelius. *The Imaginary Institution of Society.* Translated by Kathleen Blamey. Cambridge, MA: MIT Press, 1987.
Cayley, John. "The Code Is Not the Text (Unless It Is the Text)." *Electronic Book Review* (2002). http://www.electronicbookreview.com/thread/electropoetics/literal.
Chabon, Michael. *The Amazing Adventures of Kavalier & Clay: A Novel.* New York: Picador, 2000.
Chapman, Wes. *Turning In.* Diskette. Watertown, MA: Eastgate Systems, 1997.
Cochran, Terry. *Twilight of the Literary: Figures of Thought in the Age of Print.* Cambridge, MA: Harvard University Press, 2001.
Connor, Steven. *Postmodernist Culture: An Introduction to Theories of the Contemporary.* 2d ed. London: Blackwell, 1997.
Coover, Robert. *A Night at the Movies: Or, You Must Remember This.* New York: Collier, 1988.

———. "'Nothing but Darkness and Talk?': Writers' Symposium on Traditional Values and Iconoclastic Fiction." *Critique* 31 (1990): 233–55.
———. *Pricksongs & Descants*. New York: Plume, 1969.
———. *The Public Burning*. New York: Viking, 1977.
———. "Statement." In *Statements 2: New Fiction*, edited by Jonathan Baumbach and Peter Spielberg, 7–9. New York: Fiction Collective, 1977.
———. *The Universal Baseball Association, Inc.: J. Henry Waugh, Prop.* New York: Plume, 1971.
Cornis-Pope, Marcel. *Narrative Innovation and Cultural Rewriting in the Cold War and After*. New York: Palgrave, 2001.
Costa Lima, Luiz. *The Dark Side of Reason: Fictionality and Power*. Translated by Paulo Henriques Britto. Stanford, CA: Stanford University Press, 1992.
Costikyan, Greg. "A Farewell to Hexes." http://www.costik.com/spisins.html.
Coulter, Ann H. *Slander: Liberal Lies about the American Right*. New York: Crown, 2002.
Coverley, M. D. *Califia*. CD-ROM. Watertown, MA: Eastgate Systems, 2000.
Crittenden, Charles. *Unreality: The Metaphysics of Fictional Objects*. Ithaca, NY: Cornell University Press, 1991.
Danto, Arthur. *Philosophizing Art: Selected Essays*. Berkeley: University of California Press, 1999.
Davenport, Guy. *Da Vinci's Bicycle: Ten Stories*. Baltimore: Johns Hopkins University Press, 1979.
———. *The Geography of Imagination: Forty Essays*. New York: Pantheon, 1981.
Davis, Lennard J. *Factual Fictions: The Origins of the English Novel*. Philadelphia: University of Pennsylvania Press, 1996.
Debord, Guy. *The Society of the Spectacle*. 1967. Translated by Donald Nicholson-Smith. New York: Zone Books, 1994.
Delany, Samuel R. "Is Cyberpunk a Good Thing or a Bad Thing?" *Mississippi Review* 47/48 (1988): 28–35.
———. *Shorter Views: Queer Thoughts & the Politics of the Paraliterary*. Middletown, CT: Wesleyan University Press, 1999.
Deleuze, Gilles, and Félix Guattari. *A Thousand Plateaus: Capitalism and Schizophrenia*. Translated by Brian Massumi. Minneapolis: University of Minnesota Press, 1987.
DeLillo, Don. *Libra*. New York: Viking, 1988.
Der Derian, James. "The Simulation Syndrome: From War Games to Game Wars." *Social Text* 8, no. 2 (1990): 187–92.
Derrida, Jacques. *Archive Fever: A Freudian Impression*. Translated by Eric Prenowitz. Chicago: University of Chicago Press, 1996.
———. *Speech and Phenomena and Other Essays on Husserl's Theory of Signs*. Translated by David B. Allison. Evanston, IL: Northwestern University Press, 1973.
Docherty, Thomas, ed. *Postmodernism: A Reader*. New York: Columbia University Press, 1993.
Doležel, Lubomír. "Extensional and Intensional Narrative Worlds." *Poetics* 8 (1979): 192–211.
———. *Heterocosmica: Fiction and Possible Worlds*. Baltimore: Johns Hopkins University Press, 1998.
———. "Intensional Function, Invisible Worlds, and Franz Kafka." *Style* 17 (1983): 120–41.
———. "Narrative Modalities." *Journal of Literary Semantics* 5 (1976): 5–14

WORKS CITED

DuCille, Ann. "The Occult of True Black Womanhood: Critical Demeanor and Black Feminist Studies." In *Female Subjects in Black and White: Race, Psychoanalysis, Feminism,* edited by Elizabeth Abel, Barbara Christian, and Helene Moglen, 21–56. Berkeley: University of California Press, 1997.

During, Simon. "Literature—Nationalism's Other? The Case for Revision." In *Nation and Narration,* edited by Homi K. Bhabha, 138–53. London: Routledge, 1990.

Duvall, John N. "Troping History: Modernist Residue in Jameson's Pastiche and Hutcheon's Parody." In *Productive Postmodernism: Consuming Histories and Cultural Studies,* edited by John N. Duvall, 1–22. Albany: State University of New York Press, 2002.

Eberly, Rosa A. *Citizen Critics: Literary Public Spheres.* Urbana: University of Illinois Press, 2000.

Eco, Umberto. *Travels in Hyperreality: Essays.* Translated by William Weaver. San Diego: Harcourt Brace & Co., 1986.

Elias, Amy J. *Sublime Desire: History and Post-1960s Fiction.* Baltimore: Johns Hopkins University Press, 2001.

Enck, John J. "John Barth: An Interview." *Wisconsin Studies in Contemporary Literature* 6 (1965): 3–14.

Ermarth, Elizabeth Deeds. *Sequel to History: Postmodernism and the Crisis of Representational Time.* Princeton, NJ: Princeton University Press, 1992.

Eskelinen, Markku. "Cybertext Theory: What an English Professor Should Know Before Trying." *Electronic Book Review* (2001). http://www.electronicbookreview.com/thread/electropoetics/notmetaphor.

Faulkner, William. *The Sound and the Fury.* 1929. New York: Random House, 1946.

Federman, Raymond. *Critifiction: Postmodern Essays.* Albany: State University of New York Press, 1993.

———. "Surfiction—Four Propositions in Form of an Introduction." In *Surfiction: Fiction Now . . . and Tomorrow,* edited by Raymond Federman, 5–15. Chicago: Swallow Press, 1975.

———. *Take It or Leave It.* New York: Fiction Collective, 1976.

———. *The Voice in the Closet.* Madison, WI: Station Hill Press, 1979.

Fiedler, Leslie. "Archetype and Signature: The Relationship of Poet and Poem." *The Collected Essays of Leslie Fiedler.* Vol. 1, 529–48. New York: Stein and Day, 1971.

———. *Love and Death in the American Novel.* New York: Criterion Books, 1960.

Fisher, Philip. *Hard Facts: Setting and Form in the American Novel.* New York: Oxford University Press, 1987.

Foucault, Michel. *The Archeology of Knowledge and the Discourse on Language.* Translated by A. M. Sheridan Smith. New York: Pantheon Books, 1972.

Fowles, John. *The French Lieutenant's Woman.* Boston: Little, Brown, 1969.

Franken, Al. *Lies (And the Lying Liars Who Tell Them): A Fair and Balanced Look at the Right.* New York: Dutton, 2003.

Friedman, Ellen G. "A Conversation with Kathy Acker." *Review of Contemporary Fiction* 9, no. 3 (Fall 1989): 12–22.

Friedman, James. Introduction to *Reality Squared: Televisual Discourse on the Real,* edited by James Friedman, 1–22. New Brunswick, NJ: Rutgers University Press, 2002.

Frow, John. *Time and Commodity Culture: Essays in Cultural Theory and Postmodernity.* Oxford: Clarendon Press, 1997.

Fuller, Matthew. *Media Ecologies: Materialist Energies in Art and Technoculture.* Cambridge, MA: The MIT Press, 2005.

Gaggi, Silvio. *From Text to Hypertext: Decentering the Subject in Fiction, Film, the Visual Arts, and Electronic Media.* Philadelphia: University of Pennsylvania Press, 1997.

Gallagher, Catherine. *Nobody's Story: The Vanishing Acts of Women Writers in the Marketplace, 1670–1820.* Berkeley: University of California Press, 1994.

Galloway, Bruce. *Fantasy Wargaming.* New York: Stein and Day, 1981.

Gibson, William. "Johnny Mnemonic." In *Burning Chrome,* 1–22. New York: Ace, 1986.

———. *Neuromancer.* New York: Ace, 1984.

Gilbert, Sandra, and Susan Gubar. *The Madwoman in the Attic: The Woman Writer and the Nineteenth-Century Literary Tradition.* New Haven, CT: Yale University Press, 1979.

Graff, Gerald. *Beyond the Culture Wars: How Teaching the Conflicts Can Revitalize American Education.* New York: W. W. Norton, 1992.

———. "Mythotherapy and Modern Poetics." *TriQuarterly* 11 (Winter 1968): 76–90.

———. *Professing Literature: An Institutional History.* Chicago: University of Chicago Press, 1987.

———. "Under Our Belt and Off Our Back: Barth's *Letters* and Postmodern Fiction." *TriQuarterly* 52 (Fall 1981): 150–64.

Gray, Chris Hables, ed. *The Cyborg Handbook.* New York: Routledge, 1995.

Greenwood, Ed, Skip Williams, Sean K. Reynolds, and Rob Heinsoo, eds. *Forgotten Realms Campaign Setting.* Renton, WA: Wizards of the Coast, 2001.

Guillory, John. "Canon." In *Critical Terms for Literary Study,* edited by Frank Lentricchia and Thomas McLaughlin, 233–49. 2d ed. Chicago: University of Chicago Press, 1995.

Gunn, Giles. *Thinking Across the American Grain: Ideology, Intellect, and the New Pragmatism.* Chicago: University of Chicago Press, 1992.

Gygax, Gary. *Advanced Dungeons & Dragons Dungeon Masters Guide.* Lake Geneva, WI: TSR Games, 1979.

———. *Advanced Dungeons & Dragons Monster Manual.* 3d ed. Lake Geneva, WI: TSR Games, 1978.

———. *Advanced Dungeons & Dragons Player's Handbook.* Lake Geneva, WI: TSR Games, 1978.

Gygax, Gary, and Dave Arneson. *Dungeons & Dragons: Rules for Fantastic Medieval Wargames Campaigns Playable with Paper and Pencil and Miniature Figures.* 3 vols. Lake Geneva, WI: Tactical Studies Rules, 1974.

Gygax, Gary, and Jeff. Perren. *Chainmail: Rules for Medieval Miniatures.* 3d ed. Lake Geneva, WI: TSR Rules, 1975.

Gysin, Brion. "Cut-ups: A Project for Disasterous Success." In *The Third Mind,* by William S. Burroughs and Brion Gysin, 42–51. New York: The Viking Press, 1978.

Habermas, Jürgen. *The Structural Transformation of the Public Sphere: An Inquiry into a Category of Bourgeois Society.* Translated by Thomas Burger. Cambridge, MA: MIT Press, 1989.

Hakim, Eleanor. "Jean-Paul Sartre: The Dialectics of Myth." *Salmagundi* 1, no. 2 (Winter 1966): 59–94.

Halberstam, Judith, and Ira Livingston, eds. *Posthuman Bodies.* Bloomington: Indiana University Press, 1995.

Hansen, Mark. *Embodying Technesis: Technology beyond Writing.* Ann Arbor: University of Michigan Press, 2000.

Haraway, Donna J. *Simians, Cyborgs, and Women: The Reinvention of Nature.* New York: Routledge, 1991.

Harries, Elizabeth W. "'Out in the Left Field': Charlotte Smith's Prefaces, Bourdieu's Categories, and the Public Sphere." *Modern Language Quarterly* 58 (1997): 457–73.

Hassan, Ihab. *The Dismemberment of Orpheus: Toward a Postmodern Literature*. 1961. 2d ed. Madison: University of Wisconsin Press, 1982.

——. "Ideas of Cultural Change." In *Innovation/Renovation: New Perspectives on the Humanities*, edited by Ihab Hassan and Sally Hassan, 15–38. Madison: University of Wisconsin Press, 1983.

——. *Paracriticisms: Seven Speculations of the Times*. Urbana: University of Illinois Press, 1975.

——. *Radical Innocence: Studies in the Contemporary American Novel*. Princeton, NJ: Princeton University Press, 1961.

Hauser, Marianne. *The Talking Room: A Novel*. New York: Fiction Collective, 1976.

Hayles, Katherine. "What Cybertext Theory Can't Do." *Electronic Book Review* (2001). http://www.electronicbookreview.com/thread/electropoetics/ecumenical.

Hite, Molly. *The Other Side of the Story: Structures and Strategies of Contemporary Feminist Narrative*. Ithaca, NY: Cornell University Press, 1989.

Hoff, Benjamin. *The Tao of Pooh*. Illustrated by Ernest H. Shepard. New York: Dutton, 1982.

Hogue, W. Lawrence. "Historiographic Metafiction and the Celebration of Differences: Ishmael Reed's *Mumbo Jumbo*." In *Productive Postmodernism: Consuming Histories and Cultural Studies*, edited by John N. Duvall, 93–110. Albany: State University of New York Press, 2002.

Howell, Robert. "Fictional Objects: How They Are and How They Aren't." *Poetics* 8 (1979): 129–77.

Hume, Kathryn. "Robert Coover's Fiction: The Naked and the Mythic." *Novel* 12 (1979): 127–48.

Huntington, John. "Newness, *Neuromancer*, and the End of Narrative." In *Fiction 2000: Cyberpunk and the Future of Narrative*, edited by George Slusser and Tom Shippey, 133–41. Athens: University of Georgia Press, 1992.

Hutcheon, Linda. *A Poetics of Postmodernism: History, Theory, Fiction*. New York: Routledge, 1988.

Huyssen, Andreas. *After the Great Divide: Modernism, Mass Culture, Postmodernism*. Bloomington: Indiana University Press, 1986.

Irwin, William. "Computers, Caves, and Oracles: Neo and Socrates." In *The Matrix and Philosophy: Welcome to the Desert of the Real*, edited by William Irwin, 5–15. Chicago: Open Court, 2002.

——, ed. *Seinfeld and Philosophy: A Book about Everything and Nothing*. Chicago: Open Court, 1999.

Irwin, William, Mark T. Conard, and Aeon J. Skoble, eds. *The Simpsons and Philosophy: The D'oh! of Homer*. Chicago: Open Court, 2001.

Iser, Wolfgang. *The Fictive and the Imaginary: Charting Literary Anthropology*. Baltimore: Johns Hopkins University Press, 1993.

Jackson, Shelley. *Patchwork Girl*. CD-ROM. Watertown, MA: Eastgate Systems, 1995.

Jacobs, Naomi. *The Character of Truth: Historical Figures in Contemporary Fiction*. Carbondale: Southern Illinois University Press, 1990.

Jameson, Fredric. *The Cultural Turn: Selected Writings on the Postmodern, 1983–1998*. London: Verso, 1998.

——. *The Geopolitical Aesthetic: Cinema and Space in the World System*. Bloomington: Indiana University Press, 1992.

———. *Postmodernism: Or, the Cultural Logic of Late Capitalism*. Durham, NC: Duke University Press, 1991.
Jay, Gregory. *American Literature and the Culture Wars*. Ithaca, NY: Cornell University Press, 1997.
Jenkins, Henry. *Textual Poachers: Television Fans & Participatory Culture*. New York: Routledge, 1992.
Johnny Mnemonic. Directed by Robert Longo. Tristar, 1995.
Johnson, Dane. "The Rise of Gabriel García Márquez and Toni Morrison." In *Cultural Institutions of the Novel*, edited by Deidre Lynch and William B. Warner, 129–56. Durham, NC: Duke University Press, 1996.
Jones, Steven. "The Book of *Myst* in the Late Age of Print." *Postmodern Culture* 7, no. 2 (1997). http://muse.jhu.edu/journals/pmc/v007/7.2jones.html.
Joyce, Michael. *Afternoon: A Story*. Diskette. Watertown, MA: Eastgate Systems, 1987.
Juul, Jesper. "Games Telling Stories? A Brief Note on Games and Narratives." *Game Studies* 1, no. 1 (July 2001). http://www.gamestudies.org/0101/juul-gts/.
Katz, Steve. *Creamy and Delicious: Eat My Words (in Other Words)*. New York: Random House, 170.
———. *The Exagggerations of Peter Prince*. New York: Holt, Rinehart and Winston, 1968.
Keeler, Mary. "Iconic Indeterminacy and Human Creativity in C. S. Peirce's Manuscripts." In *The Iconic Page in Manuscript, Print, and Digital Culture*, edited by George Bornstein and Theresa Tinkle, 157–93. Ann Arbor: The University of Michigan Press, 1998.
Kermode, Frank. *The Sense of an Ending: Studies in the Theory of Fiction*. London: Oxford University Press, 1967.
Kernan, Alvin. *The Death of Literature*. New Haven, CT: Yale University Press, 1990.
Kingston, Maxine Hong. *Tripmaster Monkey: His Fake Book*. New York: Knopf, 1989.
Klinkowitz, Jerome. "The Extra-Literary in Contemporary American Fiction." In *Contemporary American Fiction*. Edited by Malcolm Bradbury and Sigmund Ro, 19–38. London: Edward Arnold, 1987.
———. *Literary Disruptions: The Making of a Post-Contemporary American Fiction*. 2d ed. Urbana: University of Illinois Press, 1980.
Koch, Stephen. "Premature Speculations on the Perpetual Renaissance." *TriQuarterly* 10 (Fall 1967): 4–36.
Kostelanetz, Richard. *The End of Intelligent Writing: Literary Politics in America*. New York: Sheed and Ward, 1974.
———. "Introduction." In *Breakthrough Fictioneers: An Anthology*, edited by Richard Kostelanetz, xiii–xix. West Glover, VT: Something Else Press, 1973.
Kuntz, Robert, and James Ward. *Dungeons & Dragons Supplement IV: Gods, Demi-Gods & Heroes*. Lake Geneva, WI: TSR Games, 1976.
Laclau, Ernesto, and Chantal Mouffe. *Hegemony and Socialist Strategy: Towards a Radical Democratic Politics*. London: Verso, 1985.
Lancaster, Kurt. *Warlocks and Warpdrive: Contemporary Fantasy Entertainments with Interactive and Virtual Environments*. Jefferson, NC: McFarland, 1999.
Lauter, Estella. *Women as Mythmakers: Poetry and Visual Art by Twentieth-Century Women*. Bloomington: Indiana University Press, 1984.
Lauter, Paul. *Canons and Contexts*. New York: Oxford University Press, 1991.
Leach, James, and Christian Bravery. *The Making of Black & White*. Roseville, CA: Prima Games, 2001.

WORKS CITED

LeClair, Tom, and Larry McCaffery. *Anything Can Happen: Interviews with Contemporary American Novelists*. Urbana: University of Illinois Press, 1983.
Lemaire, Gérard-Georges. "23 Stitches Taken." In *The Third Mind*, by William S. Burroughs and Brion Gysin, 9–24. New York: The Viking Press, 1978.
Long, Steven S., John Ratelifif, Christian Moore, and Matt Forbeck. *The Lord of the Rings: Roleplaying Game: Core Book*. Norfolk, WV: Decipher, 2002.
Luhmann, Niklas. "The Differentiation of Advances in Knowledge: The Genesis of Science." In *Society and Knowledge: Contemporary Perspectives in the Sociology of Knowledge*, edited by Nico Stehr and Volker Meja, 103–48. New Brunswick, NJ: Transaction Books, 1984.
Lynch, Deidre, and William B. Warner. "Introduction: The Transport of the Novel." In *Cultural Institutions of the Novel*, edited by Deidre Lynch and William B. Warner, 1–10. Durham, NC: Duke University Press, 1996.
Lynch, Deidre Shauna. *The Economy of Character: Novels, Market Culture, and the Business of Inner Meaning*. Chicago: University of Chicago Press, 1998.
Lyons, Gene. "Report on the Fiction Collective." *TriQuarterly* 43 (Fall 1978): 635–47.
Lyotard, Jean-François. *The Postmodern Condition: A Report on Knowledge*. Trans. Geoff Bennington and Brian Massumi. Minneapolis: University of Minnesota Press, 1984.
Mackay, Daniel. *The Fantasy Role-Playing Game: A New Performing Art*. Jefferson, NC: McFarland, 2001.
Mailer, Norman. *Armies of the Night: History as a Novel, the Novel as History*. New York: New American Library, 1968.
———. "Children of the Pied Piper: Mail on 'American Psycho.'" *Vanity Fair* 54 (March 1991): 154–59, 220–21.
Major, Clarence. *Necessary Distance: Essays and Criticism*. Minneapolis: Coffee House Press, 2001.
———. *Reflex and Bone Structure*. New York: Fiction Collective, 1975.
Manovich, Lev. The Language of New Media. Cambridge, MA: MIT Press, 2001.
Marcuse, Herbert. *Eros and Civilization: A Philosophical Inquiry into Freud*. Boston: Beacon, 1955.
Margolin, Uri. "Individuals in Narrative Worlds: An Ontological Perspective." *Poetics Today* 11 (1990): 843–71.
Martínez-Bonati, Félix. *Fictive Discourse and the Structures of Literature: A Phenomenological Approach*. Translated by Philip W. Silver. Ithaca, NY: Cornell University Press, 1981.
———. "Towards a Formal Ontology of Fictional Worlds." *Philosophy and Literature* 7 (1973): 182–95.
The Matrix. Directed by Larry Wachowski and Andy Wachowski. Warner, 1999.
McCaffery, Larry. "The Desert of the Real: The Cyberpunk Controversy." *Mississippi Review* 47/48 (1988): 7–15.
———. "The Fictions of the Present." In *Columbia Literary History of the United States*, edited by Emory Elliott, 1161–77. New York: Columbia University Press, 1988.
———. "An Interview with William Gibson." *Mississippi Review* 47/48 (1988): 217–36.
McCormick, Peter J. *Fictions, Philosophies, and the Problems of Poetics*. Ithaca, NY: Cornell University Press, 1988.
McGann, Jerome. *Black Riders: The Visual Language of Modernism*. Princeton, NJ: Princeton University Press, 1993.
McGurl, Mark. *The Art Novel: Elevations of American Fiction after Henry James*. Princeton, NJ: Princeton University Press, 2001.

McHale, Brian. *Constructing Postmodernism*. New York: Routledge, 1992.
———. "Postmodernism, or the Anxiety of Master Narratives." *Diacritics* 22, no. 1 (1992): 17–33.
———. *Postmodernist Fiction*. New York: Methuen, 1987.
McLuhan, Marshall. *Understanding Media: The Extensions of Man*. 1964. Cambridge, MA: MIT Press, 1994.
Memmott, Talan. *Lolli's Apartment*. http://www.heelstone.com/meridian/memmott.html.
Metal of Honor: Allied Assault. CD-ROM. Redwood City, CA: EA Games, 2002.
Michael, Magali Cornier. *Feminism and the Postmodern Impulse: Post-World War II Fiction*. Albany: State University of New York Press, 1996.
Michaels, Walter Benn. *The Gold Standard and the Logic of Naturalism: American Literature at the Turn of the Century*. Berkeley: University of California Press, 1987.
Miller, Rand, and Robyn Miller. *Myst*. CD-ROM. Novato, CA: Brøderbund, 1993.
Miller, Stephen Paul. *The Seventies Now: Culture as Surveillance*. Durham, NC: Duke University Press, 1999.
Montfort, Nick. "Cybertext Killed the Hypertext Star." *Electronic Book Review* (2000). http://www.electronicbookreview.com/thread/electropoetics/cyberdebates.
Montfort, Nick, and Stuart Moulthrop. "Face It, Tiger, You Just Hit the Jackpot: Reading and Playing Cadre's *Varicella*." *Fineart Forum* 17, no. 8 (August 2003). http://nickm.com/if/varicella.pdf
Morrison, Toni. *Jazz*. New York: Knopf, 1992.
Murray, Timothy. "Digital Incompossibility: Cruising the Aesthetic Haze of the New Media." *Ctheory* (2000). http://ctheory.net/text_file.asp?pick=121.
Myst III: Exile. CD-ROM. San Francisco: Ubi Soft, 2001.
Nealon, Jeffrey T. *Double Reading: Postmodernism after Deconstruction*. Ithaca, NY: Cornell University Press, 1993.
Nemerov, Howard. *Journal of the Fictive Life*. 1965. Chicago: University of Chicago Press, 1981.
Newman, Charles. "Foreword." *TriQuarterly* 1 (Fall 1964): 3–5.
———. *The Post-Modern Aura: The Act of Fiction in an Age of Inflation*. Evanston, IL: Northwestern University Press, 1985.
Norris, Christopher. *What's Wrong with Postmodernism: Critical Theory and the Ends of Philosophy*. Baltimore: Johns Hopkins University Press, 1990.
Nussbaum, Martha C. *Poetic Justice: The Literary Imagination and Public Life*. Boston: Beacon Press, 1995.
Okrent, Daniel. "The Year George Foster Wasn't Worth $36: An Introduction to Rotisserie League Baseball." In *Rotisserie League Baseball*, edited by Glen Waggoner, 3–7. Toronto: Bantam, 1984.
Paulson, William. *Literary Culture in a World Transformed: A Future for the Humanities*. Ithaca, NY: Cornell University Press, 2001.
Pavel, Thomas G. *Fictional Worlds*. Cambridge, MA: Harvard University Press, 1986.
Paz, Octavio. "The Dialectic of Solitude." *Evergreen Review* 5, no. 20 (September/October 1961): 100–13.
Pease, Donald E., and Robyn Wiegman. "Futures." In *The Futures of American Studies*, edited by Donald E. Pease and Robyn Wiegman, 1–42. Durham, NC: Duke University Press, 2002.
Pesce, Mark. *The Playful World: How Technology Is Transforming Our Imagination*. New York: Ballantine, 2000.

WORKS CITED

Peterson, Sandy, and Lynn Willis. *Call of Cthulhu: Horror Roleplaying in the Worlds of H. P. Lovecraft.* 5th ed. Oakland: Chaosium, 1995.

Pfeil, Fred. *Another Tale to Tell: Politics and Narrative in Postmodern Culture.* London: Verso, 1990.

Pierson, Michele. *Special Effects: Still in Search of Wonder.* New York: Columbia University Press, 2002.

Poirier, Richard. *A World Elsewhere: The Place of Style in American Literature.* New York: Oxford University Press, 1966.

Powell, Jim. *Derrida for Beginners.* Illustrated by Van Howell. Danbury, CT: For Beginners, 1997.

Punday, Daniel. "Involvement, Interruption, and Inevitability: Melancholy as an Aesthetic Principle in Game Narratives." *Sub-Stance* 33, no. 3 (2004): 80–107.

———. "The Local Site and Materiality: Kathy Acker's *Empire of the Senseless.*" *Genders* 27 (1998). http://www.genders.org/g27/g27_theories.html.

———. *Narrative after Deconstruction.* Albany: State University of New York Press, 2003.

———. "Texts and Tools." *Electronic Book Review* (1997). http://www.electronicbookreview.com/thread/electropoetics/spunoff.

Pynchon, Thomas. *Gravity's Rainbow.* New York: Viking, 1973.

———. *Vineland.* Boston: Little, Brown, 1990.

Radway, Janice A. *Reading the Romance: Women, Patriarchy, and Popular Literature.* Chapel Hill: University of North Carolina Press, 1984.

Rainey. Lawrence. *Institutions of Modernism: Literary Elites and Public Culture.* New Haven, CT: Yale University Press, 1998.

Reed, Ishmael. *Mumbo Jumbo.* 1972. New York: Scribner, 1996.

Reilly, Charlie. "An Interview with John Barth." *Contemporary Literature* 41(2000): 589–617.

Rein-Hagen, Mark. *Vampire: The Masquerade: A Storytelling Game of Personal Horror.* Clarkson, CA: White Wolf, 1992.

Riffaterre, Michael. *Fictional Truth.* Baltimore: Johns Hopkins University Press, 1990.

Riven: The Sequel to Myst. CD-ROM. Novato, CA: Brøderbund, 1997.

Robbe-Grillet, Alain. "A Fresh Start for Fiction." *Evergreen Review* 1, no. 3 (1957): 97–104.

Robinson, Charles. "Academia and the Little Magazine." *TriQuarterly* 43 (Fall 1978): 27–33.

Ross, Andrew. *No Respect: Intellectuals & Popular Culture.* New York: Routledge, 1989.

———. *Strange Weather: Culture, Science and Technology in the Age of Limits.* London: Verso, 1991.

Routley, Richard. "The Semantical Structure of Fictional Discourse." *Poetics* 8 (1979): 3–30.

Rubin, Joan Shelley. *The Making of Middlebrow Culture.* Chapel Hill: University of North Carolina Press, 1992.

Rubin, Louis D. Jr. *The Curious Death of the Novel: Essays in American Literature.* Baton Rouge: Louisiana State University Press, 1967.

Russ, Joanna. *To Write Like a Woman: Essays in Feminism and Science Fiction.* Bloomington: Indiana University Press, 1995.

Ryan, Marie-Laure. *Narrative as Virtual Reality: Immersion and Interactivity in Literature and Electronic Media.* Baltimore: Johns Hopkins University Press, 2001.

———. *Possible Worlds, Artificial Intelligence, and Narrative Theory.* Bloomington: Indiana University Press, 1991.

Salvatore, R. A. *The Crystal Shard*. Renton, WA: TSR, 1988.
Sartre, Jean-Paul. *The Winds*. Translated by Bernard Frechtman. New York: George Braziller, 1964.
Schick, Lawrence. *Heroic Worlds: A History and Guide to Role-Playing Games*. Buffalo: Prometheus Books, 1991.
Scholes, Robert. *The Fabulators*. New York: Oxford University Press, 1967.
Sellers, Susan. *Myth and Fairy Tale in Contemporary Women's Fiction*. New York: Palgrave, 2001.
Seltzer, Mark. *Bodies and Machines*. New York: Routledge, 1992.
Shapin, Stephen. *A Social History of Truth: Civility and Science in Seventeenth-Century England*. Chicago: University of Chicago Press, 1994.
Shapiro, Gary, ed. *After the Future: Postmodern Times and Places*. Albany: State University of New York Press, 1990.
Sherard, Tracey. "Women's Classic Blues in Toni Morrison's *Jazz*: Cultural Artifact as Narrator." *Genders* 31 (2000). http://genders.org/g31/g31_sherard.html.
Sidney, Sir Philip. *The Prose Works of Sir Philip Sidney*. Edited by Albert Feuillerat. 4 vols. Cambridge: Cambridge University Press, 1963.
Siegle, Robert. *Suburban Ambush: Downtown Writing and the Fiction of Insurgency*. Baltimore: Johns Hopkins University Press, 1989.
Siembieda, Kevin. *Rifts Game Master Guide*. Taylor, MI: Palladium Books, 2001.
The Sims. CD-ROM. Redwood City, CA: EA Games, 2000.
Siskin, Clifford. *The Work of Writing: Literature and Social Change in Britain, 1700–1830*. Baltimore: Johns Hopkins University Press, 1998.
Slavicsek, Bill, Andy Collins, and J. D. Wiker. *Star Wars Roleplaying Game: Revised Core Rulebook*. Renton, WV: Wizards of the Coast, 2002.
Sluganski, Randy. "LucasArts Speaks Out—Part 1: A Discussion with Hal Barwood." *Just Adventure*. http://www.justadventure.com/Interviews/Hal_Barwood/Hal_Barwood2.shtm.
Slusser, George. "Literary MTV." *Mississippi Review* 47/48 (1988): 279–88.
Sorrentino, Gilbert. *Imaginative Qualities of Actual Things*. 1971. Normal, IL: Dalkey Archive, 1991.
———. "Neon, Kulchur, etc." *TriQuarterly* 43 (Fall 1978): 298–316.
———. *Something Said: Prefaces by the Author*. Normal, IL: Dalkey Archive, 2001.
Spiegelman, Art. *Maus: A Survivor's Tale: My Father Bleeds History*. New York: Pantheon, 1986.
Stanhope, Philip Dormer, Earl of Chesterfield. *Letters to His Son and Others*. London: J. M. Dent, Everyman's Library, 1984.
Steiner, George. *Grammars of Creation*. New Haven, CT: Yale University Press, 2001.
Stevick, Philip. *Alternative Pleasures: Postrealist Fiction and the Tradition*. Urbana: University of Illinois Press, 1981.
Sukenick, Ronald. *Down and In: Life in the Underground*. New York: Beech Tree Books, 1987.
———. *In Form: Digressions on the Act of Fiction*. Carbondale: Southern Illinois University Press, 1985.
———. *Narralogues: Truth in Fiction*. Albany: State University of New York Press, 2000.
———. *Up*. New York: Dial Press, 1968.
Sunstein, Cass. *Republic.com*. Princeton, NJ: Princeton University Press, 2001.
Suvin, Darko. *Metamorphoses of Science Fiction: On the Poetics and History of a Literary Genre*. New Haven, CT: Yale University Press, 1979.

Tabbi, Joseph. *Cognitive Fictions*. Minneapolis: University of Minnesota Press, 2002.
———. "Toward a Semantic Literary Web: Setting a Direction for the Electronic Literature Organization's Directory." http://eliterature.org/pad/slw.html.
Tanner, Tony. *City of Words: American Fiction 1950-70*. New York: Harper & Row, 1971.
Tebbel, John. *Between Covers: The Rise and Transformation of Book Publishing in America*. New York: Oxford University Press, 1987.
Thurber, James. "The Secret Life of Walter Mitty." *My World—And Welcome To It*, 72-81. 1942. New York: Harcourt Brace Jovanovich, 1969.
Tillman, Lynne. *The Madame Realism Complex*. New York: Semiotext(e), 1992.
Todorov, Tzvetan. *The Fantastic: A Structural Approach to a Literary Genre*. Translated by Richard Howard. Ithaca, NY: Cornell University Press, 1975.
Trachtenberg, Alan. *The Incorporation of America: Culture and Society in the Gilded Age*. New York: Hill and Wang, 1982.
Turkle, Sherry. *Life on the Screen: Identity in the Age of the Internet*. New York: Simon & Schuster, 1995.
Twain, Mark. *A Connecticut Yankee in King Arthur's Court*. Edited by Allison R. Ensor. New York: Norton, 1982.
Vaihinger, Hans. *The Philosophy of "As If": A System of the Theoretical, Practical and Religious Fictions of Mankind*. 1911. Translated by C. K. Ogden. 2d ed. London: Routledge & Kegan Paul, 1935.
Venturi, Robert, Denise Scott Brown, and Steven Izenour. *Learning from Las Vegas*. Rev. ed. Cambridge, MA: MIT Press, 1977.
Wachowski, Larry, and Andy Wachowski. *The Matrix: The Shooting Script*. New York: Newmarket Press, 2001.
Walker, Alice. *In Search of Our Mothers' Gardens: Womanist Prose*. San Diego: Harvest, 1984.
Wallace, Michele. *Invisibility Blues: From Pop to Theory*. London: Verso, 1990.
Warhol, Andy. *The Philosophy of Andy Warhol (From A to B and Back Again)*. San Diego: Harcourt, 1975.
Watkins, Evan. *Work Time: English Departments and the Circulation of Cultural Value*. Stanford, CA: Stanford University Press, 1989.
Waugh, Patricia. *Feminine Fictions: Revisiting the Postmodern*. London: Routledge, 1989.
———. *Metafiction: The Theory and Practice of Self-Conscious Fiction*. London: Routledge, 1984.
Weber, Samuel. *Institution and Interpretation: Expanded Edition*. Stanford, CA: Stanford University Press, 2001.
Wesseling, Elizabeth. *Writing History as a Prophet: Postmodernist Innovations of the Historical Novel*. Amsterdam: John Benjamins, 1991.
White, Hayden. "The Modernist Event." In *The Persistence of History: Cinema, Television, and the Modern Event*, edited by Vivian Sobchack, 17-38. New York: Routledge, 1996.
Wilde, Alan. *Horizons of Assent: Modernism, Postmodernism, and the Ironic Imagination*. Philadelphia: University of Pennsylvania Press, 1987.
Williams, Raymond. *Culture and Society, 1780-1950*. New York: Columbia University Press, 1983.
Wimsatt, W. K. *The Verbal Icon: Studies in the Meaning of Poetry*. Lexington: The University Press of Kentucky, 1954.
Wolfe, Tom. "The New Journalism." In *The New Journalism*, edited by Tom Wolfe and E. W. Johnson, 3-52. New York: Harper & Row, 1973.

Zavarzadeh, Mas'ud. *The Mythopoeic Reality: The Postwar American Nonfiction Novel.* Urbana: University of Illinois Press, 1976.

Žižek, Slavoj. *The Fragile Absolute: Or, Why Is the Christian Legacy Worth Fighting For?* London: Verso, 2000.

——. *The Sublime Object of Ideology.* London: Verso, 1989.

——. *Welcome to the Desert of the Real: Five Essays on September 11 and Related Dates.* London: Verso, 2002.

INDEX

Aarseth, Espen, 181n5, 194n25
Abish, Walter, 90–92
accidental, 77–78, 81–82, 84. See also occasion
Acker, Kathy, 54–55
Adorno, Theodor W., 53
Afternoon (Joyce), 197
Age of Empires, 189
agency, 157, 162–67, 169–70, 173–76, 179, 182–83, 185–87
Aldiss, Brian, 128
All the President's Men, 91
allegory. *See* postmodernism
The Amazing Adventures of Kavalier & Clay (Chabon), 44n27
American imaginary. *See* civil imaginary
American McGee's Alice, 178, 184–87
American Psycho (Ellis), 208–9

American studies, 84–85
Anderson, Benedict, 83–84
Anderson, Margaret, 102
Anderson, Perry, 142
Anderson, Walter Truett, 1
Andrews, Jim, 179–85
archive, 65, 67–68, 70, 85. *See also* fictionality
Arteroids (Andrews), 179–85
Aristotle, 6, 42
Auerbach, Erich, 174
Auerbach, Nina, 210n5
Auster, Paul, 88

Baeten, Jan, 187n13
Baldur's Gate, 188
Ballard, J. G., 128

Balsamo, Anne, 139–40
Barth, John, 27, 37–57, 59, 87, 99, 125, 152, 176, 192, 203, 210
Barthelme, Donald, 44, 144
Barthes, Roland, 49, 52, 174–75
Bartlett, Laura, 131–32
Barwood, Hal, 190–91
Baudrillard, Jean, 3, 80, 129–31, 133, 134–35, 212
Baumbach, Jonathan, 104n22
Beardsley, Monroe, 95
Beat movement, 31n3
becoming-fictional, 82–85, 212
Bellamy, Joe David, 144
Bender, John, 191
Bennett, David, 21n39
Berlant, Lauren, 76
Bertens, Hans, 20, 27
Berubé, Michael, 146
Bhabha, Homi, 83–84
Birkerts, Sven, 216–17
Black & White, 188–92
Blade Runner, 128–29, 134
Blanchot, Maurice, 49
Bloom, Allan, 15
Bloom, Harold, 14–15
Bolter, Jay David, 187
book. *See* page space
Book-of-the-Month Club, 19
Boorstin, Daniel J., 2, 10
Bourdieu, Pierre, 23, 24, 26, 36, 72–73, 74, 118, 183, 211–12, 214, 215
Brinker, Menachem, 175n46
Brown, Homer, 24–25, 36
Brown, Norman O., 47
Burroughs, William, 105, 141, 179–80
Butler, Judith, 76–77
Byers, Thomas, 131–32

Califia (Coverley), 192–95, 196–97, 198, 201, 203
Call of Cthulhu, 159n13, 160
Campbell, Joseph, 48n42
canon, 14–15, 27–28, 60–61, 62, 66–67, 146, 176, 177, 210, 215. *See also* postmodernism
Capote, Truman, 116–18

Carby, Hazel, 64–65, 68
Castoriadis, Cornelius, 24
Cayley, John, 181
Chabon, Michael, 44n27
Chainmail, 153–54
Chapman, Wes, 197–200, 201, 203
Chesterfield, Lord (Philip Dormer Stanhope), 7–8
"Charlie in the House of Rue" (Coover), 109–110
Chimera (Barth), 38, 40, 210
civil imaginary, 24, 28, 59, 69, 75–77, 82–84, 212
Civilization, 189
CliffsNotes, 213
Cochran, Terry, 26
cognitive mapping, 126–27
computer game, 178, 200, 217; appeal to historical artifacts, 187–88; god game, 189–91
concrete poetry, 35, 101. *See also* page space
Connor, Steven, 14
Coover, Robert, 19–20, 31n1, 44, 104, 109–110, 120–23, 156–57, 203, 215
Cornis-Pope, Marcel, 100
Costikyan, Greg, 158n10
Coulter, Ann, 13n26
Coverley, M. D., 192–95, 196–97, 198, 201, 203
Creamy and Delicious (Katz), 44n27
creativity, 165–66
Crittenden, Charles, 171n39
cyberpunk, 28–29, 134–40, 147–50, 216; and politics, 139–40
cyborg, 147–50

Dada, 33, 104, 165
Danto, Arthur, 105n24
Davenport, Guy, 107n30
Davis, Lennard, 11–12, 36
Debord, Guy, 2, 10
"Defense of Poesie" (Sidney), 6–8
Defoe, Daniel, 169–71
Delany, Samuel, 128, 135n19, 137–39, 140, 141, 148
Deleuze, Gilles, and Félix Guattari, 54, 82

INDEX

DeLillo, Don, 88, 90
Der Derian, James, 126
Derrida, Jacques, 42–43, 65, 68, 70, 85, 87–88, 127, 213, 214
Dick, Philip K., 128–29
Dickens, Charles, 210n5
Docherty, Thomas, 53
Doctorow, E. L., 100
Doležel, Lubomír, 168–75
D'Souza, Dinesh, 146
Duchamp, Marcel, 33, 84, 105, 165–66
duCille, Ann, 61
Dungeons and Dragons, 152–61, 200, 214
During, Simon, 76
Duvall, John, 52–53, 143

Eberly, Rosa, 208–210, 214
Eco, Umberto, 167, 200
The End of the Road (Barth), 38, 45
electronic writing, 30, 67n11, 118, 178–206, 216–17; defined, 178n1
Elias, Amy, 100
Ellis, Bret Easton, 208–209
Empire of the Senseless (Acker), 54–55
Ermarth, Eliabeth, 128n9
Eskelinen, Markku, 181n5
The Exagggerations of Peter Prince (Katz), 106–112, 114, 115, 119, 123, 124, 205, 215, 216
existentialism. *See* literary culture

fake book, 116–23, 196
fan fiction, 167
fantasy, 69–71, 72, 80, 90–91, 93, 117–18
Faulkner, William, 9, 90
Fear of Flying (Jong), 208
Federman, Raymond, 100, 113–16, 119, 123; on surfiction, 9, 10, 36–37, 144
Fiction Collective, 19–20, 32, 104
fictional world theory. *See* possible world theory
fictionality: and archive, 61, 65, 68, 77, 81–85, 87, 149, 152–53, 192–95, 205–206, 210; and assemblage, 151–76, 200–202, 205, 210, 215; and folk culture, 56–57, 60–61, 64–65, 84, 177; and history, 6; and hypothetical, 5, 28–29, 134; and lying, 6–7, 13n26, 28, 63–64, 87–123, 149, 195–97, 198, 203, 205–206; and myth, 4, 24, 27, 38–57, 87, 149, 152–54, 176, 177, 188–92, 203, 205–206, 215; and science, 5–6, 7; and style, 125–50, 152–53, 176, 197–200, 204, 205–206; as strands, 23, 30, 175–76, 177–78, 188, 203–206, 213; as tool, 5, 9; in American culture, 16–20; in law, 5; in science fiction, 125–26, 134; of corporations, 18–19. *See also* institutions
Fiedler, Leslie, 46–47, 50
Fisher, Philip, 66n10
folk culture. *See* fictionality
Foucault, Michel, 11n23, 54
Fowles, John, 191
Franken, Al, 13n26
Frankenstein (Shelley), 200, 202
Frankl, Viktor, 45
fraud, 92–93
The French Lieutenant's Woman (Fowles), 191
Freudian theory, 28, 46–47, 53, 89, 93–94, 99n8
The Friday Book (Barth), 27, 38–43, 192, 210
Friedman, James, 22–23n41
Frow, John, 21, 51
Frye, Northrop, 46n36
Fuller, Matthew, 217n19
Further Fridays (Barth), 45n30

Gaggi, Silvio, 194n25
Gallagher, Catherine, 35–36
Galloway, Bruce, 160n17
"The Gernsback Continuum" (Gibson), 139
Gibson, William, 28, 128, 135, 136–41, 147, 148
Gilbert, Sandra, 44–45n29
Giles Goat-Boy (Barth), 37–38, 50, 54
Graff, Gerald, 15, 16–17, 51, 52n51
Gravity's Rainbow (Pynchon), 44, 148–49
Gray, Charles Hables, 148n47

Greenwood, Ed, 159n12
Grusin, Richard, 187
Gubar, Susan, 44–45n29
Guillory, John, 67
Gunn, Giles, 143–44
Gygax, Gary, 155n5, 155n6, 160n18, 164
Gysin, Brion, 105

Habermas, Jürgen, 211–12, 214
Hakim, Eleanor, 45–46
Halberstam, Judith, 148n47
Hansen, Mark, 217n17
Haraway, Donna, 147–50, 150
Harries, Elizabeth, 211–12
Hard Times (Dickens), 210n5
Hassan, Ihab, 47–50, 53n56, 127
"The Hat Act" (Coover), 110
Hauser, Marianne, 110–11, 112
Hayles, Katherine, 181n5
He, She, and It (Piercy), 148
Heath Anthology of American Literature, 60–61, 67, 84
Hite, Molly, 55n64
Hoff, Benjamin, 210, 214
Hogue, W. Lawrence, 121–22
Horkheimer, Max, 53
How German Is It? (Abish), 90–91, 92
Howell, Robert, 168n31
Howells, William Dean, 17
H.D. [Hilda Doolittle], 45n31
Hume, Kathryn, 44n26, 203n32
Huntington, John, 136
Hurston, Zora Neale, 59–68, 69, 70, 71, 81
Hutcheon, Linda, 33–34, 52–53, 100, 107–108n31, 142–44
Huyssen, Andreas, 33
hypertext. *See* electronic writing

Imaginative Qualities of Actual Things (Sorrentino), 94–99, 107, 108, 112, 114, 115
improvisation, 34
In Cold Blood (Capote), 117–18
intertextuality, 29

institutions, 3, 10–20, 21, 35–36, 65–66, 72; and computer games, 179–88; and the future, 67; and materialization, 24; and work, 72–73; as multiple, 23–27, 145–47, 180, 188, 211–17; marginal position, 82–85, 125, 176; positions outside of institutions, 60, 66, 125, 145–47, 152, 167–68, 175–76, 208–209, 216. *See also* literary culture in America; publishing; suture
invention, 165–66, 175
Irwin, William, 213n10
Iser, Wolfgang, 8–9

Jackson, Shelley, 200–202, 203
Jacobs, Naomi, 100
Jameson, Frederic, 13–14, 34, 91, 126–27, 142–44
Jay, Gregory, 15n31
jazz, 34–35
Jazz (Morrison), 56
Jenkins, Henry, 167n29
Johnny Mnemonic, 140
Johnson, Dane, 56n65
"The Joker's Greatest Triumph" (Barthelme), 44n26
Jones, Steven, 204n34
Jong, Erica, 208
Journal of the Fictive Life (Nemerov), 88–94, 102
Joyce, James, 9, 208
Joyce, Michael, 197
Juul, Jesper, 183

Katz, Steve, 44n27, 106–112, 114, 115, 119, 123, 124, 205, 215, 216
Keeler, Mary, 112n35
Kermode, Frank, 4, 8
Kernan, Alvin, 118–19
The King (Barthelme), 44
Kingston, Maxine Hong, 119–20, 123
Klinkowitz, Jerome, 100n12, 127
Koch, Stephen, 31
Kostelanetz, Richard, 35, 35n14
Kulchur, 103–104

Lacan, Jacques, 30, 180–81
Laclau, Ernesto, 30, 181
Lancaster, Kurt, 154n3
Lauter, Estella, 45n31
Lauter, Paul, 60, 67
Lemaire, Gérard-Georges, 105
LETTERS (Barth), 38, 41–43
Libra (DeLillo), 90
Lima, Luiz Costa, 9n16
literary culture in America, 9, 13–16, 205–206; and capitalism, 17–18; and popular reading, 23–24; and postmodernism, 211; division into subgroups, 177; existentialism in, 27, 38, 45–46, 54, 61, 87–88; formation of American literature, 16–17; in broader public sphere, 207–217; mass readership, 102; middlebrow culture, 19; opposition to occasion in Barth, 40–44; relation to game culture, 202, 204. *See also* institutions; postmodernism
"The Literature of Exhaustion" (Barth), 40–41, 51–52, 144–45
Little Review, 102
Livingston, Ira, 148n47
Lolli's Apartment (Memmott), 195–97, 198, 203
The Lord of the Rings (role-playing game), 159n13
Lost in the Funhouse (Barth), 38
Luhmann, Niklas, 7n13
lying. *See* fictionality
Lynch, Deidre, 25–26, 184n9, 191n21
Lyons, Gene, 104n22
Lyotard, Jean-François, 87–88, 142–43

Machen, Arthur, 18
Mackay, Daniel, 154n3, 158, 160–61
Mailer, Norman, 116–119, 208–209
Major, Clarence, 99n8, 112–13
Manovich, Lev, 187n13, 193
Marcuse, Herbert, 47
Margolin, Uri, 171
Martínez-Bonati, Félix, 170n35, 171
materialization. *See* fictionality
The Matrix, 28, 128–34, 135, 141, 149–50, 212–13
The Matrix and Philosophy, 213–15
Maus (Spiegelman), 214
McCaffery, Anne, 148
McCaffery, Larry, 134–38, 141
McCormick, Peter J., 170n36
McGann, Jerome, 101–102
McGurl, Mark, 31n5, 115n41
McHale, Brian, 32, 34, 91–92n4, 142, 147
McLuhan, Marshall, 2
media culture, 1–3, 10, 21, 69–70, 72, 78–81, 117, 129–30, 217. *See also* literary culture
Memmott, Talan, 195–97, 198, 203
metafiction, 38, 41–42, 50, 99, 100, 101, 107, 109, 115n41, 119
Metal of Honor: Allied Assault, 187, 204, 216
Michael, Magali Cornier, 55n64
Michaels, Walter Benn, 18–19
mimeograph publishing, 103
Miller, Henry, 208
Miller, Jacques-Alain, 180–81
Miller, Stephen Paul, 10
modernism, 101–102, 105–106, 115n41, 116, 145n43, 148
Molyneux, Peter, 189, 190
Monroe, Harriet, 102
Montfort, Nick, 181n5
Morris, William, 101, 104
Morrison, Toni, 27, 55–57, 59–60, 62, 100
Moufee, Chantal, 30, 181
Mumbo Jumbo (Reed), 121–23
Murray, Timothy, 187n13
Myst, 30, 203–206, 214
Myst III: Exile, 205
myth. *See* fictionality

Nealon, Jeffrey, 61
Nemerov, Howard, 88–94, 100, 102
Neuromancer (Gibson), 135, 138, 148
New Criticism, 46, 95–99
new journalism. *See* nonfiction novel
Newman, Charles, 141–42
News. *See* media culture
nonfiction novel, 53, 116–19

Norris, Christopher, 3
Norris, Frank, 19
Norton Anthology of American Literature, 60
novel; early history, 11–12, 35–36, 184n9; institution of, 24–26; novelism (Siskin), 12–13
Nussbaum, Martha C., 209–10, 214

occasion, 39–43, 60, 192. *See also* accidental
Okrent, Daniel, 161–62
Oulipo, 104

page space, 28, 99–116, 216–17; and whole book, 116–23, 186–87, 204. *See also* concrete poetry
Patchwork Girl (Jackson), 200–202, 203
Paulson, William, 215, 217
Pavel, Thomas, 170n36, 172–73, 174n43
Paz, Octavio, 47n39
Pease, Donald, 84–85
performance, 71–72, 75, 76–77, 78, 83, 110, 120, 160–61
Pesce, Mark, 22n40
The Philosophy of Andy Warhol (Warhol), 59–62, 68–85
Pierce, Charles Sanders, 112n35
Piercy, Marge, 128, 148
Pierson, Michele, 131
Plato, 6
poetry, 94–97, 101–102; contrasted to fiction by Barth, 40
Poetry, 102
Poirier, Richard, 48n43
Powell, Jim, 213
Pokémon, 154
Populous, 189
possible world theory, 30, 152, 168–76; extensional and intensional worlds, 169; modality, 171–72
postmodernism, 3–4, 13–14, 20–21, 28, 31–57, 80, 87–88, 105–106, 118, 123, 126–28, 129–30, 192; and architecture, 145; and history, 90–92, 100, 108, 128n9; and popular culture, 33, 146–47; as definition of culture, 51–52, 141–47, 149–50; as medium independent, 33–34; canonization of postmodernist fiction, 44–45, 49–50, 61, 210; as scenic in fiction, 109–111; feminist responses to postmodernist canon, 44–45, 50n47, 55; use of allegory, 53. *See also* literary culture
poststructuralism, 27, 50, 54, 61, 87
printing, 163. *See also* page space
Proust, Marcel, 9
psychoanalysis. *See* Freudian theory
The Public Burning (Coover), 120–23
public debate, 3
public nature of literary work, 95–99
public relations. *See* media culture
publishing, 36, 39, 49, 88, 99, 100–116, 215
Punday, Daniel, 55n63, 94–95n5, 185n11, 194–95n26
Pynchon, Thomas, 44, 120, 148–49

Radway, Janice, 167
Rainey, Lawrence, 102n16
reality television, 22
Reed, Ishmael, 35, 121–23
Rein-Hagen, Mark, 166n26
Riffaterre, Michael, 3, 66
Robbe-Grillet, Alain, 9
Robinson, Charles, 103
Robinson Crusoe (Dafoe), 169–71
role-playing games, 22, 29, 151–76, 200, 203, 205, 210, 216; and agency, 157; and literary texts, 158–61; and possible world theory, 169–70; and race, 154–55; as a form of narrative, 152; as structured by objects, 155–56; early history, 153–55; hit-point, 154; psychological appeals, 166n26; summary of, 151–52
Ross, Andrew, 139, 145
Routley, Richard, 168
Rubin, Joan Shelley, 19
Rubin, Louis D., 9

INDEX

Rushdie, Salman, 100
Russ, Joanna, 50n47, 128, 148
Ryan, Marie-Laure, 168, 171n40, 190, 194–95n26

Sabbatical (Barth), 40
Salvatore, R. A., 159n12
Sartre, Jean-Paul, 45–46
Schick, Lawrence, 153n1, 158
Scholes, Robert, 53–54
science fiction, 28–29, 125–50
"The Secret Life of Walter Mitty" (Thurber), 90–91
Sellers, Susan, 44n28
Seltzer, Mark, 162–65, 167
Sidney, Sir. Philip, 6–8
Siegle, Robert, 55
Siembieda, Kevin, 157n9
SimCity, 189
The Sims, 126, 161n19
Shapin, Stephen, 7–8
Shelley, Mary, 200, 202
Sherard, Tracey, 56n67
The Simpsons and Philosophy, 213
Siskin, Clifford, 12–13, 50
Slusser, George, 139, 140
Snow White (Barthelme), 44
Sorrentino, Gilbert, 94–99, 100, 103–104, 105, 107–108n31, 112, 114–15, 125
The Sot-Weed Factor, 37
Sound and the Fury, The (Faulkner), 90
spectacle, 1, 10
Spiegelman, Art, 214
Star Wars Roleplaying Game, 159n13
Steiner, George, 165–66, 175
Sterling, Bruce, 128
Stevick, Philip, 34
structuralism, 173
Sukenick, Ronald, 31n3, 34–35, 42–43n24, 100, 104, 105–106n26, 113, 209
Sunstein, Cass, 13n26
Survivor, 22
surrealism, 33
suture, 30, 180–88, 191–92, 197, 199–200, 205–206, 212

Suvin, Darko, 126

Tabbi, Joseph, 67n11, 148
Take It or Leave It (Federman), 113–16
Tanner, Tony, 48n43
The Tao of Pooh (Hoff), 210, 214
Tebbel, John, 103
Terminator, 134
Thurber, James, 90–91
Tillman, Lynne, 112n36
Todorov, Tzvetan, 126n2
Trachtenberg, Alan, 17
Tripmaster Monkey (Kingston), 119–20, 123
TriQuarterly, 49
Tropic of Cancer (Miller), 208
Turkle, Sherry, 166n26
Turning In (Chapman), 197–200, 201, 203
Twain, Mark, 163
Typography. *See* page space

Ulysses (Joyce), 208
The Universal Baseball Association (Coover), 156–57, 203, 215
university in American literary culture, 32n5, 38, 49n45
Up (Sukenick), 113

Vaihinger, Hans, 5–6, 11, 22, 68
Vampire: The Masquerade, 155, 160
Venturi, Robert, 145
video game. *See* computer game
Vineland (Pynchon), 120
The Voice in the Closet (Federman), 116

Walker, Alice, 28, 59, 62–71, 81–85, 87–88, 99, 125, 176, 195, 215
Wallace, Michele, 61
Warhol, Andy, 28, 33, 36, 37, 59–62, 68–85, 87, 88, 105n24, 125, 145, 183, 212
Warner, William, 25–26, 184n9

Watkins, Evan, 74
Waugh, Patricia, 55n64, 107
Weber, Samuel, 16
Wesseling, Elisabeth, 128
White, Hayden, 3-4
Wiegman, Robyn, 84-85
Wilde, Alan, 34, 110
Williams, Raymond, 25

Wimsatt, W. K., 95, 101-102, 115
Wolfe, Tom, 116-19
work, 50, 71-77, 80, 81, 212

Zavarzadeh, Mas'ud, 53n57
Žižek, Slavoj, 79-80, 129, 135, 181

www.ingramcontent.com/pod-product-compliance
Lightning Source LLC
Chambersburg PA
CBHW021839220426
43663CB00005B/310